COMPARATIVE AMERICAN IDENTITIES

This volume of Essays from the English Institute is the first in the new series to be published by Routledge.

Since 1944, the English Institute has presented work by distinguished scholars in English and American literatures, foreign literatures, and related fields. A volume of papers selected from the previous year's meeting is published annually.

Comparative American Identities

RACE, SEX, AND NATIONALITY
IN THE MODERN TEXT

EDITED WITH AN INTRODUCTION BY
HORTENSE J. SPILLERS

ESSAYS FROM THE ENGLISH INSTITUTE

ROUTLEDGE   NEW YORK AND LONDON

Published in 1991 by

Routledge
An imprint of Routledge, Chapman and Hall, Inc.
29 West 35 Street
New York, NY 10001

Published in Great Britain by

Routledge
11 New Fetter Lane
London EC4P 4EE

Copyright © 1991 by The English Institute

Printed in the United States of America

All rights reserved. No part of this book may be reprinted or reproduced or utilized in any form or by any electronic, mechanical or other means, now known or hereafter invented, including photocopying and recording, or in any information storage or retrieval system, without permission in writing from the publishers.

Library of Congress Cataloging in Publication Data

Comparative American identities : race, sex, and nationality in the
 modern text / edited by Hortense J. Spillers.
     p. cm.
   ISBN 0-415-90349-1 (hb). — ISBN 0-415-90350-5 (pb)
   1. America—Literatures—History and criticism. 2. Race in literature. 3. Sex in literature. 4. National Characteristics in literature. I. Spillers, Hortense J.
PN843.C66 1991
813.009'355—dc20   90-19918

British Library Cataloguing in Publication Data

Comparative American identities : race, sex and nationality
 in the modern text. — (The English Institute).
 1. United States. Cultural processes
 I. Spillers, Hortense II. Series
 306.0973

ISBN 0-415-90349-1
ISBN 0-415-90350-5 pbk

Contents

1. Introduction: Who Cuts the Border? Some Readings
   on "America" 1
   HORTENSE J. SPILLERS

2. The Unquiet Self: Spanish American Autobiography and the
   Question of National Identity 26
   SYLVIA MOLLOY

3. Developing Diaspora Literacy and *Marasa* Consciousness 40
   VÈVÈ A. CLARK

4. Toni Morrison's *Beloved:* Re-Membering the Body
   as Historical Text 62
   MAE G. HENDERSON

5. Re-Weaving the "Ulysses Scene": Enchantment, Post-Oedipal
   Identity, and the Buried Text of Blackness in Toni Morrison's
   Song of Solomon 87
   KIMBERLY W. BENSTON

6. National Brands/National Body: *Imitation of Life* 110
   LAUREN BERLANT

7. A Small Boy and Others: Sexual Disorientation
   in Henry James, Kenneth Anger, and David Lynch 141
   MICHAEL MOON

8. *Walden's* Erotic Economy 157
   MICHAEL WARNER

9. Fear of Federasty: Québec's Inverted Fictions 175
   ROBERT SCHWARTZWALD

   Contributors 197

1.
Introduction: Who Cuts the Border? Some Readings on "America"

HORTENSE J. SPILLERS

For Roberto and Maddie Marquez

The January 10, 1891 edition of *La Revista Illustrada* carried the initial publication of José Martí's celebrated essay, "Our America."[1] Later, almost exactly a year to the day, "El Partido Revolucionario Cubano"—the Cuban Revolutionary Party—was created, with Martí acknowledged as "its leading spirit, inspirer, and organizer."[2] The compressed background of historical events that Philip Foner provides in the Introduction to the second of four English-language volumes of Martí's writings[3] reacquaints readers in the United States with a larger-than-life romantic instance, whose initiating moments date back to one's childhood and its ephemeral encounters with symptoms of the heroic: Simón Bolívar, Father Hidalgo and "the cry of Dolores," alongside Martí, are entailed with the same fabric of cultural memory and a curiously elided time-space continuum that threads the name of A. Philip Randolph with the successes of the Brotherhood of Sleeping Car Porters and the heady political maneuvers of Adam Clayton Powell, Jr. It remains, then, a matter of surprise that, even as one eventually grasps the reasons why, Martí's "our" and "America" do not usually embrace US at all—except by the logic of a clearly defined dualism of antagonists, who, in the febrile imagination of his writings, must contend, in effect, for the right to name and claim "America." As Foner observes, that vast stretch of formidably organized political power (at which site all nine of the essayists writing here live and work, if not originate), ninety miles north of the island and nation of Cuba, demarcates, for Martí, that "other America," neither "*his* America," nor "Mother America" of Martí's dream of wholeness.[4] About seventy years following the writing of the lectures that comprise *The Philosophy of History*,[5] G.W.F. Hegel himself might have been offered occasion for surprise at the exemplary boldness of one José Martí:

> The European university must bow to the American university. The history of America, from the Incas to the present must be taught in clear detail and to the letter, even if the archons of Greece are overlooked. Our Greece must take priority over the Greece which is not ours. We need it more. Nationalist statesmen must replace foreign statesmen. Let the world be grafted onto our republics, but the trunk must be our own. And let the vanquished pedant hold his tongue, for there are no lands in which a man may take greater pride than in our long-suffering American republics. (p. 88)

Interestingly enough, Martí and Hegel, inhabiting either end of the nineteenth century, posited, for radically different reasons and toward radically different and reversed ends, two contrastive "Americas." For Martí, as the excerpted passage suggests, "Our America," of indigenous historical currents, fires, on the one hand, the profoundly figurative polemic of his revolutionary moment and impulse, those "long suffering American republics, raised up from among the silent Indian masses by the bleeding arms of a hundred apostles, to the sounds of battle between the book and the processional candle" (p. 86). On the other hand, the "other America," the United States, "this avaricious neighbor who admittedly has designs on us,"[6] arouses Martí to the visionary urgencies of an Armageddon. Perhaps the longest syntactic chain in "Our America" throws forth immitigable linkage between "since/then," *post hoc, ergo propter hoc,* embedded in oppositional ground:

> And since strong nations, self-made by law and shotgun, love strong nations, and them alone; since the time of madness and ambition—from which North America may be freed by the predominance of the purest elements in its blood, or on which it may be launched by its vindictive and sordid masses, its tradition of expansion, or the ambitions of some powerful leader . . . since its good name as a republic in the eyes of the world's perceptive nations puts upon North America a restraint that cannot be taken away by childish provocations or pompous arrogance or parricidal discords among our American nations—the pressing need of Our America is to show itself as it is, one in spirit and intent . . . (p. 93)

Though far too schematic, one learns, to exhaust, or even adequately account for, the range of Martí's thought,[7] his rhetorical binary, nonetheless, subtends one of the chief critical functions of his solidary political and intellectual engagement.

Martí's expressly dramatic protocol of pronouns is neither more nor less presumptuous than Hegel's implied one, which also distinguishes "America," New World, from the "United States of North America, but an emanation from Europe" (p. 82). Hegel's "other America" "has always shown itself physically and psychically powerless, and still shows itself so" (p. 81). These aboriginal societies "gradually vanished at the breath of European activity" (p. 81); we needn't add that such "breath" ferociously animated the winds of multiple violence—epistemic, linguistic, iconographic, genocidal. Hegel's European-emanated United States, with its "republican constitution," its Christian sects of Protestant enthusiasm, its "Universal protection for property" belongs, finally and dismissively, for Hegel, to an American "future," "where, in the ages that lie before us, the burden of the World's History shall reveal itself—perhaps in a contest between North and South America" (p. 86).

That Hegelian "perhaps" is borne out, amazingly so, in hemispheric wars of national liberation, so far, including Cuba, (in its First and Second Wars of Independence) and Cuba again, under the successful insurgency of Fidel Castro, shortly past the mid-point of the twentieth century. No one can fail to read current affairs in Ibero-Hispanic America and the Caribbean—from Sandinista Nicaragua, to post-Noriega Panama—outside an ironized perspective on this "future" and the culture texts inscribed and unfolding about it.

Ensnared, then, between Old World and New, past and future, the contrary ideas of "America" instantiate the text and the materiality on a historico-cultural ground long fabled and discursive in acts of European invention and intervention. It is as if the Word, for Europe, engenders Flesh. Peter Hulme argues, for example, that the discourse of English colonialism arises fundamentally on the career of two key terms—"hurricanes" and "Caribbees"—that mark relatively new lexemes in the English language. "Not found before the middle of the sixteenth century," these terms do not settle into "their present forms before the latter half of the seventeenth."[8] Both originate in Native American languages, and "both were quickly adopted into all the major European languages" (p. 58). Raymond Williams's *Keywords* does not carry entries on either term, but it is rather startling that as innocuous as they might appear in the lexicon, "hurricanes" and "Caribbees/Caribbean," especially the latter, have achieved keyword status over a significant spate of modern intellectual history. Any subsequent addenda that we might devise on Williams's project concerning the evolution of terministic cruxes "in the West" might well inaugurate around "Caribbean" and its own emanations.

Contemporary Cuban intellectual, Roberto Fernández Retamar—poet, essayist, and distinguished editor of *Casa de las Americas*—offers, in his classic essay, a highly informative synthesis[9] of the history of related terms—"Caribbean/Caribbees/Caliban." As background and framework that situate Retamar's reading of culture in "Our America," this rich congruence of terms is biographically reinscribed in the exemplary instance of Martí's public life and career. Retamar tracks "Caribbean" from its eponymous Carib community of Native Americans, who, we are told, valiantly resisted European incursion in the sixteenth century, to its philosophical and terministic transformations, by way of "Caliban," in the contemporary period, with specific reference to the works of Aimé Césaire, Frantz Fanon, and O. Mannoni.[10] As if a moment of phantasmogoria that perfectly mirrors the Freudian formula of media cross-dressing—the dream as *visual* transliteration of the day's *grammar* events—"Carib" is translated as a "deformation" and "defamation" into "cannibal." The latter generates an anagram in "Caliban," as Shakespeare had already made use of "cannibal" to mean anthropophagus "in the third part of *Henry IV* and *Othello*" (p. 11).

This nested semiotic filiation, inaugurated by a reputed "look," retailed as truth to Christopher Columbus, will stage a paradigm of discursive, scopophilic behavior for colonizing and enslaving powers toward "peoples of color," and most dramatically in its duration, for Hegel's "Negro" of Subsaharan "Africa," which demonstrates "no historical part of the world," it was said; ". . . has no movement or development to exhibit," it was concluded (p. 99). For Columbus's reporters (and Hegel), anthropophagi reside on that border between nature and culture, inhabited by " 'men with one eye and others with dog's muzzles, who ate human beings.' "[11]

Would we dare, then, risk a simplistic and essentialist reduction? "Someone," perhaps, saw "something" or "someone" in a stage of cultural production long before Columbus came,[12] and even now with pure revisionary heart-work and devotion to the politics of the plural, we cannot decipher exactly what it was. Having few corrective narratives to counterpoise, the future-laden actor reenacts an analogy on a child's game: a sentence is passed along a spatial sequence, person to person, and at the end of it the garbled "message" makes only comic sense. Just so (or almost), we will not "know" now, since the "first speakers," either way, are not "available." By the time Shakespeare sifts "cannibal" through the sieve of his imagination, it is an already inspissated narrative of plenitude, crystallized in the sixteenth century by, among other sources, Thomas More's *Utopia* (1580) and Michel de Montaigne's "De los Caníbales" (1580); the translation of Montaigne's work by way of Giovanni Floro's *Essays* was available to Shakespeare, Retamar observes (p. 14).

The construction and invention of "America," then—a dizzying concoction of writing and reportage, lying and "signifying," jokes, "tall tales," and transgenerational nightmare, all conflated under the banner of Our

Lord—exemplify, for all intents and purposes, the oldest game of *trompe de l'oeil,* the perhaps-mistaken-glance-of-the-eye, that certain European "powers" carried out regarding indigenous Americans. *Misprision,* therefore, constitutes law and rule of "Our America" in its "beginnings" for Europe. "Made up" in the gaze of Europe, "America" was as much a "discovery" on the retinal surface as it was the appropriation of land and historical subjects.

From what angle does one insert the "United States but-an-emanation from Europe" into this picture, or perhaps, more ambitiously, a series of perpendicular pronouns—the "I's"/"eyes" of this collection of writings on the New World?

At least one thing is doubtless: At whatever point one cuts into this early modern discourse on what will become, quite by accident, by arbitrary design, by the most complicated means of economic (and otherwise) exchange, and the entire repertoire of genetic play and chance, her space, his space, of central habitation in the unimagined "future" of World History, the initial news is hardly good for anyone. "Physically and psychically powerless" and overcome by men who *eat* (the) other(s), this orientalized, Europe-fabled "America" could not be salvaged by even the hippest stunts of the televisual media, except that a Martí, for one, will reclaim it as a necessary project of historical demolition and reconstruction. But the United States, carved out of this New World ground, must be read, just as it is intimately connected, with this unfolding historical text of unpromise. The seams will show now, but that is also part of the picture. This ground is broken—by culture and "race," language and ethnicity, weather and land formation, in generative and historical time, as more or less gendered "situation-specificities,"[13] in various postures of loves and hungers, cohabit it—even though, given any point at which the multiple "I"/"We" are positioned on its axes, it appears to be monolithic ground. Retamar, pursuing the implications of Martí's "mestizo America," identifies as *the* "distinctive sign of our culture," those ". . . descendants both ethnically and culturally speaking, of aborigines, Africans, and Europeans" (p. 9). He goes on to interrogate, in rhetorical accents sometime reminiscent of Martí's own writings: "From Túpac Amaru . . . to Nicolás Guillén, to Aimé Césaire, to Violeta Parra, to Frantz Fanon—what is our history, what is our culture, if not the history and culture of Caliban?" (p. 24).

It seems clear that at great expense to the national "pursuit of happiness," a United States culture text/praxis, in the dreamful flattening out of textures of the historical, would repress its calibanesque potential, just as we would amend Retamar's strategy of evocation to account for at least one other strand of the "sixties without apology."[14] If, for instance, Bartolomeo Las Casas and José Martí touch my life-line at some distant point of reverberation, then certainly Isabella Baumfree, become "Sojourner Truth," and

Rosa Parks, Malcolm El-Hajj Malik, and Martin Luther King, Jr., among others, must sound through Retamar's at no greater distance. The problem of the pronouns—and *we* mustn't mistake this, as the late sixties taught—cannot, will not resolve itself in a too-easy "hands around the world" embrace among hemispheric cross-cultural communities. But if one concedes "Caliban" as a joining figure, then by virtue of what set of moves is the notion applicable along a range of culture practices in light of the hegemonic entailment of operations out of which certain US communities express relations to "Our America"? In other words, in order to disrupt the homogeneous narrative that the United States, as an idea-form, or that "other America" provokes in Martí's, or Retamar's view, or even George Bush's view, the contradictions of proximity must be brought further out: Some of US render unto Caesar, more or less, is not simply locutional.

Apparently everywhere one might look on this massive scene of heterogeneous historical attitudes, it seems that "Caliban" designates a copulative potential by way of the Atlantic system of slavery—the ownership of man by man (Virginia's "chattels personal," say), man's ownership of "private property" (Cuba's seigneurial ownership of the sugar product, say), and the captive communities' occasional revolt in the teeth of it (Canada's Caribbean marronage, for example). In the sociopolitical arrangements here stipulated, "man," wherever he appears in the bargain, articulates with juridical, axiomatic, historical, ontological, and local *specificity*. "America," with its US, locates a prime time of "the fruits of merchant capital"[15] as a stunning chapter in the modern history of patriarchal law and will. In other words, America/US shows itself as a "scene of instruction" in the objectifying human possibility across an incredibly various real estate and human being. This vulgar oxymoron of purposes and motivations insists on the combo—human-as-property—and there, in all the astonishing foreclosures of certainty, "English," among other Indo-European languages, enters its currency in the "execrable trade."

It would seem highhanded, then, to read this Real as *a discourse,* but certainly the conceptual narratives around "cannibal"/"Caliban"—a colonial topos, common to the seventeenth century, Hulme argues, projects slavery "as the necessary stage between savagery and civilization" (p. 62). "Caliban" designates itself a moment of convergence between Old World and New, inasmuch as the idea-formation demonstrates "features of both the Mediterranean wild man, or classical monster . . . with an African mother, whose pedigree leads back to Book X of *The Odyssey*" (p. 70). Further, Caliban, as the issue of Sycorax,[16] entertains "particular connection with the moon . . . whose signs the Caribs could read . . ." (p. 70). Need we be reminded here of the "intersections of blood and the moon, the mother and home: towards that terrain which traditionally has been given and denied the name of 'woman' "?[17]

When Martí invokes "Mother America," one imagines that he means the formulation of "mother" in relation to nurture and security, but the term might also mark, under the precise historical circumstance upon which his vision of "America" is raised, the *silence* bred by defeat. If Columbus's *Diaries,* compounded of report, offered the explorer a useful fiction for entering New World communities, then that available discourse evinces a remarkable instance of "rhetorical enargeia," which Patricia Parker describes as "convincing description or vivid report, [containing] within it the same visual root as the name of "Argus," sent with his many eyes to spy."[18] The Columbian reporters, for example, were not only providing "promotional narratives," but "a 'blazing,' or publishing of the glories of this *feminized* New World, of the possibilities of commercial abundance and 'return' " (emphasis mine; p. 141). Perceiving a link here between language and spectacle, Parker speaks of discursive inventiveness as a "transgressive uncovering, or opening up of a secret place, of exposing what was hidden in the womb of a feminized Nature . . ." (p. 142). These "ocular proofs," giving rise to discursive elaboration, as we have observed in the Caliban/Caribbean/cannibal semiosis, yoke the gaze and the profit in a rhetorics of property (p. 147).

The inventory of both the American land and the figure of Caliban—"ugly, hostile, ignorant, devilish"—inscribes a "rhetorical and an economic instrument, one way of controlling the territory in question . . ." (p. 150). Even though Sycorax is given no script in *The Tempest,* as we recall, her "absence," except in comminatory provocation, confirms the "unrepresentability" of Caliban, the mothered-womaned, to a spectator-audience.[19] A not-sayable offers a strategy for describing the "future," which is always a pregnant possibility in the now.

Hulme describes the locus of *The Tempest* as an "extraordinary topographical dualism" because of its "double series of connotations"—the Mediterranean and the Caribbean. This scene of double inscription is borne out further in "tempest" itself, from the Mediterranean repertoire, and Gonzolo's "plantation," from the Atlantic repertoire (p. 71). But practically speaking, beyond the "rarified latitudes" of Shakespeare's art, the "discovery of America" may be read as "a magnetic pole compelling a reorientation of traditional axes." Superimposing two planes—a palimpsest, "on which there are two texts" (p. 72), "America" juxtaposes "two referential systems" that inhabit "different spaces except for that area which is the island [neither here nor there] and its first native Caliban" (p. 72). As a "geometrical metaphor," Caliban intermediates a "central axis about which both planes swivel free of one another." As a "textual metaphor," Caliban inscribes an "overdetermination," "peculiarly at odds with his place of habitation which is described as an 'uninhabitable island' " (p. 72). Caliban translates the "monstrous" in his mediating posture "between two sets of connotations" and a "compromise formation . . . achieved . . . only at the expense of distortion elsewhere" (p. 72). Precisely metaphorical in the collapse of distinctive features of contrast, Caliban can "exist only within discourse . . . fundamentally and essentially beyond the bounds of representation" (p. 72).

Or is it the *bonds,* the *bonds* of representation? William Faulkner's Luster, the grandson of his "enduring" Dilsey,[20] tries to recall to young Quentin Compson, his proximate age-mate, the name of the wild male child now installed in the shadows of "Sutpen's Hundred"[21] and decides that his not-so-ready-to-hand last name exemplifies a "lawyer's word": "what they puts you under when the Law catches you" (p. 215). Inflected from "Bon," by way of his paternity in Charles Etienne de Saint Valery Bon and a maternity situated by Faulkner's narrator as a "gorilla" of a woman, "Jim Bond" stands free, if not emancipated, in his US/African/European/Americanity as an embodied instance of the "ferocious play of alphabets,"[22] but not unlike Caliban, "he" also marks a would-be place, or a "geometrical metaphor" on the verge of being in an American wilderness—fictitious Jefferson, Mississippi (trapped in a once dark pastoral frame) after the "fall" of the South. Verging on past and future, Jim Bond, a live-wire instance of the law's most persistent social invention, assumes the status of deictic, or nonverbal marker, *here* and *there, this* and *that,* as the conventions of discourse out of which he arises proffer him no claim to a "present/presence," except as the unkinned "monster," feared and despised, from Caliban, to Bigger Thomas. Though I am suggesting here a narrative of filiations across a broad swatch of Western discourse, there are, admittedly, considerable differences between these "impression-points": If we accept the argument of Hulme and others that Caliban describes sheer and fateful discursivity that evades the trammels of representation, then what must we make of a figure like Jim Bond whose representability prescribes and provokes *all* that he is?

Both cultural vestibularity and an after-word, "America/US," from Caliban's perspective and that of his diverse relations, must come upon Language and the Law (and in a sense, they overlap the same item from the store of Europe's hardy "beneficence") as the inimical "property" of "civilized man." ("You taught me language, and my profit on't/Is, I know how to curse. The red plague rid you/For learning me your language.") This place, this text, as Jim Bond embodies it, as the European interventionist/invader might have imagined, orchestrates representation as the already-coded "future." Some of US know this process—in discourse and discourse/politics—as history as *mugging.*

This overdetermined representability, or texts overwritten, locates authority on an exterior, as the seizing of discursive initiative seems to define a first order of insurgency wherever it appears in the New World. Colonial North America as the final port-of-call on a trajectory that starts up the triangular trade all over again would mute its involvement in the narratives of Caliban, as we have observed before, by the fateful creation of "minority" communities in the United States, but it is the ascribed task of such communities to keep the story of difference under wraps through the enactments and reenactments of difference in the flesh. The single basis for a myth of national unity is raised, therefore, on negation and denial that would bring a Jim Bond to stand in the first place. In that space—like the return to the scene of a crime—we can recite the triangulation of a particular mapping that might demonstrate new ground for the workings of Hulme's "geometrical metaphor."

The historic triangular trade interlarded a third of the known world in a fabric of commercial intimacy so tightly interwoven that the politics of the New World cannot always be so easily disentangled as locally discrete moments. Nowhere is this narrative of involvement more pointedly essayed than in Faulkner's *Absalom, Absalom!* that choreographs Canada, the Caribbean, Africa, Europe, and the United States as geographical and/or figurative points of contact in this fictive discourse. If Caliban as a narrative paradigm links American communities in a repertoire of sporadic historico-cultural reference, then we might traverse its play in *Absalom, Absalom!*.

In this layer upon layer of "graphireading,"[23] Faulkner never quite comes to the point, but puts it off again and again in the successful evasion of closure. The tales that converge on "Thomas Sutpen," both the narrated and the sign-vehicle that starts up the narrative and sustains it, are related by speakers who recall the character from some vantage of time long past (as Rosa Coldfield), or, at even greater narrative remove, the recollections of others' *inherited* recollection of Sutpen (as Quentin Compson). At the intersection of a plurality of texts, Sutpen aptly demonstrates the notion of character as a structure of assumptions that reading embodies and, not altogether unlike the orientalized Carib/cannibal formation, is concocted in the imaginings of each speaker from a repertory of rancor, grudging admiration, gossip, rumor, hearsay, and more or less stabilized impression. The work plunders and reworks itself as narrators not only elaborate what they cannot have known, but also correct passed-down information, fill in gaps, piece together disparities, disprove or improve inherited conclusions, assume identities, even invent new ones, that the novel has not embedded. For instance, Quentin Compson's Canadian roommate Shreve McCannon/McKenzie (also "transported" from *The Sound and the Fury* to *Absalom, Absalom!*) posits a quite likely character of a lawyer to the mother of Charles Bon and offers an intercessory "gift" that the "author," we're led to imagine, had not thought of. We also learn from McKenzie that Thomas Sutpen could not have been born in *West* Virginia, if he were 25 years old in Mississippi in 1833, which would establish his birth year as 1808 (p. 220). Having acquired his "American history" in a western Canadian classroom, Shreve, after all, a Harvard man, knows very well that West Virginia was not admitted to the Union until 1863. But the traditional reading on Sutpen, as Quentin receives it down the paternal line, requires him to have been born "in West Virginia, in the mountains." Reading in the interstices, we surmise that Sutpen "comes from" nowhere that an early US map would have articulated.

Essentially originless, if the continuities of kinship and place of birth, relatedly, mean anything, Thomas Sutpen, reminiscent of the colonized European subject before him, "arises" in "Old Bailey" and a criminality inscribed in notary's ink. But achieving the means to efface these corrupt "beginnings" founds both the desire of Sutpen's own fictional biotext and "Sutpen's Hundred," the 10 square miles of virgin land carved out of north Mississippi. The shadow of Sutpen's imputed desire falls between two poignant moments, collapsed into a single, dreaded economy of recall and forgetfulness. The homeless prepubescent boy, wandering the surrounding country with an unspecified number of siblings and a drunken father, learns very slowly (in the tempo of the Faulknerian sentence) what hierarchy and difference are and how they work: "He had learned the difference between white men and black ones, but he was learning that there was a difference between white men and white men, not to be measured by lifting anvils, gouging eyes or how much whiskey you could drink then get up and walk out of the room" (p. 226).

As the story is interpreted by Quentin and Shreve, somewhere in Harvard yard, Sutpen's memory so freezes on these scenes that it would be plausible to think of them as analogous to birth trauma. But if one's "second birth" marks the coming to "consciousness," then the second time around for Sutpen is doubly painful, engendered by the outraged shame of *being-looked-at.* The drunken father has somehow landed work on a plantation whose owner lives in the "biggest house [Sutpen] had even seen" (p. 227). This man who owns things—"all the land and the niggers"—spends "most of the afternoon . . . in a barrel stave hammock between two trees, with his shoes ["that he didn't even need to wear"] off . . ." (pp. 227–28). When young Sutpen, bearing an unread message from his father to the man in the Big House, arrives at the front door, something quite astonishing takes place: ". . . the monkey-dressed nigger butler kept the door barred with his body while he spoke . . ." (p. 231), and "even before [Sutpen] had had time to say what he came for," the butler tells him "never to come to that front door again but to go around to the back" (p. 232).

Sutpen's "birth" in the moment strikes with such force that the narrator insinuates it as *rupture:* Even before the butler completes the message, Sutpen "seemed to kind of dissolve and a part of him turn and rush back through the two years they had lived there" (pp. 229-30). The rip in the fabric of memory occurs, so to speak, over the bar of the black body, standing in the doorway so that the enormous privation in young Sutpen is abruptly named, materialized, and objectified in the butler's own impeding presence. Suddenly, the boy gets an inkling of what he looks like to a momentarily superior other, denied by the statistical recurrence of the lexemes "nigger," "monkey-nigger," "niggers," that overtakes the passage, but be that as it may, Sutpen gets the point and it sticks: This *face,* and "he was unable to close the *eyes* of it—was looking out from *within* . . . just as the man who did not even have to wear the shoes he owned . . . looked out from whatever *invisible place* he (the man) happened to be at the moment, at the boy *outside* the barred door in his patched garments and *splayed bare feet* . . ." (emphasis mine; pp. 234-35).

"Outside" the bar defines precisely that moment of negation from which meaning can work, since, in the positing of a not-"inside" and a not-"within," Sutpen brutally discovers who is/not. Not only is he "born" to himself then, but commences to read his "history" as it is rendered through the borrowed gaze of his profoundest beholders: ". . . he himself seeing his own father and sisters and brothers as the owner . . . must have been seeing them all the time"—

as cattle, creatures heavy and without grace, brutely evacuated into a world without hope or purpose for them, who would in turn spawn with brutish and vicious prolixity, populate, double treble compound, fill space and earth with a *race* whose future would be a succession of cut-down and patched and made-over garments bought on exorbitant credit because they were white people. . . . (emphasis mine; p. 235)

It is fair to say that the young Thomas Sutpen "gets" his culture's sociotext violently and all at once through the ventriloquized medium of others' seeing, as "race"—now objectified *for* him by way of a barred doorway—and the threat of castration—in the hint of male bonding and hierarchy—become the power drive of his fundamental hunger. "Splayed bare feet" and "shoes," projecting a theory here from off the ground, let's say, not only address the downcast, "cut-down" detail, but also flirt with the missing phallus. "Niggers" will take on a certain usefulness of social economy for Sutpen, as it is surprising to him and the reader that "they" are not "inside" the bar so much as its moment of substantiation to be transcended. Sutpen is marked, then, by the "discovery" of "race," or more pointedly, by the striking news that he "has" "race," as the message is hammered home by the crucial marker of difference in a US Real—the vital sign of "Africanity" itself. In a very real sense, this coming to manhood, in all the brutality of ungentle revelation, fixes Thomas Sutpen in the inescapable madness of his own veritably now-felt difference. Mattering even less in the relay of gazes than that "monkey-dressed nigger," who is "given . . . garments free" (p. 235), Sutpen instantiates the barefoot, bareass white boy who will spend his fictional career overcoming.

Since human valuation is posited in this narrative as the distance between privation and gratification, we observe that the young Sutpen also comes upon the efficacies of "class" in this episode, but features of the sociotext are so carefully intertwined here that "race," "class," and masculine (hetero) "sexuality" are represented as a single bundle of nerves. For sure, the character, as imputed to him, grasps a human psychology and sociometry under the auspices of *lack,* as the latter offers its unsaid name to a far more sophisticated, covering notion—*desire* writ large and, in this particular instance, inscribed in the balloon face of the Negro butler. To say that Sutpen imposes, in time, the weight of his rage on "peoples of color" will not surprise; indeed, we can anticipate it with a good degree of certainty, but *how* it is so (inasmuch as the African-American person has very little to do with him in the historical situations that we come to accept as "true") focuses the puzzle of US "race" magic itself: We might suggest now that the ideology of "race" in the New World text is founded on the fundamental suspicion that one is *not* a "man," if, as in Sutpen's case, castration fear and the mark and knowledge of "race" can be said to belong to the same stuff of cognition/recognition. The utter ruthlessness of "class," then, with its relegation of women, period, though for radically different reasons, to the circuit of exchange, not only describes the violence that is interrupted by nothing at all, but does not bear distinction as a discrete feature of the socionom[24] from "race" and "sexuality." Thomas Sutpen, in the course of things, will efface his "race" (as the myth of the "land of opportunity" requires the ascendant "race" to do) and take on a new "class" (the displacement of "race" onto "property"), but in order to do so, he must not only run away from those viciously spawned siblings, but must "split" the unmapped countryside and the unfinished cartographies of the new nation.

To make an interminable story quite a bit shorter (Faulkner, after all, was trying to capture the whole world between "a cap and a period"[25]): Sutpen, and *how* he does so is about as clear as the involuted syntax of the narrative can be, lands on a "little island set in a smiling and fury-lurked and incredible indigo sea, which was the halfway point between what we call the jungle and what we call civilization, halfway between the dark inscrutable continent . . . and the cold known land to which it was doomed . . ." (p. 250). The narrative remains ignorant of the proper name of this "little island," but plants symptoms of it, as if the name itself were a postponed expectation, just as that mountainous region of Virginia, where Sutpen was born, will come to be called *West* Virginia. In effect, this generalized nominative order—"in a latitude which would require ten thousand years of equatorial heritage to bear its climate" (p. 251)—cannot be named in its global dispersion insofar as it revolves in a "heart of darkness" that cannot read itself. (This conjecture is aided by our knowledge that Sutpen is semi-literate at best.) To that extent, Conrad's Marlowe/Kurtz and Faulkner's Sutpen/Quentin/Shreve—variously positioned in the scale of literate-being—encounter the same massive display of a self-generated phantasm that bites back. Sutpen nonetheless falls in the binary between that "dark inscrutable continent" on the one hand and that "cold known land . . . the civilized land and people which had expelled some of its own blood and thinking and desires that had become too crass to be faced and borne longer . . ." on the other hand (pp. 250-51). In this romance of the "bloods," the narrator does not actually approach a geopolitical order that could be thought of as a mimesis of some "real" place, but Sutpen's role in the scheme as an overseer and "the incredible paradox of peaceful greenery and crimson flowers and sugar cane sapling size and three times the height of a man" gesture symptomatically toward the notion of the colonial/plantation system of the Hispanic and Francophone Caribbean; that "cold known land" seems to look toward Europe, as ambiguity of reference delineates the entire passage in paroxysms of modification.

In this fret and fever of telling, layers of other narratives "migrate" to the different context and signify on Faulkner's semantic surface, but at least one of the convergent texts (or shades of it) is rewritten here to establish Sutpen as an apprentice-factotum of Law and Order: The revolt of the little island's by-now indigenous black population is put down, *singlehandedly*, in John Wayne style, by Sutpen, who "[walks] out into the darkness and [subdues] them, maybe by yelling louder, maybe by standing, bearing more than they believed any bones and flesh could or should . . ." (p. 254). The most celebrated revolution in the colonial African Diaspora, or, perhaps, within this complex at *any* time, records quite a different outcome: "The slaves defeated . . . the local whites and the soldiers of the French monarchy, a Spanish invasion, a British expedition of some 60,000 men, and a French expedition of similar size under Bonaparte's brother-in-law."[26] Historian C.L.R. James is referring here, of course, to the San Domingo struggle (1791-1803), which established Haiti as the modern world's first black nation-state. Sutpen's "creators," however, are not only constructing/reconstructing Sutpen's biotext through willful and wishful distortions that posit the deeds of an "identity," but even at the risk of parody, insinuating an exalted and aggrandized figure. This economy of narrative means dwarfs the background and its particularities, as the "hero" is dramatically foregrounded at all costs.

But there is still something on Thomas Sutpen's mind. That face with eyes that "he was unable to close" acquires obsessive force, *is* the all-over memory that repeats like a rhetorical tic. Here, in an ambiguous space,

Sutpen, searching for one of the missing house servants, "the half breeds," "hunts" for two days, "without even knowing that what he was meeting was a blank wall of black secret faces, a wall behind which almost anything could be preparing to happen and, as he later learned, almost anything was . . ." (p. 252). This "text," which Sutpen can neither read, nor erase, overlaps the tale of the butler, as both episodes share their common source in a weave of related textures—from some secret and invisible posture, a putative subject of an interior generates unspecified, unspecifiable power that Sutpen can only guess. In both instances, he, we might say, intimates his own production *as* knowledge-for-another, so that in his own eyes, he has taken on objectness, "double-consciousness," or the seeing himself as an interiorized other (to his "outsiderliness") might see him. The founding of "Sutpen's Hundred," with its handcrafted, baronial mimicries, is vexed by a habit and poetics of pathos that now seem clearer to the grasp—"Home" breaches the blank wall; the barred doorway. Gaining "Home" offers him the key and extraordinary imperative.

One final piece: Sutpen's first-born son, Charles Bon, who is the father, in turn, of Charles Etienne de St. Valery Bon, is given birth to in the ambiguously fictionalized space—the son of Eulalia Bon, the daughter of the Haitian sugar plantation's owner.[27] When Sutpen, discovering his new wife's suspect racial origins, descends, finally, on Mississippi, Eulalia and child have been installed in New Orleans, perhaps, and in a more or less morganatic arrangement—at least this is the plausible text that Quentin and Shreve co-hatch. The meeting of Henry Sutpen, the "true" son and legitimate heir of Thomas by Ellen Coldfield, and Charles Bon (whom—like Sutpen—we never actually "see," except as the splendidly regressive, sartorial, and eroticized narrative object of desire in others) provides the vertiginous motions that take the reader toward the storm center of the US culture text—"race" as that awful moment of incestuous possibility *and* praxis, yearning *and* denial, refusal *and* accomplishment, wild desire *and* repression, that cannot be uttered and that cannot *but* be uttered: Jim Bond, the grandson of Charles, outside the burning ruins of an impossible and impassable history, with "Africa," "Europe," and "African-America" coursing his veins, abrupts the "return" that Sutpen wished to repress altogether. At the embodied intersection of heteronomies—and they are just about all there in the play of demography, geography, history, ethnicity, sexuality, the declensions of "class," and the signs of repression and difference in "race"—Jim Bond, in the flesh, installs a reading on the paralogisms[28] of US in "Our America."

It seems that Sutpen has been perfectly poised for this tale of contingency by way of a great-grandson whom he could not/would not have *recognized*, starting in the son. Going back to keywords in his early fictive biotext, we would try to tease out a meaning as to the *how* in recourse to three scattered resonances: 1) ambiguity; 2) evacuate/evacuation; 3) blank wall/barred entry. It will not be surprising that "blankness" does not describe a not-written upon so much as it locates a site for new, or over-inscriptions—Lillian Hellman's "pentimento,"[29] Hulme's "palimpsest." The screen, or canvas, or framed circumstance carries traces of preceding moments that alter the contemporaneous rendition, making the latter both an "originality" and an "affiliated," or the initiation of a new chain of signifying as well as an instance of significations already in intervened motion. The descriptive discourse attributed to Sutpen's dream of the "nigger" (which arises *persistently* after the fact of his coming into knowledge of self-division and "race") is laden with notions of surface and masking. It could be said that Sutpen's first and and most significant hodological instruments[30] are "flashed" by the "monkey-dressed nigger," who sends him spinning in negative self-reflection. But I think that in this particular instance, it would be too easy to dismiss the occurrence of the butler as simple mirroring, or the surface upon which young Sutpen is played back to himself. (The latter case would identify more precisely the cultural production of minstrelsy, wherein the "blank wall" of faces is "made up" in hideous, even pornotrophic, caricature. The segregation of lips, teeth, eyes, and hair, for instance, in the facial contour would fit any number of artistic programs, but wed to a scheme of [over] representation—both "over and over again," and "written" on top of, designed to reenforce instances of sociopolitical dominance—the surreal strategies of minstrelsy exact a fatal mockery of art and entertainment.) In Sutpen's case, contrastingly, the commotions stirred up on the interior *posit* an "inward." I actually mean to say that the commotions *are* the coming about of, the markings of, an interior space. (A wedge that is driven between a Real and an Imaginary, even though the verb here is perhaps too volitional?) Sutpen's "blank" describes, then, the moment of tension between a "self-created" and a "self-alienated," or the moment when he "realizes" that he is not who he thought he was; *as* he thought he was. This enablement occurs under the auspices of ignorance (a conundrum that he cannot read) and impedence (his stalled movement forward). *Blocking* and *puzzlement* compel him—literally—to *flight* and the alienated "inwardness."

This thematics might be positioned to gather up "ambiguity" and "evacuate/evacuation" as contrastive movements of a local narrative etiology. Since "evacuate" is itself a figure of ambiguity in juxtaposing double meaning, it works well to describe Sutpen's new "moment of being" (an emptying out of contents) and the "his-story" that he wears on his feet (those "cattle, creatures heavy . . . without grace . . . brutely *evacuated* . . ."). Trapped always between pre- and co-eval texts, Sutpen himself is nowhere to be found, "in person," in Faulkner's work, but those symptoms of "him," dreadfully, densely read through the various narrative devices of *Absalom,*

Absalom!, suggest that such as "he" still haunts the memory of a nation that commits the Sutpen error: Bearing the weight of knowledge, one cannot act *otherwise*, or *simply*. (Can he?) Sometimes, one's cultural project mandates the tracking down his own contingent "ambiguous" that was "written" long before.

So, who cuts the border? This question is not as mysterious as it might sound. It arose from a real circumstance around my house last summer when we wondered out loud who was responsible for cutting the border of grass on the edge of our property, simultaneous with the church's, south of the house. For several days the grass grew there, making neat quarantine in the midst of mowed lawn all around it. Small, local "wars" must start that way and massive, international ones, too, concerning the touchy question of borderlines. An instanteous household narrative lays hold here of a broader purpose: We might ask not only where the Sutpens belong in an American/US order of things, but by what finalities of various historico-cultural situations are we frozen forever in precisely defined portions of culture content?

The ways and means of negotiating borders and centers virtually constitute a new area studies in the liberal arts curriculum in the US today. (Professor Valerie Smith calls this ascendent discipline "doing" "otherness.")[31] This different economy of emphasis seems to offer an important critical tool for the chase of contradictions: Surmising from Foner's edition of Martí's writings, we guess that *La Revista Illustrada* might have been published in New York, as Martí spent several crucial years in the city and wrote many of his essays, including "Our America," on that site of contingencies. Even in the discursive play of the binary, Martí reflects in his biography certain elements of the ambiguous—at "home" in "exile," forging a revolutionary praxis in the very heartland of the "enemy" and its various culture-stuff. It would seem, then, that no "real" biotext (and/or culture text, for that matter) ever achieves much more than an unstable relationship to some abidingly imagined, or putative, centrality, even though one is surely loathe to admit *that* possibility. By the same token, "America/US" presents various faces to the world concerning, precisely, a contents in flux (and often enough, indeterminate). Landing on the smallest point, one might say, then, regarding the shifting position of the socionom, that there are days when her household cuts the border, then there are days when someone else's does.

The essays in this volume of writings, gathered from three separate panels of the 48th annual meeting of the English Institute, offer a cross-hemispheric inquiry into various aspects of culture work, e.g., the novel, the film, the autobiography, in sustained intertextual address to *comparative* American identities. Agitated to try and orchestrate "America" into a more exact cultural instance of naming, we read "America" here in a fairly broad concert of national and linguistic manifestations. Writing from various viewpoints on and in "Our America," the writers here are our colleagues across the United States and Canada in the university's departments of languages. It is noteworthy that the English Institute, in requesting this configuration of work, acknowledges its own borders with zones of French, Creole, Spanish, and American English. As the designated editor to this project by the Supervisory Committee of the organization, I should like to imagine that we have sketched here a "unified field theory" of culture studies in "Our America"/US. But such claim would be false, even as it was written down. The writings here do attempt, however, to stake out some of the salient questions that would be broached by such a project. In its weave of historical attitudes, conceptual inquiries, and authorial voices, *Comparative American Identities* situates the contemporary eye, once again, in the serendipities of "division," heterogeneity, lack of fixity, and other aspects of the repertorial, "piecing" thematic.

As VèVè Clark's "Developing Diaspora Literacy and *Marasa* Consciousness" here implies, New World culture always "dances" between the stationary points in the absolute abeyance of closure. Engaging in her essay a comparative study of three women writing—Maryse Condé, Paule Marshall, and Rigoberta Menchú—from the Francophone Antilles, the Anglophone emigrant Caribbean, and the Native Central/Hispanic Caribbean, respectively—Clark evolves an interpretive paradigm of "diaspora literacy" on the basis of the ritual twins—"*Marasa*"—in Haitian Vodoun ceremonies of initiation. Clark's myth-embedded theorization of textual relationships offers the Divine Twins—in the tradition of the gods Iwa and Legba—as a model that holds out new possibilities for consciousness beyond the binary, i.e, master/slave, patriarchy/matriarchy, domestic/maroon, rural/urban. When applied to Caribbean cultures, for example, "*marasa* Consciousness . . . ," Clark argues, "redirects our concerns beyond the syncretism of already existing binary codes, toward the identification and analysis of cultural and political practices resulting from these interactions." Clark's new model of diasporic literary studies renews our interest in the issues that gather about the Indigenist, the Négritude, and "New Negro" movements of the 1920s and 1930s. We might reread these chapters of diasporic literary history in light of Clark's "*marasa* Consciousness."

If Clark penetrates deep inside the ethnographic and religious texture of the indigenous cultural layer, then Sylvia Molloy, in the opening essay of the volume, "The Unquiet Self: Spanish American Autobiography and the Question of National Identity," turns, similarly, toward the socius to reflect on the ideological crisis embedded in "the very fabric of Spanish American self-figuration." The notion of the "autobiographical" is understood here along new lines of emphasis, as Molloy's work highlights the tension between "public" imperative and the "private" project that throws the text of Spanish American "self-life-writing" as a genre into stressful ambiguity. Closely reading into features of the biotexts of Domingo Faustino Sarmiento, Argentine writer-statesman of the nineteenth century, and José Vasconcelos, Mexican writer and statesman in the twentieth, Molloy articulates the "crisis of authority" that culminates in Spanish America, brought on by the influence of the Enlightenment and independence movements away from Spain. Molloy seeks to effect here two fundamental moves: "to allow the preoccupation with national identity (undeniably present in Spanish American self-writing) to reverberate in the text as an ever-renewed scene of crisis necessary to the rhetoric of self-figuration" and "to see it as a critical space, fraught with the anxiety of origins and representation, within which the self stages its presence and achieves ephemeral unity."

As questions raised by VèVè Clark and Sylvia Molloy instigate a larger national scene against which the particularities of texts might unfold, "nation" itself comes to be understood as a massive instance of slippage across discursive borders. Two other essays here resituate the "crisis" thematic in the US culture text by looking at some of the work of Toni Morrison—Kimberly W. Benston's "Re-Weaving the 'Ulysses Scene': Enchantment, Post-Oedipal Identity, and the Buried Text of Blackness in Toni Morrison's *Song of Solomon*" and Mae G. Henderson's "Toni Morrison's *Beloved:* Re-Membering the Body as Historical Text." Benston's "Re-Weaving," troping on some of the sub-textual intentions of this volume, offers a richly modulated reading performance that orchestrates a number of dissonant textualities onto the novel's common ground—Ralph Ellison's *Invisible Man,* Ishmael Reed's *Mumbo Jumbo,* and several classical literary points, including the *Iliad,* the *Odyssey,* the *Satyricon,* and the oedipal complex. Tracking a discursive economy that arises fundamentally in insurgence, Benston argues that *Song of Solomon* instantiates the circulation of meaning and "desiring-producing," despite the imposition of closure and repression: "The community . . . constantly (re)composes itself in the face of the Law's effort to arrest the disseminations of black text and community alike." Morrison not only "re-weaves" the 'Ulysses Scene' of wandering/male quest/male journey, but "performs" such "re-weaving" by having the male adventurer, "Milkman" Dead, follow in the footsteps of the novel's Pilate, the "unoriginated" and navel-less, who, with a missing "omphalos," turns the phallus off. Benston goes on to argue that Morrison concludes with the interpolation and performance of the novel's own embedded double that furnishes the work with a "mode of being which realizes . . . the implications of self-enactment." This African-American post-modernist "epic" thematizes its effort to execute a radical, dislocating translation of a "buried Text of blackness." There is repetition here, but as appropriation; revision, but as inscription and projection. As another "take" on that "cut," Benston concludes that Morrison's *Song of Solomon* exacts a "cut across the fabric of discourse."

Mae G. Henderson's profound meditation on Toni Morrison's *Beloved* considers "cut" in a different register, as the marks and scarrings on the captive female body offer up the "archaeological site or memory trace" that Sethe—Morrison's central figure in the novel—seeks to transform into a narrative, a history. A fictionalized history, or a historicized fiction, *Beloved* interrogates the interrelationship between *image* and *text*. Like the historian and the writer, the character of Morrison's work would give shape to the memories, would "extract a configuration from a cluster of images or diversity of events." The marks of Sethe's ordeal in slavery are linked, then, in the construction of a personal and historical discourse. Offering a displacement of studies in slavery as an empirically dominated field of discourse, Henderson reads an "interiority" into the captive situation, as we gain through her reading of the novel another dimension of slavery's *person*. "Rememory"/"memory" comes to rest at the place of the captive situation as Henderson seeks to transform the Freudian reference into a moment of larger cultural and historical point. Here "memory" dives deep into the repertoire of the collective biotext as at least two systems of discourse come to constitute it—what Henderson identifies here as the inscriptions of the "master code" of writing and what the "literary archaeological" project might provide, both by way of the writer's fictive construct and the fictive subject's assertion of narrative desire. Working with "memory" that overlaps the historical, the fictive subject and the writer (of history and fiction) must encounter "the absent," which, "(like the historical) is only the 'other' of the present—just as the repressed is only the 'other' of the conscious. To that extent both are with us always."

A transitional essay here between the American "nations" of discourse and a few of their moments and the libidinal economies of the "nations" and a few of their moments, Lauren Berlant's "National Brands/National Body: *Imitation of Life*" works the ground between filmic text and literary text to reposition in sight the "national body" and its implications for women-bodies and black-bodies. Looking at Fannie Hurst's 1930s novel, *Imitation of Life,* and John Stahl's and Douglas Sirk's separate cinematic treatments, from the 1930s and the 1950s respectively, Berlant offers an impressive shuttling movement between disparate narratives, from the US Constitution to filmic criticism. Theorizing the interarticulations between female identification and the "national public sphere," Berlant juxtaposes Nella Larsen's *Passing* with other texts here to inquire into the origins of the US political body. As the quintessentially disembodied and abstract US political agenda, the white, property-owning male of the eighteenth century "grows up" both with his nation's coming into being and its abstraction of "being/body" into the substitutions of "citizenship." In other words, "he" "traded" a "real" body for an "alibi," as the privilege is not extended to women and to the African-American male and female in the historical instance. *Embodiedness,* then, in this essay articulates nicely with the "national public sphere." Berlant instigates a "logic of this dialectic between abstraction . . . and the surplus corporeality of racialized and gendered subjects—its discursive expressions, its erotic effects, its implications for a nationalist politics of the body. . . ." This democratic congress of textual means works back to back with another look at film's import, in Michael Moon's "A Small Boy and Others: Sexual Disorientation in Henry James, Kenneth Anger, and David Lynch."

Engaging with libidinal economies in their public impress and articulations, Michael Moon and Michael Warner (in the volume's commissioned essay, "*Walden*'s Erotic Economy") trace the flows and circuitries of "desire-producing" in their interarticulations with the socius. Michael Moon examines a cluster of US culture texts produced over the last century: Henry James's "The Pupil," and two films—Kenneth Anger's *Scorpio Rising* and David Lynch's *Blue Velvet.* Moon argues that these transmedial works all foreground "the mimed and ventriloquized qualities of the performances of ritual induction and initiation into 'perverse circles,' " rather than mute the "mimetic secondariness" of the representations. Following Mikkel Borch-Jacobsen's lead and "trumping" on René Girard's theorizing a mimetic triangulation of desire, Moon provocatively argues that sexuality— coming in the plural—is *"disoriented"* by mimesis. The "disavowed knowledge" of "ostensibly minority pleasures like sadomasochism plays constantly around the margins of perception of the 'normal' majority. . . ." If we can claim, in truth, no autonomy of desire, even, then it is unlikely that we can maintain any "ordinary 'orienting' notions of which desires we are at home with and which ones we are not." Powerfully available images of ostensibly perverse desire "disorient" prevailing assumptions and bring "home to us the shapes of desires and fantasies that we ordinarily disavow as our own." Temporary dislocations from now-current "home" sexual orientations—homo/heterosexual—are staged in Moon's reading. He suggests that the reader/viewer is "disorientingly circulated through a number of different positions on the wheel of 'perversions.' " The outcome is that we are compelled to re-attend our thinking about the dependence of high and popular culture on the "disavowed knowledges" for their (the cultures') various representational programs.

I don't believe that the Thoreau and his *Walden* presented here have been quite seen before now. This reader, at least, maintained separate rooms for Thoreau and *any* "erotic," but Michael Warner argues persuasively enough that these divorced configurations of thought will never cleave again. Desiring a "transformed libido," a new body-erotics that would break through "*the* economy to reach a total economy of sensual pleasure," Thoreau becomes our transformed, ascetic puritan man, "revisioned" in classical New England time (for a long time, the only US time that mattered, when we recall Thomas Sutpen's unoccasioned temporalities and spaces). These close readings on a heretofore antiseptic *Walden* positions Thoreau's imperative—"Have no waste. Enjoy your waste"—in line with Weber's critique of capitalism and the Protestant ethic. Playing with, abrading, the ambiguities of "waste" and anal eroticism, Warner's reading of *Walden* conduces toward a capitalist theorization that effects "a complete collapse of economic critique with a critique of sensual self-relation." The politics of sexuality, as Warner points out in the opening moves of his argument, now locates on the national scene a contestatory arena around the issues of "pornography, reproductive freedoms, arts funding, and AIDS," etc. Such proliferation of conflict makes it necessary to rethink the pluralities of the sexual. As one of this particular national moment's "most obvious consequence has been that a consensual, normal sexuality can no longer be taken for granted," we are led, in turn, to reconsider the entire "history of sexuality" as we have inherited it in the United States. Linking his interpretive moves back to Herbert Marcuse's *Eros and Civilization,* Warner, for all intents and purposes, eroticizes—joyfully—one of the "major texts" of the US literary canon.

Bringing this volume to a close, Robert Schwartzwald's "Fear of Federasty: Québec's Inverted Fictions" will educate many of its readers in aspects of a history and culture of which we have been long ignorant. Poising Denys Arcand's film, *Le Déclin de l'empire américain* at the intersection of various social economies, Schwartzwald situates moments of the modern history of Québec in relationship to a various thematics—the impact of European colonization across Canada, the Québécois anti-colonial project, and the impact of imperialism, even as it impinges on the latter. Speaking of Arcand's film as "an 'updated' anti-colonial perspective" on Québec's "rapid process of modernization over the past three decades," Schwartzwald considers the film a take-off point to initiate "a presentation on the sexual anxiety embedded in even the most radical discourses of Québécois anti-colonialism." *Le Déclin* opens the way for Schwartzwald to explore these discourses because they are "exemplary of a rhetorical strategy that has been profoundly liberatory," but at the same time, these liberational discourses, "built on the very terrain of modernist preoccupations about subjectification, convey," nevertheless, "the tragic resiliency of homophobic tropes and their consequences." Schwartzwald cogently establishes the historical background of these contemporary events, arcing through points of Québec's "Quiet Revolution" of the 1960s and 1970s and its significant journal, *parti pris*. Adopting as its motto, "Laicism, Socialism, Independence," *parti pris* "telescoped" the specific vocation of Québec's "Quiet Revolution" and effected solidarity with the "anti-imperialist and anti-colonial struggles of the period," including national independence movements in Subsaharan Africa, revolution in Cuba, and the Civil Rights crusade in the United States. "*Parti pris* was not only a journal, but a publishing house that brought out novels, essays, and poetry that sought to 'demystify' Québec's colonial situation. . . ." This discourse put to use the anti-colonial stance poised in the works of Sartre, Fanon, Mémmi, Bercque, Guevarra, and Malcolm X, as it became distinguished as a literary protocol. Despite that, the "epistemological heritage" of "homophobic oppression" hangs on, "persists at the very heart of the anti-colonial imperative to think about subjectification outside the paradigm bequeathed by imperialism." With these opposing tendencies deployed, Schwartzwald firmly situates himself not only to offer a reading of the particular matters at hand, but to echo many of the other queries that have been set in motion here—how to live with, articulate, expose, that fabric of paradox and contradiction that seems to weave through and across the hemisphere.[32]

Attempting to read this dissonant "America"/US/Canada, *Comparative American Identities* is offered in the interest of a larger and unfinished project on one of our most persistent global intersections.

NOTES

1. *"Our America": Writings on Latin America and the Struggle for Cuban Independence* by José Martí, ed. with intro. and notes Philip S. Foner. Trans. Elinor Randall, Juan de Onís, and Roslyn Held Foner (New York: Monthly Review Press, 1977), p. 94. (All quotations from "Our America" come from this edition, subsequent page numbers noted in the text.)

2. Foner, *"Our America,"* Introduction, p. 17.

3. Roberto Marquez's "Soul of a Continent" (*American Quarterly*, 41, 4 [December, 1989], pp. 695–704]) provides a very informative review of the four English-language editions of Martí's writings. All of them translated by Elinor Randall, editorially marshalled by Philip Foner, and published by the Monthly Review Press, the other volumes are: *Inside the Monster: Writings on the United States and American Imperialism* (1977); *On Education: Articles on Educational Theory and Pedagogy, and Writings for Children from the "Age of Gold"* (1979); *On Art and Literature: Critical Writings* (1982).

4. Foner's tracking of Martí's inflections of "Our," "his," and "Other America" is pointedly read on pp. 24–25 of the Introduction to *"Our America."*

5. *The Philosophy of History* by Georg Wilhelm Friedrich Hegel, with intro. Professor C.J. Friedrich; Prefaces by Charles Hegel; trans. J. Sibree (New York: Dover Publications, Inc., 1956). (All quotations from Hegel come from this edition, subsequent page numbers noted in the text.)

6. Foner, *"Our America,"* Part III—"The Second War for Independence"—"Cuba Must Be Free of the United States As Well as Spain": A Letter to Gonzalo Quesada, New York, October 29, 1889; p. 244.

7. Marquez's "Soul of a Continent" (Cf. n.3) offers a reading on Martí's life and work that would surprise any facile conclusions concerning certain of the activist's imagined loyalties. Marquez notes that Martí's attitudes about "the concept of class warfare" and "working class violence" would suggest that he did not "believe that any intrinsic or essential conflict of interest divided classes" (p. 701).

In the Preface to *Caliban and Other Essays,* Roberto Fernández Retamar engages our deepest complexities of imagination about a figure who lived 15 years (1880-1895) in the United States, yet forged the second of Cuba's revolutionary struggles in New York City. As a ring on the thematics of paradoxical change, Martí, for Retamar, became "not only the most advanced of our thinkers," because of the context out of which his Cuban struggle was solidified, "but a North American radical as well." Retamar goes on: "Although, on the one hand, he criticized with ever-greater lucidity the ills of North American society and the danger that one sector of it represented for Latin America and the Caribbean . . . on the other hand (as Juan Ramón Jiménez stated, thinking of his great essay on Whitman from 1887), 'Spain and Spanish America owe him, in large part, our poetic access to the United States' " (trans. Edward Baker; foreword by Fredric Jameson [Minneapolis: University of Minnesota Press, 1989], xv-xvi]).

8. Peter Hulme, "Hurricanes in the Caribbees: The Constitution of the Discourse of English Colonialism," in *1642: Literature and Power in the Seventeenth Century,* ed. Francis Barker, et. al. Essex Sociology of Literature Conference. Proceedings of the Essex Conference on the Sociology of Literature, July, 1980. (University of Essex, 1981), pp. 55-56. (All quotations from Hulme come from this edition, subsequent page numbers noted in the text.)

9. Roberto Fernández Retamar, "Caliban": Notes Toward a Discussion of Culture in Our America," in *The Massachusetts Review* (special issue), ed. Roberto Marquez; Vol. XV, Nos. 1/2 (Winter-Spring, 1974), pp. 7-72. Trans. Lynn Garafola, David Arthur McMurray, and Roberto Marquez.

This celebrated essay originally appeared in *Casa de las Americas* (Havana), 68(September-October, 1971).

Retamar's "Caliban" engendered a catalytic moment for a "little magazine" project in "New World Thought and Writing" that surfaced in Amherst, Massachusetts in the mid-1970s. Conceived of by Roberto Marquez, the journal was a semi-annual publication, named "Caliban," with a trial run in the special edition of the *Massachusetts Review* that Mr. Marquez edited. David Arthur McMurray and Hortense Spillers assisted Marquez in this bilingual editorial work that featured short stories, poems, essays, and graphics by writers and artists from the Caribbean, Latin America, and the Unites States. The inaugural issue of "Caliban" carried work by, among others, Edward Braithwaite, Jan Carew, Mario Benedetti, and Andrew Salkey (Vol. 1, No. 1[Fall-Winter, 1975]).

10. Retamar refers here to a repertory of significant texts that include Fanon's *Black Skin, White Masks;* Cesaire's *Discourse on Colonialism,* and Mannoni's *Psychology of Colonialism* ("Caliban," pp. 17-21).

11. Cited by Retamar from Columbus's Navigation Log Books ("Caliban," p. 11).

12. Ivan Van Sertima, *The African Presence in Ancient America: They Came Before Columbus* (New York: Random House, 1976).

13. This term offers a slight variation on "situation-specificity" which Fredric Jameson coins in his Foreword to *Caliban and Other Essays* (Cf. n. 7). In a discussion of Retamar's place in the mapping of culture work, Jameson speaks of a "situation-specificity" "for a positioning that always remains concrete and reflexive." Intervening on the "binary and invidious slogan of *difference*" (emphasis Jameson), "situation-specificity" seems to get at concisely what it evokes.

14. In reviewing the career of his essay, "Caliban," Retamar points to certain uses of the sixties ("Both decades and centuries can have their uses"). He situates here the political context in which the essay was produced and cites *The 60s Without Apology* as a "noteworthy book" (Sohnya Sayres, Anders Stephenson, et. al., eds. [Minneapolis: University of Minnesota Press, 1984]). Retamar's reading of the background for his essay appears in "Caliban Revisited" in *Caliban and Other Essays,* p. 47.

15. I borrow freely here from *Fruits of Merchant Capital: Slavery and Bourgeois Property*

in the Rise and Expansion of Capitalism by Elizabeth Fox-Genovese and Eugene D. Genovese (New York: Oxford University Press, 1983).

16. Abena Busia's illuminating discussion of the tropes and complexities of "silence" that loudly speak female "unrepresentability" in the modernist text about "Colonialism" is found in: "Silencing Sycorax: On African Colonial Discourse and the Unvoiced Female," *Culture Critique* (Summer, 1990). I am grateful to Professor Busia for sharing this text with me prior to its publication.

17. In a fascinating study of Aristotelian catharsis, John McCumber suggests a relocation of the concept—," . . . one which places it not in the masculine framework of the doctor's office or the equally masculine sanctuaries of Eleusis but in the infinitely more subtle and profound terrain of woman's body" ("Aristotelian Catharsis and the Purgation of Woman," *Diacritics*, 18, 4 [Winter, 1988], p. 58). The quotation in the text is found on p. 55.

18. *Literary Fat Ladies: Rhetoric, Gender, Property* (London: Methuen, 1987), p. 140. (All quotations from Parker come from this edition, subsequent page numbers noted in the text.) My personal thanks to Professor Parker for this wonderful gift.

19. A close examination of the history of dramatic representations of the figure "Caliban" is provided by Virginia Mason Vaughan, " 'Something Rich and Strange': Caliban's Theatrical Metamorphosis," *Shakespeare Quarterly*, 36, 4(1985); the Folger Shakespeare Library.

20. *The Sound and the Fury* pp. 390–405 (New York: Vintage Books, 1956). This edition of Faulkner's novel carries the genealogical chart of familial traits that identifies all Compson-connected characters, including house servants. The more recent Norton Edition of the work submits this material to the appendix: Ed. David Minter (New York: W.W. Norton, 1987). Professor Minter points out that the "Appendix/Compson" was not composed until the fall of 1945 for Malcolm Cowley's *Portable Faulkner* (p. 224). Even though not a part of the novel, *per se,* this trace, inaugurated in the invocation of "Ikemotubbe," hounds the reader from beginning to end. It appears to pose the same kind of problematics of reading that Eliot's "appendix" to "The Wasteland" generates.

21. *Absalom, Absalom!* (New York: The Modern Library, 1951). (All quotations from the novel come from this edition, page numbers noted in the text.)

22. This phrase is "lifted" from David Krause's close reading of aspects of *Absalom, Absalom!* in his citation of Denis Donaghue's *Ferocious Alphabets,* (London: Faber, 1981), in Krause, "Reading Bon's Letter and Faulkner's *Absalom, Absalom!, PMLA,* 99, 2 (March, 1984), pp. 225–41.

23. Krause, following Donaghue, distinguishes "epireading" and "graphireading": " 'Epireading is reading which proceeds under [the privileging of 'action and speech'], transposing the written words on the page into a somehow corresponding human situation of human persons, voices, characters, conflicts, conciliations.' " "Graphireading," on the other hand, " 'deals with writing as such and does not think of it as transcribing an event properly construed as vocal and audible' " (p. 226). One might think of "epireading," given Krause's translation, as "speech on the human tongue," as Hugh Kenner once described it—without recourse to the dictionary, etc. But the deconstructionist project has rendered such distinction, perhaps, less easy to formulate. It seems to me that Faulkner's canon straddles this debate in quite astonishing ways, inasmuch as his syntactical protocol seems dominated by the anxieties of revision and a severe oppositional movement to the uncertainties of "improvised" speech. More exactly, Faulkner's narrative devices appear to generate speaking-as-repentence, in which case, whatever one might speak at one moment becomes, on second thought, inadequate, as the latter is not effaced so much as "improved" upon and "essayed" over and over again. This seems the dominant semiotic burden of *Absalom, Absalom!* as characters "listen" to themselves talk and appear to revise and correct, aggrandize and elaborate in the moment.

24. Current critical inquiry generates quite appropriately, I think, regard for "race,"

gender," "class," "sex/sexuality," as key terms of our social fabulations. But like my colleague, Professor Amy Lang, I weary (somewhat) of the 3–4 step language device that fractures the fabulous social subject into a few Big Moments. This problem is partially addressed in "Sieving the Matriheritage of the Sociotext," by Myriam Diaz-Diocaretz in *The Difference Within: Feminism and Critical Theory,* eds. Elizabeth Meese and Alice Parker (Amsterdam: John Benjamins Publishing Company, 1989), pp. 115–49. I am suggesting "socionom" as a shorthand for those Big and small "moments" of the biotext that are both proclaimed and ignored, that loudly intrude, or slip away into the margins of the evasive. One is "also . . ." as the real and historical situation dictates, as "choice" seems available, and in connection with a complicated repertoire of means that Barbara Christian has identified under the head of "natal community."

25. Portions of Faulkner's letter to Malcolm Cowley, in answer to a question about *Absalom, Absalom!* have become a heady piece of Faulkneriana. Cited in Krause: " 'I am telling the same story over and over, which is myself and the world. Tom Wolfe was trying to say everything, get everything, the world plus "I" or filtered through "I" or the effort of "I" to embrace the world in which he was born and walked a little while and then lay down again, into one volume. I am trying to go a step further . . . I am trying to say it all in one sentence, between one Cap and one period . . . I am still trying to put all mankind's history into one sentence' " (Cf. n. 22, p. 240).

26. *The Black Jacobins: Toussaint L'Ouverture and the San Domingo Revolution* (New York: Vintage Books, 1963); from Preface to the First Edition[ix].

27. Like the "Appendix/Compson," the Modern Library edition of *Absalom, Absalom!* carries sketches of the Faulkner character. We learn from this source, for instance, that "Shreve McCannon" (Shrevlin McCannon) is a citizen of Edmonton, Alberta, Canada. This "Chronology" begins with Thomas Sutpen, "born in West Virginia mountains. Poor whites of Scottish-English stock."

28. The concept of "paralogism" is discussed in Fredric Jameson's Foreword to *The Postmodern Condition: A Report On Knowledge* (Minneapolis: University of Minnesota Press, 1984). Theory and History of Literature, 10. Trans. Geoff Bennington and Brian Massumi; xix.

29. *Pentimento: A Book of Portraits,* (Boston: Little, Brown, 1973). The "pentimento" seems to be a slightly different concept from the "palimpsest," exquisitely configured as a background idea in *Civilization and Its Discontents.* The mind as a "Rome" of impressions shows depth and layering, or dimensionality, in contrast to the surface of the "pentimento."

30. This term is taken from Sartre's *Being and Nothingness: An Essay on Phenomenological Ontology,* trans. with intro. Hazel Barnes. From "hodos," Sartre's use of "hodological" concerns one's "everyday pragmatic level of existence." We form a "hodological" map of the world "in which pathways are traced to and among objects in accordance with the potentialities and resistances of objects in the world" (from the Translator's Introduction, xiv). The reader will also recognize symptoms of Sutpen's "stroke" from the gaze as elements adopted from Sartre's "Look," Part Three, Chapter One, IV. (New York: Philosophical Library, 1956). I am suggesting here that "mirrors," like maps, constitute the "hodological" equipment—the way by which we establish who/where we think we are.

31. Second Annual Retreat in African-American Literature and Culture, "Sites of Colonialism." Convened by Professor Houston Baker and the Center for the Study of Black Literature and Culture at the University of Pennsylvania; March 15–17, 1990.

32. One of the most persuasive interventions on the traditional mythos of the "American" scene is provided in the second chapter of Houston Baker's *Blues, Ideology, and Afro-American Literature,* "Figurations for a New American Literary History: Archaeology, Ideology, and Afro-American Discourse" (Chicago: University of Chicago Press, 1984.)

2.
The Unquiet Self: Spanish American Autobiography and the Question of National Identity

SYLVIA MOLLOY

In speaking of Spanish American autobiography, it is not my intention here to tackle the paradox on which every autobiographical act is founded: how to narrate the "story" of a first person whose existence can only be confirmed in the present of its enunciation. While not ignoring the linguistic and philosophical quandary autobiographical writing necessarily poses, I choose here to address issues that are basically cultural and historical in nature; not so much to find out what the "I" is trying to do when it writes "I" but, more modestly, what are the fabulations to which self-writing resorts within a given space, a given time, and a given language, and what do those fabulations tell us about the literature and culture to which they belong.

Autobiography in Spanish America has suffered from more than a measure of neglect on the part of critics. This is not because, as has so frequently and thoughtlessly been asserted, autobiography is unusual, nor is it because Hispanic writers, due to elusive "national" characteristics, are not prone to record their lives on paper. The perceived scarcity of life stories written in the first person is less a matter of quantity than a matter of attitude: autobiography is as much a way of reading as it is a way of writing. Thus, one might say that, whereas there are and have been a good many autobiographies written in Spanish America, they have not always been read autobiographically: filtered through the dominant discourse of the day, they have been hailed either as history or fiction, and rarely considered as occupying a space of their own. This reticence is in itself significant. For the reader, in denying the autobiographical text the reception it merits, generically speaking, is only contributing to a disquiet that the text in itself harbors, at times well hidden from view, at others, more manifest. The anxiety of being translates itself into an anxiety of being in (for) literature.

In contrast with other autobiographical traditions, Spanish American autobiographies are unstable texts. They not infrequently meet with derision: Sarmiento, writing his autobiography in nineteenth-century Argentina, is denounced for engaging in "an exercise in vacuity," ridiculed as "a citizen who publishes two hundred pages and a genealogical tree to relate his life, that of all the members of his extended family and even that of his servants.[1] And, in twentieth-century Mexico, Vasconcelos's *Ulises criollo* is maliciously compared to the syrupy ballads of Agustín Lara. The difficulty with which self-writing asserts itself as a viable form turns the autobiographer into an inordinately wary writer, conscious of his or her own vulnerability and of the reader's potential disapproval. Self-writing is a form of exposure that begs for understanding, even more, for forgiveness. *Que me perdonen la vida:* the Spanish idiom used by the Argentine Victoria Ocampo to summarize her plea to her readers may be extended to many Spanish American autobiographers. Not only should the phrase be read literally—that the autobiographer's life be forgiven, that it be read sympathetically—but in its other, more drastic sense: that the autobiographer's life be spared, that his or her execution be stayed. The notion of transgression evoked by the phrase and the power it gives the reader whose forgiveness it solicits are significant. There is often a sense that what one is doing may be wrong, not morally but tactically; a sense that, given the insecure status of the genre, one may be going about self-writing in the wrong way. Spanish American autobiographers are most efficient self-censors who, within their life stories, map out silences that point to the untellable—and often tell what they feel cannot be told autobiographically in other, less compromising texts. Severo Sarduy's humorous contention that the "I" in Spanish America is in the closet, choosing forms other than the autobiographical to manifest itself, seems particularly apt.

The neglect or the misunderstanding that has greeted autobiographical writing in Spanish America make it, not surprisingly, an ideal field of study. As it is unfettered by strict classification, canonical validation, or cliché-ridden criticism, it is free to reveal its ambiguities, its contradictions, the hybrid nature of its composition. In addition, from the ill-defined, marginal position to which it has been relegated, Spanish American autobiography has a great deal to say about what is not itself. It is an invaluable tool with which to probe into the other, more visible, sanctioned forms of Spanish American literature. As that which has been repressed, denied, forgotten, autobiography comes back to haunt and to illuminate in a new light what is already there.

I have chosen to limit my comments to the nineteenth and twentieth centuries, chiefly though not exclusively for generic reasons. First-person narratives, it is true, abound in Colonial literature. Chronicles of discovery and conquest, especially those involving some measure of self-awareness on the part of their authors, might be seen as distant forms of the autobiographical mode. In the same way, self-reflexive documents (such as, for example, Juana Inés de la Cruz's *Respuesta* to the Bishop of Puebla, in the late seventeenth century, or confessional depositions before the tribunals of the Inquisition), given the defensive strategies they adopt and the vindication of self they propound, may be considered, and indeed have been considered, too, autobiographies. While not denying the preoccupation with self at work in these texts, I find that their primary concern is not autobiography—even if the latter may be one of their unwitting achievements. Furthermore, the circumstances in which these texts were written preclude, or at least considerably modify, the textual self-confrontation that marks autobiographical writing. The fact that the above mentioned texts are conceived primarily for a privileged reader (the King of Spain, the Bishop of Puebla, an ecclesiastical tribunal) who has power over writer and text; the fact, too, that the narration of self is more a means to achieve a goal than the goal itself; the fact, finally, that there is rarely a crisis of identity in this self-writing would make these texts, in my view, only tangentially autobiographical.

At the same time, of course, I am loath to declare peremptorily that Spanish American autobiography "begins" in the early nineteenth century, as I would hope to avoid the notion that autobiography in Spanish America is a form progressing from nineteenth-century clumsy hybridization to twentieth-century aesthetic perfection. This evolutionary view of literature, which has Spanish America always "catching up" with its purported European models (when the whole point of Spanish American literature is to deviate from those models), seems particularly inadequate in this case.[2] If I choose to look at Spanish American autobiography from the early nineteenth century onward, it is because I am especially interested in the peculiar awareness of self and culture brought about by ideological crisis, and because I am curious of the way in which that crisis is reflected, better yet, incorporated, into the very fabric of Spanish American self-figuration.

The crisis I speak of, brought on by the influence of the European Enlightenment and by the independence from Spain that was to mark its culmination in Spanish America, is, of course, a crisis of authority. It is no coincidence that questions about the validity of self-writing, or reflections on the goals of autobiography, should appear in Spanish America at the moment a received order is being replaced by a produced order; that it should appear, in addition, within the context of the more general debates over national identities and national cultures, debates in which relations to Spanish, and more generally European, canonical authority are forcibly renegotiated. If, in the case of Colonial writers, self-writing was legitimated by an institutional Peninsular Other for whom one wrote (the Crown, the Church), in the case of the post-Colonial autobiographer, those institutions no longer accomplish their validating function. Indeed, the very notion of institution, as it had been understood, comes under serious questioning. If one no longer writes oneself down for King or Church, for whom, then, does one write? For Truth? For Posterity? For History—the discipline that so many nineteenth-century autobiographers the world over will turn into their validating source? To this crisis of authority corresponds a self in crisis, writing in an interlocutory void. The predicament of the nineteenth-century Spanish American autobiographer, the very tentative figurations of self that he or she engages in, the constant search for reader recognition, give rise to a pattern of tantalizing ambiguities that always allude to (but never openly ask) the same question: For whom am I "I," or rather, for whom do I write "I"? The vacillation between public persona and private self, between communal representativeness and individual soul-searching, between honor and vanity, between self and country, between lyrical evocation or factual annotation of the past are but a few manifestations of the hesitancy that marked (and even now may mark) Spanish American self-writing.

While interested in the connections between self-figuration, national identity, and cultural self-awareness, and in the representational patterns that such connections, or contaminations, give rise to, I do not wish to align myself with the many attempts, within and without Spanish America, to elucidate, define—invent, finally—a "national" Spanish American essence of which literature would be an unmediated manifestation. Nor do I entirely share the view that all Spanish American texts, however "private" in appearance, are really, and invariably, national allegories and should specifically be read as such.[3] This view might not seem inappropriate at first glance to consider certain Spanish American autobiographers intent on merging self and nation into one, memorable *corpus gloriosus*. It supposes, however, unchanging modes of textual production in Spanish America, ignores the fact that, as politics diversifies its discursive practices, so does literature—and, indeed, so does autobiography. The "I" speaks from more than one place. Reliance on either view—the text as national essence or as national allegory—cuts critical reflection short instead of opening it up and channels the text into one, exclusive reading. What seems more profitable, instead, is to allow the preoccupation with national identity (undeniably present in Spanish American self-writing) to reverberate in the text as an ever-renewed scene of crisis necessary to the rhetoric of self-figuration; to see it as a critical space, fraught with the anxiety of origins and representation, within which the self stages its presence and achieves ephemeral unity.

I shall consider two examples to make myself clear: in the nineteenth century, Domingo Faustino Sarmiento, probably the most forceful Argentine writer of the period, the prototype of the writer statesman so frequent then (and frequent even now) amongst Latin American intellectuals, who wrote two autobiographies, *Mi defensa* (1843) and *Recuerdos de provincia* (1850); in the twentieth century, the Mexican José Vasconcelos, definitely less at ease in the same dual role—writer and statesman—who wrote his four-volume autobiography in the 1930s.

Sarmiento is one of those early autobiographers who had trouble validating his exercise. A self-taught intellectual, a brilliant essayist, a questionable historian, he claims the same public utility for his self-writing as for his purportedly well-documented biographies. His *Recuerdos de provincia* begins, for example, with an eloquent evocation of Sarmiento's native province, San Juan, laid culturally bare by Spain's slothful colonial system. San Juan—by extension, Argentina—offers the autobiographer-turned-archivist only "frail and deteriorated historical holdings." There are three palm trees that, since "there is no written history, serve as reminders, as monuments to memorable events (p. 42); there is a door to a Jesuit monastery from where the embossed lead lettering has been gouged out; finally, there is a file, labeled as containing the history of San Juan, but emptied of its contents. The message is clear: San Juan is vacant, a barren place where there are no letters, where history has become mute.[4] A worthy disciple of Michelet, Sarmiento takes it upon himself to make the silent speak. Resorting to individual recollection is useful and necessary *because* the file is empty and the palm trees mute. Memory, his own personal memory becomes a valid source for history, of which autobiography, in his view, is a form. It is not so much a privilege of the solipsistic self as it is a civic duty: one remembers so that a communal past not be lost.

This clear parallel established between individual *bios* and a provincial, would-be national *ethos* is not devoid of epic overtones: Sarmiento harbors an heroic image of himself which he would gladly pass on to his readers. Yet the bond he stresses is of an even more intimate nature. It is not merely that Sarmiento pictures himself as an exemplary Argentine: he *is* Argentina, forming with his country one, inseparable body. "I was born in 1811, the ninth month after the 25th of May" (p. 160), he writes, unambiguously establishing the genetic link, having the moment of his gestation coincide with the date of his country's first move to secede from Spain. If San Juan— a *tabula rasa* awaiting signs—is a synecdoche of the country, so is Sarmiento, as subject of his autobiography: he will *be* the writing on the blank page.

This national incarnation informs personal memory and imposes strictures on the way it functions within the text. If some form of preconception invariably governs the unfolding of autobiography—that preconception that Gide calls "un être factice préféré"[5]—dictating the rearrangement of the past, then one may say that Sarmiento's factitious being is the very country his text contributes to found. This national factitious being, however, has more than one face. A quick look at *Mi defensa,* the autobiographical piece antedating *Recuerdos* by seven years and written very early in Sarmiento's career, reveals that the figuration guiding the text is, not surprisingly, that of the self-made and self-taught hero. If autobiographical writing may be seen as an oscillation between dandyism and seduction—the desire to inscribe the unique on the one hand while, on the other, the need to attract others to the autobiographical persona—then *Mi defensa* clearly stresses the first mode (while *Recuerdos* concentrates on the second). In *Mi defensa,* Sarmiento forgoes all reference to lineage (the word *solo* recurs obsessively in the text), devotes the briefest of presentations to his immediate family and then turns the focus on himself as the self-taught head of the household—a precocious and watchful *pater familias* from age fifteen on. This image of the self-made citizen is clearly one that Sarmiento wishes to foster. Indeed, it will increasingly pattern his self-writing, as one of the choice figurations that represent his bond with Argentina: Sarmiento, father of the country. The only lineage that is mentioned in this first autobiography is the one privileging cultural inheritance, connecting Sarmiento to the great chain of books and associating him, not unproblematically, to a European (mostly French) canon. "Books are the memory of mankind, covering thousands of years. With a book in our hand, we remember . . ."[6] It is indeed with a book in his hand—Villemain, Tocqueville, Guizot, Pierre Leroux (and also Benjamin Franklin)—that Sarmiento will write himself and write his country. Reading, writing, translating are for him modernizing gestures and extensions of self: they will allow him to "re-letter" the blurry, illegible, or blank pages of the colony Spain left behind.

Seven years later, Sarmiento rewrites his autobiography. In the new text, *Recuerdos de provincia,* the factitious national being that triggers his self-writing has changed; nonetheless, it is once more determined by what Martínez Estrada has so aptly called Sarmiento's "domestic sensibility,"[7] that is, the recasting of family romance in an ideological, precisely political mold. Abandoning the role of precocious family leader and solitary hero, he now beholds himself not alone but *en famille,* a son many times over, heir to a distinguished patriotic lineage and the product of a community. As a result, these new recollections, calculatingly dedicated "to my compatriots only,"[8] emphasize family ties instead of short-circuiting them. In addition, far from limiting himself to the immediate family group, Sarmiento chooses to create an extended family out of prestigious figures from his native San Juan who came before him. Where he once, in *Mi defensa,* had needed to stand alone, he now must appear accompanied.

This genealogical necessity responds to a conscious, ideological posture and to a new political plan.[9] The bellicose *Mi defensa,* written by a quite young Sarmiento, needed to sell the image of a relative newcomer to the national scene: thus the arrogant figuration of the maverick intellectual reading French books to which few had access, of the self-styled young father who, singlehandedly, could bring order to a chaotic family and, by extension, to his country. Seven years later, it is a more secure Sarmiento who writes *Recuerdos,* one who allows himself to widen his scope, well aware that even when he speaks of others he speaks of himself; well aware, too, that while the image of the lonely, self-made intellectual with a privileged connection to European Enlightenment might have helped project him onto the national scene, a less "original" figuration, as member of a family and, by extension, of a cultural community, might serve him better to achieve his new goal, that of presidential candidate.

The national icon that Sarmiento creates in his combined autobiographies—father of the country, son of the country, the country itself, the country's necessary leader—was extremely effective. Generations of Spanish American readers, falling prey to the illusion of referentiality which had them confuse the historical man with his self-serving strategies, were unable (or unwilling) to read him against the grain: they read him—both admirers and critics—precisely as he intended to be read. Not only effective for Sarmiento, the national icon became authoritative: it was a model that would prove remarkably enduring in Spanish America. If Sarmiento did not invent the conflation between man and country for the purpose of self-portraiture, he gave it a breadth and a power of conviction unmatched till then in Spanish America. He also carried the strategy to its limits, dangerously hovering on the borders of self-parody. One wonders if Sarmiento was aware of this. One wonders if he who so confidently asserted in the opening pages of *Recuerdos de provincia* that he was "bequeathing a statue to posterity" thought back to that phrase when, in the last letter he wrote before his death, he stated: "I am just an empty, battered old can." One might see Sarmiento's legacy, as autobiographer, as that hollow can: a mold, a form, masking a representational void. This does not mean that the mold was not used but precisely the contrary. On reading Benjamin Franklin's autobiography, Sarmiento states he wished to be "a little Franklin"—*un Franklincito.* By extension, many admiring readers of Sarmiento strived to be "little Sarmientos." José Vasconcelos, writer and politician in the Mexico of the 1930s, is perhaps the most notorious of these followers, adapting Sarmineto's strategy to the needs of a fascinating new masquerade.

Vasconcelos writes his autobiography in the 1930s, at the end of a period in his life that includes remarkable literary and political achievements: as one of the principal ideologues of the Mexican revolution's cultural program, he has preformed brilliantly as Minister of Education in the Obregón administration in the twenties; as essayist and self-styled philosopher, he has already published two decisive and quite controversial books, *Indología* and *La raza cósmica*. That period of success ends, however, in resounding defeat: a presidential candidate in 1929, Vasconcelos loses a (probably fraudulent) election, and goes into exile to write an autobiography that is very much a product of the Mexican Revolution. Interweaving personal history with the history of Mexico in the first two decades of this century, the four volumes read indeed like a huge mural, much like the ones Vasconcelos himself, as Minister of Education, commissioned from Diego Rivera and others. A mural that includes him as narrator, participant, and even protagonist, it does not, however, dwarf him. Rather (since I have resorted to the perhaps facile but tempting metaphor), in the same way that he turns Mexico into a mural,[10] Vasconcelos "muralizes" himself, presenting a gigantic self-image that overshadows that of Mexico while feeding off it, an image that Vasconcelos, through a sleight of hand, would transform into Mexico itself.[11]

There are unmistakable echoes of Sarmiento in Vasconcelos's representation. Yet Sarmiento had used the willful conflation of self and country projected in *Recuerdos de provincia* prophetically, not only to present the man he had been but the politician he would be, if given a chance. In the context of the Argentine nineteenth century, the image fully retained its efficacy. Vasconcelos, instead, uses the image in his *Ulises criollo* retrogressively (and, it could be argued, anachronistically) to voice a lament. He presents an image not of a man who might one day be president but of one who, had his country been wiser, would have attained that office. This was, in fact, the image that he had presented in 1929 when running as a presidential candidate against the *caudillo* Calles, but it had proved unconvincing. To quote Carlos Monsiváis:

It was History as representation: Calles would be Caliban, Doña Bárbara, the ferociousness and primitive nature of an unredeemed people; Vasconcelos would be Ariel, Santos Luzardo, the culture of the West reduced to a mirage: the Spirit would defeat the Sword.[12]

But the Spirit did not and Vasconcelos lost the election. The exaggerated national icon that had failed in the political arena would become, in the autobiographical project, a compensatory spectacle of monumental proportions. *Ulises criollo* (the title, *Creole Ulysses,* speaks for itself) and the other three volumes were an attempt to infuse a dead rhetoric of messianic nationalism with new life, recycling it on the level of personal myth. The opportunity of reconstruction that Vasconcelos felt had been denied him in the presidential elections would now constitute the basis for his self-writing: what had not worked for Mexico would work for him. And curiously enough, for all the shrillness of the representation he left behind, work, in an unexpected way, it did.

Vasconcelos does not claim, or at least does not primarily claim, as did Sarmiento, historical status for his autobiography. When referring to the conception of *Ulises criollo,* he describes it as "a novel, and what better novel than one dealing with one's own adventures and passions?"[13] Now it is obvious that *Ulises criollo* is not a novel, although critics, hesitating to accept it as an autobiography, have, on occasion, characterized it as such. (And then have promptly dismissed it as a "bad novel.") Vasconcelos's use of the word *novel,* although in appearance inadequate, is not, I venture, frivolous. It seems to indicate not so much what the book is as what the book is not. In an exact reversal of Sarmiento, who had written of his autobiography "this is not a novel," thereby implying that it was history, Vasconcelos implies that *Ulises Criollo* is not exactly history by calling it, precisely, a novel. But if it then turns out not to be a novel, what is it? The foreword to the first edition indicates that Vasconcelos is conscious of the work's hybrid nature. On the one hand, he points to the book's autobiographical, even confessional, nature: "It contains the experience of one man and it aspires not to exemplarity but to awareness" (I, p. 8). On the other, however, when explaining the choice of the title, *Ulises criollo,* he proposes a less personal reading and points to loftier designs:

> The name that I have given the whole work [i.e. *Ulises criollo*] is explained by its contents. A destiny that rises like a comet, suddenly radiates, then goes out during long periods of darkness, and the turbulent atmosphere of present-day Mexico, justify the analogy with the *Odyssey.* As for the adjective *criollo,* I chose it as a symbol of the defeated ideal of our country. . . . *Criollismo,* that is to say, a culture of a Hispanic type, in its ardent, unequal struggle against a spurious *Indigenismo* and an "Anglo-Saxonism" disguised in the trappings *[que se disfraza con el colorete]* of the most deficient civilization known to history: these are the elements that have battled in the soul of this *Mexican Ulysses* as in that of each of his compatriots. (I, p. 8)

There appears to be some contradiction here. Is this autobiography about personal awareness and the individual man, or is it about exemplarity and a mythical hero embodying virtues his national community holds dear? It is, in a way, both. Vasconcelos, in the twentieth century (unlike Sarmiento, in the nineteenth), works with two diverging, even conflicting modes of self-representation. In fact, one could argue that there are two narrative lines, two different stories being told, in each of the books composing this autobiography. For example the first book, *Ulises criollo,* is the story of the hero's quest for national identity, more precisely for a national revolutionary identity. But it is no less the story of another quest, sexual in nature, conducted through an impassioned, at times disturbingly intimate bonding with the mother—a bonding few critics of Vasconcelos, too caught up in the national figuration, are willing to discuss.[14]

Vasconcelos's story of sexual discovery (an obsessive narrative that clearly *needs* to be told) runs counter to, or at least seriously interferes with, the model inherited from Sarmiento. The latter form of national self-figuration produced economical, contained texts and had little use for expenditure and dispersion, sexual or otherwise. *Ulises criollo* resolves that difference in a striking manner, combining the national and the sexual in the complex figure of the mother. That figure is, quite literally, an erotic and ideological matrix. The first recollection in *Ulises criollo,* at the beginning of the text, registers, in fact, this maternal duplicity where the physical and the political become one. Brought up in the frontier town of Piedras Negras, in constant fear of real invasion by the Apaches and ideological invasion by the "Yankees," Vasconcelos remembers himself in symbiosis with a protective mother who holds him tightly—"I felt myself a physical extension of her, a section barely severed from a warm, protecting, nearly divine presence" (I, p. 9)— and who reads to him from a book she holds on her lap. The mother's body, as object of desire, will thereon structure one narrative line of *Ulises criollo;* the mother's book, purveying culture, instructing the son in the Catholic faith and in "things of my nation," giving him a highly idealized (and notoriously biased) version of Mexico, structures the other narrative line. To privilege one story over the other—say, to read the bombastic "national" Vasconcelos as one might the monolithic "national" Sarmiento, to the detriment of a "sexual" Vasconcelos—would definitely impoverish this autobiography. What is of interest here, precisely, is to read the two combined; to see how Mexico and the sense of the national becomes eroticized in this autobiography through the figure of the mother and, conversely, to see how that very same mother, a guardian of Mexican spirituality mutes sexual promiscuity by projecting the erotic onto a higher plane. The mother allows for the union of what one could loosely term the lyric "I" in Vasconcelos (in this case, the child in love with his mother), and his epic "I" (the hero who, through that mother, will *be* Mexico).

Vasconcelos's double image was greeted by contradictory reviews and in general did not go over well. The candor, the audacity even, with which sexuality was referred to, coupled with the heroic national self-image, made, in the eyes of most readers, for an unstable combination. The autobiography had, above all, a *succès de scandale*. Perhaps because of those mixed reactions and doubtlessly because of the sharp turn to the right in his personal politics, Vasconcelos (like Sarmiento before him) undertook a new self-representation. He did not, however, as had his precursor, write a second autobiography but instead resorted to scissors and paste. In 1958, at the peak of his ultramontane pamphleteering, Vasconcelos expurgated his book. Explicitly courting an entirely new readership, the "I" of this new *Ulises criollo* recomposes himself through erasure, imposes a new outlook—a new recollective pattern, that is, retrospectively, a new memory—on the material that had formerly constituted the very substance of his past: "not a few of the events and scenes I had to relate then arouse a strong repulsion in me now. However, since it is no longer possible to destroy what was, at least the possibility remains to erase what is unworthy of recollection."[15]

In name of the new image of himself and of the new readers he wishes to reach, Vasconcelos corrects the past. Proposing, retroactively, the image of autobiographer as penitent, he proceeds to savage his life story with a censor's zeal.[16] Specific references to sexual encounters are suppressed, the more salient aspects of Vasconcelos's boastful promiscuity are done away with, whole chapters, whole sequences are excised from the text. As with many censoring jobs arising more from impassioned prejudice than systematic ideological strictures, this one is often arbitrary, not to mention careless, both in substance and in narrative form. The reader is not presented, pace Vasconcelos, with a new "I," nor is the "possibility to erase what is unworthy of recollection" a viable one here. The expurgated text is not simply a "new" story; it is the same old story, crisscrossed with badly healed scars. However, what strikes today's reader as the most daring revelation of *Ulises criollo,* the obsessive passion for the mother, remains intact. It is as if Vasconcelos, uncomfortable with the double narrative line of his hybrid autobiography—the national hero and the erotic quester—had renounced the latter in order to consolidate the former. Yet by leaving the mother's story intact he merely reduced the explicitness of the erotic, not defused its charge in the text.

The consequences of this erasure were decisive: today, the expurgated version of *Ulises criollo,* published by the archconservative Editorial Jus, has more readers than the original. Unlike the other, unexpurgated version of Vasconcelos's *Ulises,* usually grouped in a volume with his other autobiographical works, this one may be purchased independently; in addition, it may be purchased at a relatively low price.

Sarmiento and Vasconcelos are, unquestionably, two extreme cases in which national self-figuration, for reasons both historical and personal, is perceived as an imperative. The two men were, after all, politicians as well as writers, politicians *at the same time* they were writers. (one wonders, for example, how Vargas Llosa, after losing the presidential election in Peru, will rewrite *Aunt Julia and the Scriptwriter* in years to come.) It is also true that, in both Sarmiento and Vasconcelos, the conflation of self and country was used as an ideological tool against an imperialistic other—Spain, whose obscurantism Sarmiento corrects with his enlightened republican self; the United States whose influence Vasconcelos battles with his Mexican persona. If not always so urgent, so confrontational, the need for such a figuration is nonetheless present in other Spanish American autobiographers. In the same way that Vasconcelos rereads and modifies the "original" Sarmientian mold, other twentieth-century autobiographers repair, consciously or not, to a model of national representativeness they appropriate and adjust to their purposes. It may be faithfully imitated, as a cliché, in purely utilitarian autobiographies; in more thoughtful texts, it may be accepted as a problematic model and ultimately questioned; or, more drastically, it may be denounced for its vacuous rhetoric and resented as an imposition: "Rien ne vous tue un homme comme d'être obligé de représenter son pays, " writes Cortázar, quoting Jacques Vaché, in the epigraph to the autobiography he does *not* write, that is, his novel *Hopscotch*. If the heroic, monumentalist conception of a national "I" is on the wane (except perhaps in purely political autobiographies, like Eva Perón's *La razón de mi vida),* one might say that it has left its trace in the consistent anxiety of representativeness so often manifest in Spanish American autobiographies. While "I" is no longer a synecdoche for a country, it may be a synecdoche for a group, a community, a gender. The latter seems particularly true of autobiographies written by women or by members of minority groups, that is, by those whose presence has routinely been ignored.

The testimonial stance continues to mark autobiographical writing in Spanish America. If not always perceiving him- or herself as a historian (that perception seems to lose ground as generic difference becomes more specific in Spanish American literature), the autobiographer favors the role of the witness. The fact that the testimony is often endowed with the aura of terminal visions—the autobiographer bearing witness to that which is no more—not only aggrandizes the author's individual figuration but reflects the communal dimension sought for the autobiographical venture. Much of Spanish American self-writing is an exercise in memory doubled by a ritual of commemoration, in which individual relics (in Benjamin's sense of the term) are secularized and re-presented as shared events.

While on the one hand this perception of self restricts the individual scrutiny so frequently associated in other literatures with autobiography (a view, one should not forget, that applies to just *one* type of autobiography), on the other, it has the advantage of capturing a tension between self and other, of generating a reflection on the fluctuating place of the subject within its community, of allowing for other voices, besides that of the "I," to be heard in the text. Even those cases which seem to favor one of the poles of this oscillation between self and community to the apparent exclusion of the other—say, on the one hand, Mariano Picón Salas's first person plural in *Regreso de tres mundos,* so deliberately "representative" that it becomes an abstraction, and, on the other, the defiantly private "I" of Norah Lange's *Cuadernos de infancia*—even those cases allow, unsuspectingly perhaps, for that tension. So, although it might be tempting to see in Spanish American autobiographical texts a subject, enmeshed in different tactics of repression (what cannot be told) and self-validation (what must be told in a way acceptable to a nation or at least to a community), that has not yet come into its own (i.e. the story of the self "alone"), it would be ill-advised to conclude that progress towards introspection, from the constraints of the document to the freedom of fiction, is a desired goal for these texts. Given the history of the genre, the components that gradually, secretly, have come to integrate what one might term a Spanish American autobiographical tradition, such an evaluation would not only be unwarranted, it would impose extraneous demands on the texts. If, in the nineteenth century, a very tentative autobiographical subject, in order to give itself texture, resorted to tactics of self-validation that included claims to national representativeness, to group bonding, to testimonial service—claims, in short, that opened the self to a community—by the twentieth century, those tactics have been naturalized, have been incorporated into an autobiographical rhetoric. No longer forcibly considered a historical necessity, strictly speaking, they nonetheless continue to inform the discourse of self-representation in Spanish America, have become an intrinsic part of the writing subject's perception of self.

NOTES

1. Juan Bautista Alberdi, *Cartas quillotanas*. Preceded by an explanatory letter by D. F. Sarmiento (Buenos Aires: Ed. La Cultura Argentina, 1916), pp. 133-34. All translations, except when otherwise noted, are my own.

2. For discussion of a similar evolutionary view of nineteenth- century North American literature prompting "pangs of cultural inadequacy," see William C. Spengemann in his *A Mirror for Americanists* (Hanover and London: University Press of New England, 1989), pp. 7-27.

3. Fredric Jameson, "Third-World Literature in the Era of Multinational Capitalism," *Social Text,* 15 (1986), pp. 65-88. For an effective critique of Jameson's position, see Aijaz Ahmad, "Jameson's Rhetoric of Otherness and the 'National Allegory,' " *Social Text,* 17 (1987), pp. 3-25.

4. For the role of the Romantic historian as interpreter of a mute past, see Lionel Gossman's illuminating "History as Decipherment: Romantic Historiography and the Discovery of the Other," *New Literary History,* 18, 1 (1986), pp. 23-57. For Sarmiento's views on French historiography, see his "Los estudios históricos en Francia," *Obras,* II (Buenos Aires: Imprenta y Litografía Mariano Moreno, 1896), p. 199.

5. André Gide, *Journal 1889-1939* (Paris: Gallimard, La Pléiade, 1955), p. 29. Gide adds: "One might say the following, which I see as a sort of inverted sincerity (in the artist): He must tell his life not in the way he has lived it but must live his life in the way he will tell it. In other words: that the portrait of himself that is his life be identical to the ideal portrait he desires. More simply: that he be the way he wants himself to be."

6. Sarmiento, "El monitor de las escuelas primarias," *Obras completas,* IV (Buenos Aires: Imprenta y Litografía Mariano Moreno, 1896), p. 411.

7. Ezequiel Martínez Estrada, *Sarmiento* (Buenos Aires: Sudamericana, 1969), p. 18.

8. Sarmiento cleverly alerts two sets of readers, to a point exclusive of each other, to the reception of *Recuerdos de provincia.* Or perhaps it would be more accurate to say that Sarmiento envisages two successive and quite different readings of his text. One set of readers is composed of those *compatriots* to whom he dedicates the book, who, as his contemporaries,

will understand his references to "circumstances of the moment" and sympathize with his position. The others, to whom he alludes indirectly in his introduction, will read the text after his death and will not fully understand those references. For them Sarmiento sets up the exemplum, the "statue for posterity." I have tried to show how these two sets of readers are foreseen by the two, divergent epigraphs to *Recuerdos,* in my "Inscripciones del yo en *Recuerdos de provincia*" (*Sur,* 350-351 [1982], pp. 131-40). For a helpful discussion of the different kinds of readers a text can summon see, on the subject of Montaigne's *Essais,* Claude Blum, "La peinture du moi et l'écriture inachevée," *Poétique,* 53 (1983), pp. 60-71.

9. For a solid analysis of the change in attitude from *Mi defensa* to *Recuerdos de provincia,* see Tulio Halperín Donghi, "Sarmiento: su lugar en la sociedad argentina postrevolucionaria," *Sur,* 341 (1977). For additional, very insightful comments on Sarmiento's presentation of himself in *Recuerdos* as a political candidate, see Carlos Altamirano and Beatriz Sarlo, "Una vida ejemplar: la estrategia de *Recuerdos de provincia,*" in their *Literatura y sociedad* (Buenos Aires: Hachette, 1983), pp. 163-208.

10. Or as Carlos Monsiváis notes, speaking of Vasconcelos's efforts to explore the different manifestations of cultural nationalism: "What is important is to produce symbols and myths, to imagine a heroic past and to people it, in a Wagnerian manner, with twilight gods like Cuauhtémoc." "Notas sobre la cultura mexicana en el siglo XX," in *Historia general de México,* IV (Mexico: El Colegio de México, 1977), p. 349.

11. On the composition of self for symbolic purposes, so patent in Vasconcelos and Sarmiento, one may usefully consult Daniel Arasse, "*La prudence* de Titien ou l'autoportrait glissé à la rive de la figure," *Corps ecrit,* 5 (1983), pp. 109-15, in which, following Panofsky, the author studies self-depiction as an "allegorical support."

For the specific nationalistic twist given the symbolic composition of self, see Robert F. Sayre, "Autobiography and the Making of America," in *Autobiography: Essays Theoretical and Critical,* ed. James Olney (Princeton: Princeton University Press, 1980). Sayre sees national intent as a distinctive trait of American autobiography: "American autobiographers have generally connected their own lives to the national life or to national ideas. . . . From the times of Columbus, Cortez [sic], and John Smith, America has been an idea, or many ideas" (pp. 149-50). Despite the allusion to the Spanish conquest, Sayre's observations are limited to a certain type of autobiography written in the United States. This annoying parochialism notwithstanding, his remarks are useful to approach certain Spanish American autobiographies.

12. Carlos Monsiváis, "Notas sobre la cultura," p. 355.

13. José Vasconcelos, *Memorias,* II (Mexico: Fondo de Cultura Económica, 1982), p. 1141. The four books of Vasconcelos's autobiography—*Ulises criollo, La tormenta, El desastre,* and *El proconsulado*—have been collected in the two volumes of this edition. Quotations from *Ulises criollo* refer to this edition and page numbers are given directly in the text.

14. There are exceptions. In an excellent article on Vasconcelos, referring to other notorious Oedipal ties in Mexican literature, mainly in the work of poets, Enrique Krause writes: "Vasconcelos' prose Oedipus has gone by unnoticed, when it is doubtlessly more profound, more significant and more complex [than the others]. He devotes a third of *Ulises criollo* to evoking it. The first love story [Vasconcelos] tells in his memoirs is not the passion for Adriana but the passion for his mother, Carmen Calderón. All of Vasconcelos's lives issue from and lead back to this bond." Enrique Krauze, "Pasión y contemplación en Vasconcelos," *Vuelta,* 78 (1978), p. 12.

15. José Vasconcelos, *Ulises criollo* (Mexico: Editorial Jus, 1958), p. 5.

16. In an early passage referring to his mother's relation to books, Vasconcelos tells how her devoutness made her suspicious of books that in any way questioned the teachings of the church. In an unforgettable scene, after the departure of an uncle whose ideas differ from hers, she has her very young son build a fire in the yard and burn up, in "a pyre of printed words," all the books the uncle left behind.

3.
Developing Diaspora Literacy and *Marasa* Consciousness

VÈVÈ A. CLARK

The New Negro, Indigenist, and Négritude movements of the 1920s and 1930s constitute the grounded base of contemporary Afro-American, Caribbean, and African literary scholarship. Critics return repeatedly to this textual field as if to embrace a heralded center, familiar and stable. Skepticism regarding presentations of the era as a coherent whole has inspired redefinitions of the period's demarcations, classic works as well as national and transnational intertextualities.[1] Bearing in mind the discontinuities, one must acknowledge, however, that among other achievements, the new letters movements provided an epistemological break away from the predominance of Euro-American influences on black texts, the discursive agendas previously defining textual production particularly in nineteenth- and early twentieth-century Caribbean writing.[2] New letters works became communal property to be read and revised across national boundaries. Antilleans and some Hispanics, for instance, embraced texts by Langston Hughes and Claude McKay and were challenged by the Afro-American example to respond in stylistic kind.[3] Unlike any other epoch of African-American expression, new letters shared a common ideology: writing regional, ethnic, and peasant experiences into existence. Their very articulation signified protest directed against cultural repression on the one hand and racial self-hatred on the other. The paradox of such a posture is suggested by Jean Price-Mars's use of the term *collective bovaryism* to describe in retrospect his generation's capitulation during the American Marine Occupation of Haiti (1915–1934). From the Haitian contradictions emerged defensive political, cultural, and textual agendas as of 1927 which paralleled the black revolts of Harlem and Paris but were determined by the particular circumstances provoking their enunciation.[4]

Even as the predominantly male new letters voices were materializing in the Caribbean, their narrative and discursive strategies were being redefined in terms of gender by women novelists the likes of Suzanne Lacascade and Annie Desroy whose texts inaugurated "la littérature féminine" in the Guadeloupe and Haiti of 1924 and 1934, respectively.[5] Scholars consistently overlooked these early texts primarily because none of the authors participated in either Indigenism or Négritude.[6] A separate tradition developed for over five decades and was not recognized as such until Maryse Condé published her study of Antillean novelists, *La Parole des femmes* in 1979.[7] Recent scholarship, however, has rekindled interest in this body of literature whose intertextual and comparative relationships I shall explore across national boundaries in theoretical discussions devoted to Maryse Conodé's *Hérémakhonon* (1976), Paule Marshall's *Praisesong for the Widow* (1983), and Rigoberta Menchú's, *I, Rigoberta Menchú* (1983), texts representing the Francophone Antilles, the Anglophone emigrant Caribbean, and the Native Central/Hispanic Caribbean respectively.[8] Their analysis as a unit suggests the need for new theories within comparative literature and revised definitions of the diaspora in African-American scholarship.[9]

The new letters movements invented a construct, *the African diaspora*, referring to the phenomenon and history of African-American displacement in the New World beginning with Columbus's settlements in coastal Hispaniola during the sixteenth century.[10] Demographic, cultural, and class differences among the slaves exported to North America and the Caribbean were reconstructed by merchants, colonists, and early colonial historians as an essentialist tale of shared experience. The differences which had not disappeared were used as means of preventing slave solidarity on a given plantation, particularly through the practice of separating captives who spoke the same language.[11] Centuries later, the new letters recognition of an African diaspora in part reclaimed the differences and rhetorically redefined unity in transnational terms.

Alain Locke's *The New Negro* (1925) belongs to a radical conception of black identity and expression. Three decades prior to African and Caribbean independence, he addressed the international consequences of America's emancipation of its slave populace and the racial awareness it unleashed. Moreover, Locke predicted that the then colonized territories would undergo a similar de-mastering process in the future.[12] His was a visionary pronouncement directed as much to the politics of decolonization as it was to Afro-American literary expression whose counterparts were soon to emerge in Port-au-Prince and Paris. Essentially, new letters invited readers into a sphere of cultural difference which required a command of what I have termed *diaspora literacy* if the texts were to be understood from indigenous, cultural perspectives beyond the field of Western or westernized signification. From the 1930s through independence, African diaspora texts were bound to exoticism for mainstream readers and would remain so until Ethnic Studies entered elite, academic institutions to challenge the limited ethnicity of the canon.[13]

DIASPORA LITERACY

Diaspora literacy defines the reader's ability to comprehend the literatures of Africa, Afro-America, and the Caribbean from an informed, indigenous perspective. The field is multicultural and multilingual, encompassing writing in European and ethnic languages.[14] In the current textual environment, diaspora literacy suggests that names such as *Popul Vuh,* Legba, Bélain d'Esnambuc, Nanny, José Martí, Bigger Thomas, and Marie Chauvet represent mnemonic devices whose recall releases a learned tradition. This type of literacy is more than a purely intellectual exercise. It is a skill for both narrator and reader which demands a knowledge of historical, social, cultural, and political development generated by lived and textual experience. Throughout the twentieth century, diaspora literacy has implied an ease and intimacy with more than one language, with interdisciplinary relations among history, ethnology, and the folklore of regional expression. Only recently has literary theory applied to Afro-Caribbean texts become indispensable.[15]

Representations of African diaspora history and culture have assumed a binary formation—us and the Others—a residual construction surviving from the master/slave heritage. Houston Baker in his *Modernism and the Harlem Renaissance* (1987) re-examines the binary oppositions existing between the ideologies of Booker T. Washington and W.E.B. Du Bois. From that encounter two intriguing discursive strategies have been identified—mastery of form/deformation of mastery. As I read Baker's work, I was aware that a third principle might well exist beyond the oppositional framework within which we have interpreted new letters.[16] I have termed that third principle *the reformation of form,* a reduplicative narrative posture which assumes and revises Du Bois's double consciousness. In the wider field of contemporary literary criticism, this reformative strategy approximates the deconstruction of mastery. The consciousness accompanying the revision in which many of us participate has no name. It may well be that peasants engaged in Vodoun ceremonies in Haiti and its diaspora have provided a figure and frame through which African diaspora criticism might establish a theory of comparative literature based on the vernacular.[17]

Black music has provided examples of contextual and formal re-presentations by mastering form/deforming mastery and reforming form. John Coltrane's "My Favorite Things" masters the text by replicating its melody, deforms that same text by sounding on it and the listener's implied identification with Broadway fantasy and through improvisation reforms the conflicting registers it has established in the process of their articulation.[18]

MARASA CONSCIOUSNESS

Marasa is a mythical theory of textual relationships based on the Haitian Vodoun sign for the Divine Twins, the *marasa*. The sign itself lures a viewer into interpretation limited only and obviously by the reader's degree of literacy. At the fundamental level, the *marasa* represent biological twins born to peasant families who may react quite differently to unexpected births. Twins are feared in some cultures throughout Africa and the Caribbean and adored in others.[19] Generative readings of the sign also include the child born sequentially after twins, the *dossu* (male) and *dossa* (female)—symbolically represented as a unit termed the *marasa trois* in Vodoun signification. In this *bosal* (uninitiated) interpretation, the sign derives from familial relationships and the anxieties accompanying two more mouths to nurse and feed or the belief that twins, despite the hardships their births have occasioned, will bring good fortune to the family compound.

Among Vodoun initiates instructed in the interpretation of signs, the performance of ritual, and the proper interactions with the *lwa* (ancestral and nature spirits), the *marasa* are invoked in the *Prière Guinée* after Legba, Loko, and Ayizan. Legba is the first *lwa* whose presence in a Vodoun ceremony must be acknowledged before ritual practice commences. He not only "opens the doors" for interaction with the spirits through drum, dance, and song, but also figuratively stands at the gates of literacy.[20] Loko the butterfly of wisdom (in the air) linked to his "wife" Ayizan, earth and keeper of goods and markets, are the metaphorical symbols of opposition devolving from Legba. In fourth place appear the *marasa* restating the binary oppositions commonly associated with the principal Haitian *lwa* (the ebb and flow of the waters—Agwé and Erzulie or the serpent above and below—Damballah and Ayida), as well as the third principle formed by the sequence of Legba/Loko/Ayizan invocations. *Marasa* states the oppositions and invites participation in the formulation of another principle entirely. Those of us accustomed to the Hegelian dialectic would seek in comparable environments resolution of seemingly irreconcilable differences: slave/master, partriarchy/matriarchy, domestic/maroon, rural/urban, and the like when the *marasa* sign, like others produced in agrarian societies, has another more "spiralist" agenda in mind.[21]

Marasa consciousness invites us to imagine beyond the binary. The ability to do so depends largely on our capacities to read the sign as a cyclical, spiral relationship. On the surface, *marasa* seems to be binary. My research

Sign for the Marasa Trois

of Haitian peasant lore and ritual observance has revealed that the tension between oppositions leads to another norm of creativity—to interaction or deconstruction as it were. In Vodoun, the philosophical and environmental contrasts embedded in the *marasa* sign and the belief system it represents are danced into another realm of discourse during Vodoun ceremonies.[22]

Marasa is derived from creation myths among the Fon/Ewe in Ancient Dahomey (present-day Benin) which are non-patriarchal in character. *Marasa* is the Haitian version of Mawu (female)-Lisa (male) whose divine powers emanate from the non-gender-specific being, Nananbuluku. Mawu-Lisa populated the world through the figure of Legba, the chief guardian of language and literacy.[23] Representations of the *marasa* in the form of vèvè assume uniformity at the horizontal and vertical crossroads thereby insuring a stable field of interaction with the *lwa;* improvisations on the grounded form, left and right, top and bottom encourage originality. Our contemporary notions of unity and difference in Caribbean writing find their reflection in the *marasa trois*.[24]

Marasa denotes movement and change and may serve as a metaphor representing the profound differences in environment, social organization, and language encountered by slaves in the Americas. Moreover, the *marasa* principle points to the transformation of cultural oppositions in plantation societies. Relief from contradictions was certainly not guaranteed and persists in many sectors of Caribbean societies to this day. Movement beyond the binary nightmare occurred on several levels of experience, thereby transforming Caribbean society: indigenous religious practices (Vodoun, Santería, Candomblé, Shango); bought freedom; marronage and Back-to-Africa movements; interracial marriage or the mulatto phenomenon, as well as new letters movements. Marasa consciousness is a sign of the textual times in the Caribbean. So much of the writing features displacement: 1) environmental disruptions such as hurricanes, floods, and volcanos; 2) departures from home ground due to seasonal labor, rural-urban drift, exile, and emigration; 3) radical socio-political change through coups d'état, independence agendas, and strikes; 4) double consciousness due to color, class, and educational differences experienced by one individual. Degrees of bilingual or diglossic dissonance in the Caribbean are at the very root of the problem requiring transformation. In neo-colonial societies, the standard of literacy and the official language of its articulation is Other—French, English, Spanish rather than Creole or a native language. Literacy is therefore reckoned on an evolutionary chain from rural to urban or urban to hexagonic metropole. The toll on the individual's double consciousness at the level of language is deeply unsettling because out of place, signifying upon return to the regional landscape (if return does occur) an imagination out of mind. The past two decades of Creole revival and defense in the Anglophone, Francophone, and Dutch Caribbean have transformed the previously inferior status of amalgamated, New World languages into an increasingly valued form of written expression.[25] Social, textual, and linguistic transformations in Caribbean cultures and literatures when analyzed within the context of binary oppositions remind us that movement rather than false notions of stability are mandated if, indeed, stability signifies domination by a minority (whether old planters, békés, or military dictators).

Coming to *marasa* consciousness in the twentieth century is a third stage in diasporic development, the first two representing the racially conscious new letters movements followed in Africa and the Caribbean by anti-colonial, anti-repression writing. This third position looks back at the contradictions of new letters and liberation movements by commenting upon the results in an environment of continuous change. In the late twentieth century, we are witnessing not only the inclusion of the Other in the Academy, the extension of the notion of learning to include world civilizations, but also theoretical discussions based on the once disparaged vernacular. Henry Louis Gates's successive explications of the Signifying Monkey as a hermeneutics of black criticism culminating in *The Signifying Monkey* is a fine example of the shift in critical theory.[26] Similar use of vernacular figures and frames have occurred in Caribbean literature, notably in my brief essay, "Marassa: Images of Women from the Other Americas" (1984) and Maximilien Laroche's *Le Patriarche, Le Marron et La Dossa* (1988).[27] Laroche seeks to establish a flexible reading of the Haitian novel from its inception in the nineteenth century with Eméric Bergeaud's *Stella* (1859) through to contemporary texts of the 1980s. Laroche's approach considers twin relations in a single novel (e.g., Manuel/Gervilien; Délira/Annaise in Jacques Roumain's *Masters of the Dew* [1944]), but is primarily concerned with the entry of women writers into the history of Haitian letters beginning with the publication in 1934 of Annie Desroy's *Le Joug*. Beyond the Caribbean, twinning relationships surface in Afro-American critical theory as in Gates's analyses of *Their Eyes Were Watching God, Mumbo Jumbo,* and *The Color Purple* which suggest to me an intertextual *marasa*.[28] Although the *marasa* figure is specifically Haitian, traditions of imagining beyond difference appear in various ritual practices throughout the Caribbean.[29] I shall use the *marasa* principle to illustrate intertextual readings of Marie Chauvet and Maryse Condé and comparative approaches to three scenes in texts by Condé, Marshall, and Menchú. In the latter, we are observing the protagonists as they develop diaspora literacy; we become voyeurs reading the characters reading events: Veronica Mercier attending the "Allegiance to the Revolution" gathering in West Africa; Avey Johnson dancing in the drum fête on Carriacou; and Rigoberta Menchú participating in a Labor Day strike in the capital city of Guatemala.

DECIPHERING THE DIFFERENCES

Intertextual relationships between Marie Chauvet's trilogy, *Amour, Colère et Folie* (1968) and *Hérémakhonon* have been overlooked in the increasingly sophisticated criticism devoted to Condé's work. Revision of *Amour* occurs in Condé's portrayals of the protagonist's sexual behavior as a strategy for drawing the reader into the political repression concealed in the narrative. To borrow Henry Louis Gate's term, Condé is Signifyin(g) on Claire Clamont, the central figure in *Amour* and on Chauvet's detached narrative technique.[30] Chauvet's text exposes a system of dictatorship in the Haiti of the Marine Occupation uncovered by the sheltered, unmarried Claire.[31] Her repressed sexuality becomes the metaphor for repressed desire generally among the bourgeois citizens of her town and by association the nation as a whole. Claire's alienation from her family and the political context, for reasons due to color and class antagonisms, does not prevent her from slaying the representative of oppression—Commandant Calédu—by the novel's end. Reaction against political oppression is accomplished through a *crime passionnel* whose motivations are confusing given Claire's peculiar detachment from social and sexual relationships. Chauvet's strategy ultimately protects Claire and the reader from narrative complicity in the very clandestine operations she discloses.

By contrast, Condé uses Veronica's sexual encounters as a device by which to educate the uninformed, implied reader presumably unfamiliar with the silences surrounding sexual and political repression within the diaspora. Veronica reacts against the sexual prejudices of her black, bourgeois relatives in Guadeloupe by sleeping with their socio-cultural enemies, as it were—a mulatto from a respected family and a Frenchman. Condé is not simply restating Fanon's *Black Skins, White Masks* in the narrative nor is she defending the Mayotte Capécias of the Caribbean,[32] rather she creates a text in which a black woman's sexuality is defined in prescriptive fashion—by class, color, race, and culture—limited according to the men with whom she *cannot* have a relationship. Clearly, the disclosure of sexual repression among Caribbean women is not the principal agenda in *Hérémakhonon*. The text is concerned primarily with another more secretive area of diaspora culture, access to which Condé provides through Veronica's sexuality. Her affair with Ibrahima Sory, the Minister of the Interior in a recently liberated West African nation occupies the narrative center—former relationships in Guadeloupe and Paris are recalled in flashback. Veronica and the uninformed, implied reader enter together the spaces of post-Independence, Islamic West Africa. Condé presumes that not unlike her protagonist, the reader is highly literate regarding the new letters movements, shares her pride in black culture and esteem for African liberation struggles. All three of these presumptions are challenged by the narrative, the latter more seriously indicted. Essentially, Veronica's brief three-month sojourn and her relationship with Ibrahima Sory unravel her own rigid apolitical posture as a teacher of philosophy who only begrudgingly agrees to include ideological works by Fanon and Nkrumah in her syllabus. At the Lycée she encounters members of the disenfranchised Opposition Party whose assertions regarding State repression she conveniently ignores. Her sexual relationship with Sory—once it becomes apparent to members of the Opposition—compromises the non-partisan position she has adopted. The implied reader, too, is compromised, having witnessed at close quarters the governing party's deliberate silencing, imprisonment, and (perhaps) murder of one of three persons who befriended Veronica and whose fate, rather than whose rhetoric, convinces Veronica and the reader that repression exists in independent Africa. Claire's detached sexual behavior in *Amour* is revised by Condé in such a way that Veronica's *liaisons dangeureuses* reveal black-on-black bias and political repression within the diaspora during the early 1960s—at a time when in North America and South Africa struggles for civil rights assumed that racial or ethnic conflict superseded issues of class and gender, and defined anti-colonial resistance.[33]

The differences in portrayal of a woman deciphering the sub-text of political repression may seem coincidental from *Amour* to *Hérémakhonon*. When Maryse Condé critiqued part two of Chauvet's trilogy in *La Parole des femmes,* she suggested grounds for intentional revision:

As in *Amour,* the reader might well regret the fact that power relationships are simply represented as a malevolent force, as Absolute Evil. We would have preferred to witness the system of repression dismantled in a manner more immediately apparent. However, such was not the novelist's intention. She wanted to convey the atmosphere of mourning which had engulfed the entire country; no amount of logic or rationalization could clarify the situation. Evil Incarnate does not allow for any kind of revolt at all.[34]

In apparent opposition to Chauvet's text, Condé reveals the insidious machinations of government repression in detail. At the discursive level, *Hérémakhonon* deforms the mastery of one of the most important political novels by a woman author in Caribbean literature.

Hérémakhonon is a paradoxical text at odds with itself. Its contradictory nature derives from Condé's resolve to write of her coming-to-political consciousness in Guinea during the early 1960s from the narrative perspective of an apolitical *anti-moi.*[35] Consequently, the text is double-voiced and the strategy particularly revealing in the "Allegiance to the Revolution" scene—one of Veronica's earliest exercises in reading the political sub-text.[36] In free direct discourse, Veronica describes the ritual nature of the gathering at Party Headquarters. Within the interstices of that narration, she admits her inability to decipher the objectives motivating public, political enactments of this nature.

Through a veil of irony and sarcasm, an acutely observant "I" examines the setting in terms of gender relationships of power and acquiescence—the ruling male elites seated on a raised platform above, the women militants grouped at right angles in the audience below. The narrator views the assembly as mock service where praise, testimony, and the taking of oaths confirm one's loyalty to the ruling party. The voice here is skeptical: "Play-acting? Sincere? Does the crowd fall for it?" (p. 77/46). Through another "I," Condé presents the scene quite differently in asides inserted into Veronica's enlightened readings of the gathering. The other "I" fails to comprehend the scene in its entirety, in part due to the narrator's ideology of non-commitment. Primarily, though, Veronica is confused because she does not understand the languages other than French in which the participants speak. She has entered a diglossic situation; "I do not/can't understand," repeated at intervals, describes a major barrier to diaspora literacy which Veronica obviously does not seek to overcome.

Contradiction arises in the text through the tension between diaspora literacy and delusion. *Hérémakhonon* clearly celebrates the meticulous learning of a displaced intellectual whose knowledge is affirmed by the often hermetic allusions sprinkled throughout the narrative.[37] Veronica's literacy is deceptive, having failed to evolve beyond the 1950s, and is further compromised by her indulgence in sentimental images of the noble revolution and the African homeland embraced by New World blacks.[38] As Françoise Lionnet observes in a penetrating critique, *Hérémakhonon* indicts " 'neurotics from the Diaspora' (p. 52)—who come to Africa in a selfish search for personal fulfillment, remaining safely uninvolved in the revolutionary struggles of the local population."[39] Condé's deformation of mastery is doubly focused on images of black revolutionary purity and an Africa recreated by the new letters movement. That agenda is clear in the ironic use of the Malinké *here* (happiness/peace) *makhonon* (await) or Welcome House—the figurative epithet with which Ibrahima Sory christens his villa. He and his extended family have occupied ruling space once occupied by French colonial administrators as they await post-revolutionary calm. Welcome House is also a metaphor for the mythical Africa invented by Négritude writers against whose call to come home Condé has frequently argued:

The proponents of Négritude made a big mistake and caused a lot of suffering in the minds of West Indian people and black Americans as well. We were led to believe that Africa was the source; it is the source, but *we believed that we would find a home there, when it was not a home.* Without Négritude we would not have experienced the degree of disillusionment that we did. (Emphasis added)[40]

Ironically, it is through disillusionment that the reader's diaspora literacy develops into post-colonial consciousness in *Hérémakhonon*.

Praisesong for the Widow and *Hérémakhonon* represent *marasa* of textual resonance and dissonance. Avey Johnson and Veronica Mercier are both seeking a welcome house; their "narratives of apprenticeship"[41] in Carriacou and West Africa figure as third and ultimate points in a triangular quest for lost identity. Both Avey and Veronica are seeking to weave together disparate memories surviving their childhoods and adulthoods. Avey's triangle is shaped by experiences among black cultures in southern coastal America, New York, and Grenada/Carriacou in the Caribbean. Veronica's begins in her native Guadeloupe, extends to Paris and later Guinea. Moreover, the texts are infused with a host of cultural allusions that challenge the reader's literacy. Linguist Velma Pollard has identified six of Marshall's recognizable culture references; of the six, interaction with Legba and the communal dances for the ancestors relate to *Hérémakhonon*.[42] Near the end of the "Allegiance" gathering, Veronica admits her frustrations at not being able to read the scene or intervene:

I have to admit, I'm lost. They have their problems that I can no longer ignore. I need a guide, an interpreter, a chief linguist to make offerings and have the message from the oracle decoded. (p. 80/48)

The chief linguist whose services she requires is Legba. Veronica's retreat into mythology is very much out of character; the allusion functions, therefore, as an ironic invocation whose recall masks her lack of political sophistication. For Avey Johnson, Legba is a figure actualized. During the drum fête Lebert Joseph, the elderly, crippled figuration of Legba, dances Avey into diaspora literacy. He helps her decode the messages of solidarity and difference which stimulate her reading of events as they unfold and her participation in the mastery of form.

Marshall's revision of the welcome house topos is strikingly apparent in her representation of the drum fête. It is a healing ritual in which we cannot imagine her *marasa* Veronica consenting to participate in view of her ironic persona, positivist training, and incentive to discover the political sub-text of the narrative unfolding before her. No such political climate appears in *Praisesong;* rather, Marshall reconstitutes the ethos of new letter's travelogues and ethnographies of the 1930s. Much of this writing privileged cultural exchange with the peasantry over socio-economic and political analyses of cultural retentions.[43]

"The Beg Pardon" chapter in *Praisesong* provides a compelling metaphor describing a woman, an outsider overcoming alienation, as she simultaneously develops diaspora literacy. Structurally, interaction at the drum fête when Avey joins in the Carriacou Tramp is similar to Condé's "Allegiance" gathering: the scene is set, participants delineated, landscape examined. The absence or presence of interaction is perceived as a symptom of the protagonists' alienation from or embrace of diaspora literacy within the arenas to which their interest has been drawn. Following the "Allegiance" gathering, stunned by her inabilities to comprehend, Veronica retreats into whiskey, into the promise of forgetfulness in order to soothe her alienated self; Avey, by contrast, reassembles divisive memories from her past and is, thereby, reincorporated into black world society. Condé's representation is linear and at right angles related in a hyper-verbal narrative condition. Marshall's narration of the drum fête is circular, a danced event, conducted counterclockwise in a timeless evocation of diaspora memory. Avey's entry into the moving circle of dancers completes her quest as she crosses over the ancestral waters into meta-history. The scene impresses by its non-verbal form of communication; the absence of spoken words causes the few utterances by Joseph, Rosalie Parvay, and Bercita Edwards to assume heightened significance. Intrusive and comforting phrases, introduced as residues of Avey's past (pp. 247, 248, 249) because they are contextualized in ritual practice, reveal the continuity that she is seeking during her precipitous journey to Carriacou. Intrusive voices from Veronica's past, registered as flashbacks in dissociated contexts throughout the text, do not allow her diasporic identities to knit, to heal. They remain so many allusions lacking a communal, therapeutic site in which personal growth might well have developed.

Mastery of form is the narrative purpose and discursive strategy in the Carriacou Tramp scene. Avey masters the rhythms and dances (if not the songs) which tie together in practice diasporic sites in Tatem, New York, and the Caribbean. She has crossed over, she has returned. The sounding of her name at the conclusion of the Carriacou ritual recalls her grandmother's teachings:

The old woman used to insist, on pain of a switching, that whenever anyone in Tatem, even another child, asked her name she was not to say simply "Avey," or even "Avey Williams." But always "Avey, short for Avatara." (p. 251)

By casting in the past as a remembered rather than presumed response to Bercita Edwards's query, "And who you is?," Marshall leaves space at the very opening of the next section for Lebert Joseph to rename her. He is convinced that she belongs to the *Arada* (West African) ethnic nation. *Arada* is inscribed in Avey's body language and ritual posture and the renaming recognized as a sign of initiation into diaspora literacy. In the future, in answer to rare questions about her ethnic identity, she might well respond: Avey, short for Avatara *Arada* Williams-Johnson.

Marshall's intent is to develop the drum and dance literacy of her readers and that of Avey as well. The short, declarative sentences and phrases are overwhelmed with detail. There is a cinematic quality to these descriptions: close-ups of body parts, a skirt flaring here, a foot edging forward elsewhere, the narrative perspective retreating at intervals to reveal the entire community of fifty persons or one section of that same moving mass. Marshall has captured the alternating perspectives from which we as outsiders perceive a danced ritual and, from Avey's point of view, how the uninitiated outsider is drawn into the dancing whole as participant.

Paule Marshall's representation of drum/dance literacy in prose engages in a revision of synecdoche. She has not allowed the traditional fragmentation of the trope to prevail, rather she fuses this rhetorical device of substitution through ritual practice:

The dancers in their loose, ever-widening ring were no more than a dozen feet away now. She could feel the reverberation of their powerful tread in the ground under her, and the heat from their bodies reached her in a strong yeasty wave. Soon only a mere four or five feet remained between them, yet she continued to stand there. Finally, just as the moving wall of bodies was almost upon her, she too moved—a single declarative step forward. At the same moment, what seemed an arm made up of many arms reached out from the circle to draw her in, and she found herself walking amid the elderly folk on the periphery, in their counterclockwise direction. (p. 247)

Reuniting part with whole is the narrative purpose of *Praisesong,* and Marshall's metaphor for solidarity within the diaspora a memorable evocation:

And for the first time since she was a girl, she felt the threads, that myriad of shiny, silken, brightly colored threads (like the kind used in embroidery) which were thin to the point of invisibility yet as strong as the ropes at Coney Island. Looking on outside the church in Tatem, standing waiting for the *Robert Fulton* on the crowded pier at 125th Street, she used to feel them streaming out of everyone there to enter her, making her part of what seemed a far-reaching, wide-ranging confraternity. Now suddenly, as if she were that girl again, with her entire life yet to live, she felt the threads streaming out from the old people around her in Lebert Joseph's yard. From their seared eyes. From their navels and their cast-iron hearts. And their brightness as they entered her spoke of possibilities and becoming even in the face of the bare bones and the burnt-out ends. (p. 249)

Avatara-Avey-Arada embraces the *marasa* of her diasporic ethnicity constructed along axes of erasure and permanence. The contradictions of her upbringing and marriage evolve into "possibilities and becoming" signifying a consciousness no longer consumed by apparent conflicts. In opposition to Condé's text, *Praisesong* suggests the value of contextualized cultural action in transforming the colonized subject's skepticism regarding personal development and social change.

I, Rigoberta Menchú, the oral history of a young Quiché woman's coming-to-activist-consciousness, was related to Venezuelan anthropologist Elisabeth Burgos-Debray in Paris and rearranged by her for publication. Menchú is not middle class; her diaspora does not derive from Africa and, unlike Veronica Mercier and Avey Johnson, she is not involved in a personal quest for identity *per se.* Menchú was raised in an oral culture and has only recently learned to read—in Spanish, not her native Quiché; hers is a testimony and not a fictionalized rendering. The usefulness of comparing texts opposed at the levels of culture, class, ideology, and language proficiency resides in the quality of difference together they illuminate. Rigoberta Menchú's narrative challenges the limitations of the writing voice as we know it and the history of Caribbean literature by women in the process of its establishment. Her testimony revises our definitions of diaspora, literacy, narrative technique, and the implied reader.

Inherited as a culture-specific metaphor describing Jewish migrations and African displacement, the diaspora is not a term the reader generally associates with native North and South Americans. Nonetheless, resettlement of the so-called Indians sanctioned the construction of North America and the contemporary Caribbean as concepts from which the native presence has been conveniently excised.[44] I would argue that all cultures in the "New World" are diasporic. The singular memory that we "Americans" share in the hemisphere originates from histories of resettlement, emigration, and displacement. Resettlement reforms, if not eradicates, communal languages once defined in ethnic or nationalistic terms. Consequently, literacy in resettled territories implies assimilation to a master(ed) language transformed to accommodate the prerequisites of communication in a new environment.[45] When Rigoberta Menchú is forced to vacate her home in the *Altiplano* (mountains) to work as a day laborer in the *fincas* (plantations), and in the process becomes a revolutionary, she and others like her to do so because they have been terrorized by the Guatemalan army seeking to occupy lands the "Indians" claimed as their own; ironically, the Quiché give voice to their oppression in becoming literate in the language that oppresses her people. Menchú's testimony reads itself into the Spanish-speaking, *ladino* opposing camp and simultaneously "writes" into textual being a previously invisible Quiché history of resistance. Hers is an unusual illustration of diaspora literacy in whose sites the *marasa* principle of movement appears at the level of expression itself. *I, Rigoberta Menchú* creates new speech that is neither Quiché nor standard Latin American Spanish. Doris Sommer's perceptive article, " 'Not Just a Personal Story': Women's *Testimonios* and the Plural Self," addresses the diglossic language issue quite succinctly:

> Rigoberta's Spanish is qualitatively different from that of the "ladinos" who taught it to her. And her testimony makes the peculiar nonstandard Spanish into a public medium of change.[46]

In addition, the testimony and others like it, redefine literacy as an ideological rather than a purely educational pursuit. Menchú distinguishes clearly between literacy programs focused on Biblical exegesis administered, for instance, by Catholic Action (whose pedagogical intent is assimilation) and liberation theology, in which reading functions as a mode of analysis and an ideology of contestation. Literacy becomes the Indianists' "miraculous weapon," inciting political action against *ladino* landowners and government officials. The C.U.C. (Comité de Unidad Campesina/United Peasant Committee) to which Menchú and countless others belong supports in action this new definition of literacy.

In chapter thirty-two, "Strike of Agricultural Workers and the First of

May in the Capital," Menchú depicts Indianist laborers fighting back against *ladino* violence and repression in February 1980 and May 1981. The structure of the chapter and narrative relationship of the May First celebrations to the whole consistently reform the form of indigenous Quiché cultural and oral practice, as well as bourgeois narrative techniques. Recall of the strike in 1980 is situated metonymically against the May 10, 1981 Labor Day scene to which I shall refer shortly. A pattern emerges in Menchú's narration of the strike. The multiple perspectives on the event are common in orature where the storyteller situates her/himself between antagonistic characters and their habitual behavior (Bouki/Malice, Tortoise/Hare). The narrator recounts the tale from one and then the other viewpoint and comments upon the interaction of opposites, in a process comparable to the *marasa* principle—all the while improvising on an already existing scenario.[47] Rigoberta Menchú does not presume the existence of a preceding text, in fact, testimonial literature supposes ignorance on the part of the implied reader.[48] Menchú re-members the strike for fair wages from opposed positions representing defense and offense among the "Indianists": 1) sabotage of plantation machines and the building of barricades during the strike; 2) organization of the offensive and its failure. In the midst of a "plural narration," she inserts a surprisingly personal account regarding the development of leadership qualities.[49] In an oral narrative, Menchú's analysis would function as a third analytical, narrating voice:

We have learned that the role of a leader is as a coordinator more than anything, because the struggle is propelled forwards by the *compañeros* themselves. My work was mainly preparing new *compañeros* to take over the tasks that I or any of the other leaders do. In practice, the *compañeros* have to learn Spanish as I did, have to learn to read and write as I did, and assume all the responsibility for their work as I did. The reason behind this was that we're continually changing our roles, tasks, and our work. . . . we have understood that each one of us is responsible for the struggle and we don't need leaders who shuffle paper. We need leaders who are in danger, who run the same risks as the people. When there are many compañeros with equal abilities, they must all have the opportunity to lead their struggle. (p. 228)

The unspoken code here is the consistent murder of peasant leaders by the Guatemalan army. "Indianist" strategies requiring shifting directors reflects the peasants' pragmatic approach to resistance against the landowners. The three-sided representation of the strike as defense/offense and transformation of the individual stands as Menchú's ideological, narrative barricade protecting the significant event she is about to relate.

Having set the ground for an understanding of Quiché resistance in 1980 which, in retrospect, was a failure and considered a trial-run, Menchú settles into relating the May 10th, 1981 Labor Day successes. She narrates the scene as though it were a performance—structurally similar to Condé's and Marshall's approaches. Menchú's testimony is consistently time specific, remembered by dates and days in the oral manner, cast, however, in an activist, binary setting of struggle. The participants are opposed: peasant, workers, and Christian collaborators on one side; the police, authorities, army, and bracketed landowners whom they serve, on the other. No possibility of reconciliation; no liminal space is imagined, as in Condé's "Allegiance" gathering, where Veronica's perceptions stand between. Rather, Menchú draws the reader into conflict, brutal and unrehearsed. The narrative cannot be contained. The reader travels briskly about the capital city bombarded at once by the army's weaponry and a ubiquitous, plural self that Menchú's re-presentations evoke. She describes in detail interactions between these contending forces (all sorts of diversionary, peasant tactics) and ends the scene with a reflection on women's roles in the movement—a revealing, gender-specific moment in the text that may have been prompted by a question from Elisabeth Burgos-Debray:

Women have played an incredible role in the revolutionary struggle. Perhaps after the victory, we'll have time to tell our story. It is unbelievable. Mothers with their children would be putting up barricades, and then placing "propaganda bombs", or carrying documents. Women have had a great history. They've all experienced terrible things, whether they be working-class women, peasant women or teachers. This same situation has led us to do all those things. We don't do them because we want power, but so that something will be left for human beings. And this gives us the courage to be steadfast in the struggle, in spite of the danger. (p. 233)

Throughout the rememorization of May 10th, Menchú depicts the power system tactics which were so elusive to the protagonists of *Amour* and *Hérémakhonon*. Menchú's text reveals systems of oppression that cannot be described effectively from a distance, but are best analyzed in the midst of conflict by activists, some of whom may not survive the encounter. Furthermore, survivors who testify must be literate enough in a European language to insure the inscription of these events on our collective memory.

In the struggle to survive and resist, Menchú's text represents the reformation of form at several levels. The 1981 Labor Day strike's significance resides in the peasants' determination to reform *ladino*-imposed holidays into events celebrating "Indianist" activism. Moreover, testimonial literature and the language of its articulation are by nature reformative. The genre implies reformation of contradictions as Sommer has observed: ". . . In women's *testimonios,* apparently incompatible codes, such as Catholicism and communism, militance and motherhood, are syncretized to produce a flexible field of signification and political intervention."[50] *Marasa* consciousness when applied to Caribbean culture redirects our concerns beyond the syncretism of already existing binary codes, toward the identification and analysis of cultural and political practices resulting from these interactions—such as Vodoun, Carnival, and liberation theology, for example.

Much of the scholarship devoted to testimonials presumes a bourgeois, implied reader. Clearly, Menchú's testimony revises that definition by addressing itself as well as to the growing numbers of indigenous peasants literate in Spanish for whom the text represents a manual for social change. The implied reader is obviously dually constituted by the testifying voice speaking in two cultural directions at once. A disengaged reading is equally probable, as Sommer indicates:

> . . . readers can be called into the text without their assuming an identity with the writer or with her group. Identity is unnecessary and impossible in the acknowledgement of difference that testimonials impose on their readers. The reader can be linked at a respectful distance metonymically, as an extension of a collective history.[51]

Ultimately, *I, Rigoberta Menchú* and other works within the genre suggest the need to revise current literary theory through examinations of the interactions that are now occurring between newly formed indigenous readers and these new texts.

The problematic area of reader identification remains a central issue for consumers of transnational texts. Concerns expressed by the producers of indigenous texts within the multilingual Caribbean assume a different configuration. Reader identification recedes in its theoretical relevance when bilingualism and illiteracy within national boundaries subvert the establishment of a coherent, native reading public. When some of the more adventurous authors render their texts in Creole, they risk not being read in the original by both national and transnational audiences. The notion of national literacy is further complicated by alienation—a replay of Price-Mars's *collective bovaryism*—among already literate readers disinterested in indigenous, or worse, diasporic texts.[52] Although partially reconciled by the practice of simultaneous rewriting in a language more widely read, the anxiety of not reaching one's language constituency—an indigenous, implied reader—has likely stifled the efforts of more potential authors than we know. Developing diaspora literacy, then, is a progressive enterprise to which Condé, Marshall, and Menchú have devoted their narratives against the odds. Within the fluid textual climates in which these works were being produced, Menchú's testimony reformulates concepts of political and cultural literacy depicted by Condé and Marshall. The compressed space of Menchú's coming-to-consciousness and textualization of her activism have fused otherwise oppositional discursive strategies, namely the mastery of form, deformation of mastery, and reformation of form into a cohesive undertaking.

To conclude with a synthesis would undermine the principles of revision figured in the *marasa*. But conclude, I must. For readers of Francophone Caribbean literature, it may be instructive to engage the critical imagination in the process of destabilizing established intertextualities. I am referring here to acknowledged intertexts, notably Jacques Roumain's *Gouverneurs de la rosée* (1944) and Simone Schwarz-Bart's *Pluie et vent sur Telumée Miracle* (1972).[53] Has the diaspora produced a revision of the narrative fields articulated by these textual opposites? And, if so, how do we as comparatists (pre)determine and identify the configurations of textual transformation? A final comment: to defamiliarize our tidy, binary constructs is in *marasa* practice to divine: the rhythm is gonna getcha, the rhythm is gonna getcha, the rhythm is gonna getcha.[54]

NOTES

1. Scholarship devoted to new letters is extensive. For bibliographical references see Nathan Huggins, *Harlem Renaissance* (New York: Oxford University Press, 1974); Margaret Perry, comp., *Harlem Renaissance: An Annotated Bibliography* (New York: Garland Publishing, 1982); Victor A. Kramer, *Harlem Renaissance Re-Examined* (New York: AMS Press, 1987); Colette V. Michael, comp., *Négritude: An Annotated Bibliography* (West Cornwall, CT: Locust Hill Press, 1988). Although I have confined my remarks to new letters in Harlem, Port-au-Prince, and Paris, similar developments were occurring in Cuba, Puerto Rico, and Trinidad. See, for example, Martha K. Cobb, *Harlem, Haiti and Havana* (Washington, D.C.: Three Continents Press, 1979); Aníbal González Perez, "Ballad of the Two Poets: Nicolás Guillén and Luis Palés Matos," *Callaloo* 10.2 (Spring 1987):285-301; Reinhard Sander, *The Trinidad Awakening: West Indian Literature of the Nineteen-Thirties* (Westport, CT: Greenwood Press, 1988).

2. The history of nineteenth-century literary production is described in J. Michael Dash, *Literature and Ideology in Haiti* (Totowa, NJ: Barnes and Noble Books, 1981) and Léon-François Hoffmann, *Le Roman haitien: Idéologie et Structure* (Sherbrooke: Naaman, 1982).

3. On the subject of new letters influences and intertextualities, consult: Martha Cobb, *Harlem, Haiti and Havana;* Arnold Rampersad, *The Life of Langston Hughes* (New York: Oxford University Press, 1986); Robert P. Smith, "Rereading *Banjo*: Claude McKay and the French Connection," *CLAJ* 30.1 (September 1986):46-58; M.E. Mudimbé-Boyi, "Harlem Renaissance et l'Afrique: Une aventure ambigue," *Présence Africaine* 147 (1988):18-28. With meticulous detail, A.J. James Arnold documents French literary influences in Césaire's work in *Modernism and Négritude* (Cambridge: Harvard University Press, 1981); textual relations between Mallarmé and Césaire are examined in Annie Pibarot, "Césaire lecteur de Mallarmé" *Frankophone Literaturen Ausserhalb Europas*, ed. Janos Reisz (Frankfurt am Main: Peter Lang, 1987):17-27.

4. Jean Price-Mars, *Ainsi Parla L'Oncle* (Paris: Imprimerie de Compiègne, 1928). For a rereading of the ideological conflict between the Francophile, Dantès Bellegarde, and Price-

Mars, see Patrick Bellegarde-Smith, *In the Shadow of Powers: Dantès Bellegarde in Haitian Social Thought* (Atlantic Highlands, NJ: Humanities Press International, 1985). Their opposed positions deserve comparison with that of Booker T. Washington and W.E.B. Du Bois within the wider field of culture and discourse, as in Houston A. Baker's *Modernism and the Harlem Renaissance* (Chicago: University of Chicago Press, 1987) and John Brown Childs's *Leadership, Conflict and Cooperation in Afro-American Social Thought* (Philadelphia: Temple University Press, 1989). I am grateful to Andrew Parker (Amherst College) for drawing my attention to Childs's study.

5. Suzanne Lacascade, *Claire Solange, âme africaine* (Paris: Eugène Figuière, 1924) and Annie Desroy, *Le Joug* (Port-au-Prince: Imprimerie Modèle, 1934).

6. With the exception of Suzanne Césaire, Aimé Césaire's wife who edited the journal *Tropiques* with him from 1941-45, women's participation in Francophone new letters was marginal. See the two volume facsimile of *Tropiques* reprinted in 1978 by Editions Jean-Michel Place, Paris. The role of the Nardal sisters in the Négritude movement as conveners of gatherings and translators for *La Revue du Monde Noir* remains confusing despite frequent mention in literary histories. For a brief attempt at unraveling the story, see Louis T. Achille, "In Memoriam: Paulette Nardal," *Présence Africaine* 133-134 (1985):291-293.

7. Maryse Condé, *La Parole des femmes* (Paris: L'Harmattan, 1979).

8. Maryse Condé, *En attendant le bonheur: Hérémakhonon* (Paris: Seghers, 1988); Paule Marshall, *Praisesong for the Widow* (New York: E.P. Dutton, 1983); and Elisabeth Burgos-Debray, ed., *Me Llamo Rigoberta Menchú Y Así Me Nació la Consciencia* (Barcelona: Editorial Argos Vergara, 1983). English translations of Condé and Menchú are by Richard Philcox, *Hérémakhonon* (Washington, D.C.: Three Continents Press, 1982) and Ann Wright, *I, Rigoberta Menchú* (London: Verso Editions, 1984). Further references to these editions are cited by page numbers within the text.

9. Contending approaches to comparative literature methodologies within Caribbean literature appear in Albert S. Gérard, "Problématique d'une histoire littéraire du monde carîbe" *Revue de littérature comparée* 62.1 (January-March 1988):45-56; Ana Pizarro, "Reflections on the Historiography of Caribbean Literature," *Callaloo* 11.1 (Winter 1988):173-185; and llena Rodriguez and Marc Zimmerman, eds., *Process of Unity in Caribbean Society: Ideologies and Literature* (Minneapolis: Institute for the Study of Ideologies and Literatures, 1983). Regarding comparative literary theory, see Ulrich Weisstein, *Comparative Literature and Literary Theory,* trans. William Riggan (Bloomington: Indiana University Press, 1973).

10. The Christopher Columbus ventures are examined critically in Tzvetan Todorov, *The Conquest of America* (New York: Harper and Row, 1984) and Hans Koning, *Columbus: His Enterprise* (New York: Monthly Review Press, 1976).

11. Edward Brathwaite, *The Development of Creole Society in Jamaica, 1770-1820* (Oxford: Clarendon Press, 1971); Eugene Genovese, *Roll Jordan Roll, The World the Slaves Made* (New York: Vintage Books, 1972); Gabriel Debien, *Les esclaves aux Antilles Françaises, XVIIe-XVIIIe siècles* (Basse-Terre, Guadeloupe, 1974).

12. Alain Locke, *The New Negro* (New York: Albert and Charles Boni, 1925).

13. For this insight, I am indebted to Sylvia Wynter's fascinating argument in which she identifies as an epistemological recentering the entry of Black Studies into the Academy. See her article, "The Ceremony Must Be Found: After Humanism," *Boundary 2* 12.3/13.1 (Spring/Fall 1984):19-70.

14. Albert S. Gérard, ed., *European-language Writing in Sub-Saharan Africa* (Budapest: Akademiai Kiado, 1986) and *African-language Literature: An Introduction to the Literary History of Sub-Saharan Africa* (Washington, D.C.: Three Continents Press, 1981).

15. The term *diaspora literary* developed originally from my analysis of *Hérémakhonon* delivered as a paper during the African Literature Association Conference in 1984, Baltimore, Maryland. The definition here has been revised and expanded. See "Developing Diaspora

Literacy: Allusion in Maryse Condé's *Hérémakhonon,*" in *Out of the Kumbla: Womanist Perspectives on Caribbean Literature,* eds. Carole Boyce Davies and Elaine Savory Fido (Trenton, NJ: Africa World Press, 1989):315-331.

16. Houston Baker's analysis is certainly more broadly argued than my brief references would indicate. For purposes of comparing texts from the diaspora, I have found it useful to refer to his model for the study of discursive strategies rather than the Afro-American interdisciplinary sites on which the argument is grounded. In the future, similar cultural bases for analysis of Caribbean and African texts must certainly be considered.

17. Critical works by Houston Baker and Henry Louis Gates have suggested models for the vernacular approach to literary theory that I am attempting to practice in this essay. Gates's chapter, "A Myth of Origins: Esu-Elegbara and the Signifying Monkey" is exemplary; my efforts here represent a preliminary statement of the *marasa* principle within comparative literature; Henry Louis Gates, Jr. *The Signifying Monkey* (New York: Oxford University Press, 1988):3-43.

18. John Coltrane, *My Favorite Things,* Atlantic Recording CS 1361 (1981).

19. See, for instance, Peter B. Hammond, "Economic Change and Mossi Acculturation," *Continuity and Change in African Culture,* eds. William R. Bascom and Melville J. Herskovits (Chicago: University of Chicago Press, 1959) and Robert Brain, "Friends and Twins in Bangwa," *Man in Africa,* eds. Mary Douglas and Phyllis M. Kaberry (New York: Anchor Books, 1971).

20. Depictions of the *marasa* in Haitian ritual ceremony appear in a number of works. Interpretive readings may be found in Milo Rigaud's two studies, *La tradition voudou et le voudou haitien* (Paris: Niclaus, 1953) and his *Ve-Ve, Diagrammes rituels du vodou* (New York: French and European Publications, 1974); Maya Deren, *Divine Horsemen* (New York: Chelsea House, 1953/1970); Karen Brown, "The 'Veve' of Haitian Vodu: a Structural Analysis of Visual Imagery," Ph.D. dissertation, Temple University, 1976.

21. The "spiralist" agenda to which I am referring has been transferred to literary production by one of Haiti's premier authors in Creole and French. Frankétienne qualifies the aesthetics of his poetry and prose as spiralist. See the most recent publications, *Adjanoumelezo* (Haiti: Imprimerie des Antilles, 1987) and *Fleurs d'Insomnie* (Haiti: Imprimerie Henri Deschamps, 1986) among others.

22. Consult, for example, Deren's *Divine Horsemen* and Brown's "The 'Veve' of Haitian Vodu: a Structural Analysis of Visual Imagery"; and VèVè Clark, "Fieldhands to Stagehands," Ph.D. dissertation, University of California, Berkeley, 1983.

23. Melville Herskovits, *Dahomey, An Ancient, West African Kingdom* (New York: J.J. Augustin, 1938) and Herskovits with Frances S. Herskovits, *An Outline of Dahomean Religious Belief* (New York: Kraus, 1964).

24. Milo Rigaud, *Ve-Ve, Diagrammes rituels du vodou:* 35, 91, 141, 409-419. Rigaud collected and reproduced vèvès of the *marasa trois* and through his analysis introduced a figure that had been obscured in previous scholarship. The validity of his interpretations has been approached skeptically due to their mystical nature. In the current theoretical climate, Rigaud's persistent work at collecting and analysis may be re-evaluated in an atmosphere more positively disposed to his unusual interest in Vodoun, uncommon among Haiti's mulatto elite, and his eccentric approaches devalued in the wider field of cultural criticism at the time.

25. For an overview of Creole language theory, see Derek Bickerton, *Roots of Language* (Ann Arbor: Karoma Publishers, 1981) and Albert Valdman and A. Highfield, eds., *Theoretical Orientations in Creole Studies* (New York: Academic Press, 1980).

26. Cf. the earlier essay by Gates, "The blackness of blackness: a critique of the sign and the Signifying Monkey," *Black Literature and Literary Theory,* ed. Henry Louis Gates, Jr. (New York: Methuen, 1984):285-321.

27. VèVè A. Clark, "Marassa: Images of Women from the Other Americas," *Woman of*

Power 1.1 (1984):58-61; Maximilien Laroche, *Le Patriarche, Le Marron et La Dossa: Essais sur les figures de la gémellité dans le roman haitien* (Sainte-Foy, Québec: GRELCA, 1988).

28. Gates, *The Signifying Monkey*.

29. In addition to the sources cited above in note 20, the principal bibliographical references to *marasa* are collected in Gates, *The Signifying Monkey:* 3-43 and 259-264.

30. Gates, *The Signifying Monkey:* xix-xxviii.

31. Marie Chauvet, *Amour, Colère et Folie* (Paris: Editions du Seuil, 1968). The setting refers, in fact, to François Duvalier's regime (1957-1971). Allusions to contemporary politics caused the text to be censored in Haiti and Chauvet forced into exile in North America where she died soon after of cancer.

32. Frantz Fanon, *Black Skins, White Masks,* trans. Charles Lam Markmann (New York: Grove Press, 1967).

33. Jack M. Bloom, *Class, Race and the Civil Rights Movement* (Bloomington: Indiana University Press, 1987); David J. Garrow, *The Walking City: the Montgomery Bus Boycott* (Brooklyn, NY: Carlson Publishers, 1989); Ernest Harsch, *South Africa: White Rule, Black Revolt* (New York: Monad Press, 1980).

34. Condé, *La Parole des femmes:* 104. Condé is equally critical of Chauvet's *Amour* in *La Parole:* "On aimerait que Marie Chauvet démonte davantage pour notre profit la stérilité de la machine de pouvoir qui se met en branle. Elle ne le fait pas, se bornant à des notations brèves sur la misère des paysans qui augmente, les vivres qui se rarefient. Sans doute ne peut-elle pas en dire plus, puisque tout est vu à travers les yeux de Claire, la vieille fille, enfermée dans la prison de ses frustrations. On ne peut pas nier que son portrait quant à elle soit tracé de main de maître" (p. 100).

35. Condé, *La Parole des femmes:* 125; and Maryse Condé, "I Have Made Peace with My Island," with VèVè Clark, *Callaloo* 12.2 (Spring/Summer 1989):101, 119-123.

36. Condé, *Hérémakhonon:* 76-80/46-48.

37. See my discussion in "Developing Diaspora Literacy" in *Out of the Kumbla*.

38. Regarding the limitations of Veronica's literacy, I am basing these conclusions on the absence of allusions to post-Independence political writings as well as the protagonist's reluctance to teach the works of Fanon and Kwame Nkrumah in *Hérémakhonon:* 14.

39. Françoise Lionnet, "Happiness Deferred: Maryse Condé's *Hérémakhonon* and the Failure of Enunciation," in *Autobiographical Voices: Race, Gender, Self-Portraiture* (Ithaca, NY: Cornell University Press, 1989):181. From differing theoretical perspectives, Lionnet and I have arrived at similar readings of the text.

40. Maryse Condé, "I Have Made Peace with My Island": 117. Consult also Condé's articles: "Pourquoi la négritude: négritude ou révolution?" *Négritude africaine, négritude caraïbe,* ed. Jeanne-Lydie Gore (Paris: Editions de la francite, 1973):150-154, and "Négritude césairienne, négritude senghorienne, *Revue de la littérature comparée* 191-192 (July-December 1974):409-419.

41. "Narratives of apprenticeship" replaces the standard term *Bildungsroman* in Arlette M. Smith, "Maryse Condé's *Hérémakhonon:* A Triangular Structure of Alienation," *CLAJ* 32.1 (September 1988):45-54.

42. Velma Pollard, "Cultural Connections in Paule Marshall's *Praisesong for the Widow,*" *World Literature Written in English* 25.2 (Autumn 1985):285-298.

43. I owe this insight to Hazel Carby's unpublished paper "Zora Neale Hurston and the Discourse of the Folk" and to my own research on Zora Neale Hurston's and Katherine Dunham's interactions with Caribbean societies during the 1930s. These two women are certainly not the sole participants in the discursive genres of ethnography created during the 1930s. George E. Marcus and Michael M. J. Fisher's *Anthropology as Cultural Critique* (Chicago, University of Chicago, 1986) in their self-reflexive examinations provide enlightening perspectives on the field. These critiques notwithstanding, ethnography became

a more personalized discipline in the 1930s, during which time the class and gender of the observer were allowed to enter into the dynamics of observation where previously difference was perceived according to racial and cultural definitions of the outside observer.

44. For an overview of this historical process, see Todorov, *The Conquest of America*.

45. Creolizing or "seasoning" in the assimilation process is analyzed from historical and linguistic perspectives in studies noted above; see numbers 11 and 25.

46. Doris Sommer, " 'Not Just a Personal Story': Women's *Testimonios* and the Plural Self," in *Life/Lines: Theorizing Women's Autobiography*, eds. Bella Brodski and Celeste Schenck (Ithaca, NY: Cornell University Press, 1988):128. Again, Andrew Parker drew my attention to this valuable assessment.

47. Descriptive and theoretical critiques of folk narrative may be approached through Lawrence Levine, *Black Culture and Black Consciousness* (New York: Oxford University Press, 1977); Alan Dundes, ed., *Mother Wit From the Laughing Barrel: Readings in the Interpretation of Afro-American Folklore* (Englewood Cliffs, NJ: Prentice Hall, 1973) and *Sacred Narrative: Readings in the Theory of Myth* (Los Angeles: University of California Press, 1984.

48. Charles T. Davis and Henry Louis Gates, Jr., *The Slave's Narrative* (New York: Oxford University Press, 1985). On implied reader theory, consult Wolfgang Iser, *The Act of Reading: A Theory of Aesthetic Response* (Baltimore: Johns Hopkins University Press, 1978) and *The Implied Reader: Patterns of Communications in Prose Fiction from Bunyan to Beckett* (Baltimore: Johns Hopkins University Press, 1974).

49. On the notion of "an explicitly collective subject behind the first-person narrator of testimonials," see Sommer, "Not Just a Personal Story": 108–112.

50. Sommer: 130.

51. Sommer: 130.

52. See Albert Gérard's, "Problématique d'une histoire littéraire du monde caraïbe" and Condé's view of the distanced reading public that she encountered on her return to Guadeloupe in "I Have Made Peace with My Island": 111–115.

53. Jacques Roumain, *Gouverneurs de la rosée* (Paris: Editions Messidor, 1986), and *Masters of the Dew*, trans. Langston Hughes and Mercer Cook (London: Heinemann, 1978); Simone Schwarz-Bart, *Pluie et vent sur Telumée Miracle* (Paris: Editions du Seuil, 1972), and *The Bridge of Beyond*, trans. Barbara Bray (London: Heinemann, 1982).

54. "Rhythm is Gonna Get You," Gloria Estéfan and Miami Sound Machine on the album *Let it Loose*, Epic Records OET 40769.

4.

Toni Morrison's *Beloved*: Re-Membering the Body as Historical Text

MAE G. HENDERSON

Now, women forget all those things they don't want to remember. The dream is the truth. Then they act and do things accordingly. . . . So the beginning of this was a woman and she had come back from burying the dead.
Zora Neale Hurston, Their Eyes Were Watching God

We tell stories because in the last analysis human lives need and merit being narrated. This remark takes on its full force when we refer to the necessity to save the history of the defeated and the lost. The whole history of suffering cries out for vengeance and calls for narrative.
Paul Ricoeur, Time and Narrative

Upon the death of the other we are given to memory, and thus to interiorization . . . since Freud, this is how the "normal" "work of mourning" is often described. It entails a movement in which an interiorizing idealization takes in itself or upon itself the body and voice of the other, the other's visage and person, ideally *and* quasi-literally devouring them. This mimetic interiorization is not fictive; it is the origin of fiction, of apocryphal figuration. It takes place in a body. Or rather, it makes for a body, voice, and a soul which, although "ours," did not exist and had no meaning *before* this possibility that one *must* always begin by remembering, and whose trace must be followed.
Jacques Derrida, Memories for Paul de Man

. . . I had brought not a child but suffering into the world and it, suffering, refused to leave me, insisted on coming back, on haunting me, permanently. One does not bear children in pain, it's pain that one bears: the child is pain's representative and once it is delivered moves in for good. . . . [A] mother is . . . marked by pain, she succumbs to it.
Julia Kristeva, "Stabat Mater"

There is an "uncanniness" about his past that a present occupant has expelled (or thinks it has) in an effort to take its place. The dead haunt the living. The past: it "re-bites" [*il remord*] (it is a secret and repeated biting). History is "cannibalistic," and memory becomes the closed arena of conflict between two contradictory operations: forgetting, which is not something passive, a loss, but an action directed against the past; and the mnemic trace, the return of what was forgotten. . . . More generally speaking, an autonomous order is founded upon what it eliminates; it produces a "residue" condemned to be forgotten. But what was excluded. . . . re-infiltrates the place of its origin—It resurfaces, it troubles, it turns the present's feeling of being "at home" into an illusion, it lurks—this "wild," this "ob-scene," this "filth," this "resistance" of "superstition"—within the walls of the residence, and behind the back of the owner (the *ego*), or over its objections, it inscribes there the law of the other.

Michel de Certeau, *Heterologies: The Discourse of the Other*

Describing the nineteenth-century slave narratives, Toni Morrison observes, "No slave society in the history of the world wrote more—or more thoughtfully—about its own enslavement." Yet, for Morrison, the narratives with their "instructive" and "moral" force are incomplete:

Over and over, the writers pull the narrative up short with a phrase such as, "but let us drop a veil over these proceedings too terrible to relate." In shaping the experience to make it palatable to those who were in a position to alleviate it, they were silent about many things,and they "forgot" many other things. . . . [1]

We should note that "things too terrible to relate" were most often the sexual exploitation of slave women by white men. Convention allowed, indeed almost demanded, that these violations be named but not described. Morrison continues, "But most importantly,—at least for me—there was no mention of their *interior life*" (emphasis mine). The writer's "job"—as Morrison sees it—"becomes how to rip that veil drawn over proceedings too terrible to relate . . . ," to "find and expose a truth about the interior life of people who didn't write it," to "fill in the blanks that the slave narratives left, to part the veil that was so frequently drawn," and, finally, "to implement the stories that [she has] heard (110-113).

In utilizing the image of the veil, we note that Morrison draws on and revises a DuBoisian metaphor that was originally intended to suggest the division between blacks and whites in American society.[2] Rather than measuring a division *between* the races, however, Morrison's use of the veil as metaphor measures a division *within* the race—a psychic and expressive boundary separating the *speakable* from the *unspeakable* and the *unspoken*.[3] Her task as a writer, therefore, is to transgress these discursive boundaries by setting up a complementary and dialogic relationship between the "interiority" of her own work and the "exteriority" of the slave narrative.

Morrison, then, aims to restore a dimension of the repressed personal in a manifestly political discourse. In some ways, the texts of the slave narratives can be regarded as classic examples of the "return of the repressed," primarily because the events relating to violence and violation (which are self-censored or edited out) return again and again in "veiled allusions." To the degree that her work is intended to *resurrect* stories *buried* and *express* stories *repressed,* Morrison's relationship to the slave narrators, as well as the relationship of her text to its precursor narratives, can be profitably compared not only to the relationship of the historian to his or her informant, but also the analyst to the analysand.

Dedicating her novel *Beloved* to the "Sixty Million and more" who failed to survive the Middle Passage, Morrison sets out to give voice to the "disremembered and unaccounted for"—the women and children who left no written records. The epigraph from Romans 9:25 prefigures the writer's purpose to reclaim this "lost tribe":

> *I will call them my people,*
> *which were not my people;*
> *and her beloved,*
> *which was not beloved.*

In her citation of a New Testament passage that repeats with little difference a passage from the Old Testament, the author not only problematizes the nature of the relationship between the past and the present, but also thematizes the importance of historical Reclamation and Repossession. As Jehovah reclaimed the Israelites after their apostasy (figured in Hosea as spiritual adultery), so Morrison seeks to repossess the African and slave ancestors after their historic violation (figured in *Beloved* as physical rape). Further, Morrison reinscribes the tension between Old Testament Law and New Testament spirit. Significantly, it is the epistles of Paul (Romans and Galatians, in particular) which announce that the doctrine of justification by deeds under the Old Dispensation of the Law is revised through justification by grace under the New Dispensation of the Spirit.[4] Engaging the Scriptures as a kind of intertext, Morrison enacts in her novel an opposition between the Law and the Spirit, redeeming her characters from the "curse of the law" as figured in the master's discourse. In her rewriting of Scripture, Morrison ushers in an ironic new dispensation figured not by the Law of the (white) Father, but the Spirit of the (black and female) child, Beloved. Thus Morrison challenges the hegemonic status of the (primarily male) slave narratives as well as the "canonical" history embodied in the master('s) narratives in a project which seeks to make both more accountable to the "disremembered and unaccounted for."

Like several of her contemporaries, Morrison seeks to achieve these ends in a novel that both historicizes fiction and fictionalizes history.[5] The following is Morrison's recollection of the events on which the novel was based:

I . . . remember being obsessed by two or three little fragments of stories that I heard from different places. One was a newspaper clipping about a woman named Margaret Garner in 1851. It said that the Abolitionists made a great deal out of her case because she had escaped from Kentucky . . . with her four children. She lived in a little neighborhood just outside of Cincinnati and she had killed her children. She succeeded in killing one; she tried to kill two others. The interesting thing, in addition to that, was the interviews that she gave. She was a young woman. In the inked pictures of her she seemed a very quiet, very serene-looking woman and everyone who interviewed her remarked about her serenity and tranquility. She said, "I will not let those children live how I have lived." She had run off into a little woodshed right outside her house to kill them because she had been caught as a fugitive. And she made up her mind that they would not suffer the way that she had and it was better for them to die. They put her in jail for a little while and I'm not even sure what the denouement is of her story. But that moment, that decision was a piece, a tail of something that was always around. . . .[6]

Continuing, Morrison links the above story fragment to another related in James Van der Zee's *The Harlem Book of the Dead:*

In one picture, there was a young girl lying in a coffin and he says that she was eighteen years old and she had gone to a party and that she was dancing and suddenly she slumped and they noticed there was blood on her and they said, "what happened to you?" And she said, "I'll tell you tomorrow. I'll tell you tomorrow. . . ." That's all she would say. And apparently her ex-boyfriend or somebody who was jealous had come to the party with a gun and a silencer and shot her. And she kept saying, "I'll tell you tomorrow" because she wanted him to get away. And he did, I guess; anyway she died (584)

It was the newspaper clippings and Van der Zee's photostory that provided the historical or "real-life" bases for the novel. "Now what made those stories connect, I can't explain," says Morrison, "but I do know that, in both instances, something seemed clear to me. A woman loved something other than herself so much, she had placed all of the value of her life in something outside herself." Morrison's project, then, is twofold: the exploration of the black woman's sense of self, and the imaginative recovery of black women's history.

Describing her narrative strategy as a "kind of literary archeology," Morrison explains that, for her, "the approach that's most productive and most trustworthy . . . is the recollection that moves from the image to . . . text." Her task, as she defines it, is to "[move] that veil aside" in order to penetrate the "memories within." Although these memories—personal and collective—constitute the "subsoil of [her] work," she informs us that these alone cannot give "total access to the unwritten interior life. . . ." For Morrison, it is "only the act of the imagination" that can provide such access:

[O]n the basis of some information and a little bit of guesswork you journey to a site to see what remains were left behind and to reconstruct the world that these remains imply. What makes it fiction is the nature of the imaginative act: my reliance on the image—on the remains—in addition to recollection, to yield up a kind of truth. By "image," of course, I don't mean "symbol"; I simply mean "picture" and the feelings that accompany the picture.[7]

Elaborating on the relationship between picture and meaning, Morrison contrasts her own literary method (to move from image to text) to that of writers who move "from event to the image that it left": "My route is the reverse: the image comes first and tells me what the 'memory' is about."[8]

The notion of "literary archeology"—the imaginative and reconstructive recovery of the past which characterizes Morrison's fictive process—can be usefully compared with R.G. Collingwood's description of the historical process: If the novelist relies upon the *a priori* imagination to construct the *possible* story in which characters and incidents develop "in a manner determined by a necessity internal to themselves," the historian relies upon the same inferential process to construct "his" story of the *past*. In the following passage, Collingwood demonstrates that "as works of imagination, the historian's work and novelist's do not differ":

Each of them makes it his business to construct a picture which is partly a narrative of events, partly a description of situations, exhibition of motives, analysis of characters. Each aims at making his picture a coherent whole, where every character and every situation is so bound up with the rest that this character in this situation cannot but act in this way, and we cannot imagine him as acting otherwise. The novel and the history must both of them make sense; nothing is admissible in either except what is necessary and the judge of this necessity is in both cases the imagination. Both the novel and the history are self-explanatory, self-justifying, the product of an autonomous or self-authorizing activity; and in both cases this activity is the *a priori* imagination.[9]

The present essay will examine Morrison's novel in the context of some contemporary historical theory on discourse and narrativity, suggesting, where novelistic considerations warrant, a reading that links historiography and psychoanalysis.

Like Morrison, the principal character in *Beloved* is in struggle with a past that is part of white/male historical discourse. Lacking a discourse of her own, Sethe's task is to transform the residual images ("rememories") of her past into a historical discourse shaped by narrativity. These images, however, remain for a time disembodied—without form, sequence, or meaning. The challenge of the slave as victim of enforced illiteracy is similar to that of the highly literate contemporary historian or novelist—and that is to discover a way of organizing memory, of contriving a narrative configuration in the absence of written records. If it is true, as Henry Louis Gates, Jr. argues, that our sense of the self, as we have defined it in the West since the Enlightenment, "turns in part upon written records," if "our idea of the self . . . is . . . inextricably interwoven with our ideas . . . of [writing]," then what are the consequences of an absence of written records? Quite simply and perhaps startlingly, as a slave "one's sense of one's existence . . . depended upon memory." "It was memory, above all else," according to Gates, "that gave shape to being itself."[10] What these remarks do not address, however, is how one formally shapes and derives meaning from disparate memories. In other words, how does one extract a configuration from a cluster of images or diversity of events? How does one, finally, transpose memories from a visual to a diegetic, or narrative, register? Like Morrison, Sethe must learn to represent the unspeakable and unspoken in language—and more precisely, as narrative.

Morrison figures both the interiority and the exteriority of memory, that is, memory as thought and memory as material inscription.[11] In the novel, "Beloved" is the public inscription of a private memorial—seven letters chiseled into the pink headstone of a child-victim of "mother-love," a word Sethe had remembered from the preacher's funeral eulogy. If the inscription of Beloved is the trace ("the mark left behind") that initiates the novel's plot, it is also an image that haunts the text in the multiple guises of the character Beloved. As a term, "beloved" is an address conferred by the lover on the object of affection, and used in matrimonial and eulogistic discourse, both commemorative, linguistic events: the former prefiguring the future, the latter refiguring the past. The action of the novel, however, attends to the novelistic present—a present problematized by an unresolved past and an unanticipated future, a present which the past does not prefigure nor the future refigure.

When we meet Sethe at the outset of the novel, her "future was a matter of keeping the past at bay" (42).[12] Her aim has been to protect her children from "rememory"—which she describes as follows:

Someday you be walking down the road and you hear something or see something going on. So clear. . . . It's when you bump into a rememory that belongs to somebody else. Where I was before I came here, that place [Sweet Home] is real. It's never going away. Even if the whole farm—every tree and grass blade of it dies. The picture is still there and what's more, if you go there—you who never was there—if you go there and stand in the place where it was, it will happen again; it will be there for you, waiting for you. (36)

"Rememory," it would seem, is something which possesses (or haunts) one, rather than something which one possesses. (It is, in fact, that which makes the past part of one's present.) Yet, despite her best efforts to "[beat] back the past," Sethe remains, in her words, "full of it." "Every mention of her past life hurt. Everything in it was painful or lost"(58). Hayden White's description of Ibsen's Hedda Gabler would also seem apt for Morrison's Sethe: She "suffers [from] the incubus [or, in this case, the succubus] of the past—a surfeit of history compounded by, or reflected in, a pervasive fear of the future."[13]

Thus, unable to contrive a meaningful or appropriate configuration for her memories, Sethe finds herself tyrannized by unconfigured and literally disfiguring images. As a consequence of an attempted escape, she receives a savage beating, leaving her back "a clump of scars." These scars function as signs of ownership inscribing her as property, while the mutilation signifies her diminishment to a less-than-human status. Traces of the past that Sethe represses (but can neither remember nor forget) have been gouged onto her back by the master's whip and bear the potential burden of both *his*tory and *her*story. Like the inscription of Beloved and the pictorial images of the past, the scars function as an archeological site or memory trace.

If the master has inscribed the master('s) code on Sethe's back, a white woman and a black man, in an effort to decipher it offer her alternative readings. Although initially "struck dumb" at the sight of Sethe's scars, Amy, a runaway white girl who saves the fugitive's life and midwives the delivery of her second daughter, sees Sethe's back as a "chokecherry tree":

See, here's the trunk—it's red and split wide open, full of sap, and this here's the parting for the branches. . . . Leaves, too, look like, and dern if these ain't blossoms. Tiny little cherry blossoms, just as white. Your back got a whole tree on it. In bloom. (79)

Amy describes an image, but an image which prompts her to wonder "what God have in mind." In her reverie, Sethe's back remains the trace of an event whose meaning, motivation, and consequence are largely unreadable.

Alternative readings are provided by Baby Suggs, Sethe's mother-in-law, and Paul D, the last survivor of the men from Sweet Home, the Kentucky plantation where he and Sethe had met before the War. Baby Suggs perceives her daughter-in-law's back as a pattern of "roses of blood," stenciled onto the bedsheet and blanket. Paul D, however, remarks on "the sculpture [Sethe's] back had become, like the decorative work of an ironsmith too passionate for display. . . ." (By the time Paul D arrives, the open wounds have healed into an intricate filigree whose private meaning is concealed from public exposure.) Notably, the distance between these suggestively gendered readings—the chokecherry tree and blood roses on the one hand, and the wrought-iron maze on the other—signifies the distance between so-called "natural" and culturally inscribed meanings attributed to the sign.

It is the white man who inscribes; the white woman, the black man, and the black woman may variously read, but not write. Because it is her back (symbolizing the *presence* of her *past*) that is marked, Sethe has only been able to read herself through the gaze of others. The challenge for Sethe is to learn to read herself—that is, to configure the history of her body's text. If, as Paul Ricoeur contends, "the past survives by leaving its trace," then Sethe must learn how to link these traces (marks of her passage through slavery) to the construction of a personal and historical discourse.[14] Sethe's dilemma is that as a female slave without the benefit of literacy, she finds herself the written object of a white male discourse and the spoken subject of a black male and white female discourse. Significantly, Baby Suggs does *not* speak of the wounds on Sethe's back. "Baby Suggs hid her mouth with her hand" (93). Instead, she concentrates on the ritual of healing: "*[W]ordlessly,* the older woman greased the flowering back and pinned a double thickness of cloth to the inside of the newly stitched dress" (emphasis mine, 93). The presumption is, of course, that black women have no voice, no text, and consequently no history. They can be written and written upon precisely because they exist as the ultimate Other whose absence or (non)being only serves to define the being or presence of the white or male subject. The black woman, symbolizing a kind of double negativity, becomes a *tabula rasa* upon which the racial/sexual identity of the other(s) can be positively inscribed.

Sethe's back is numb ("the skin on her back had been dead for years"), signifying her attempts to repress the past. (But the return of Paul D and, later Beloved, signal the return of the repressed.) For Sethe, these scars constitute traces of past deeds too horrible and violent either to forget or remember (a situation which Morrison describes elsewhere as "a perfect dilemma"). The brutal whipping she receives as punishment for her attempt to run away is only part of a cluster of events which Sethe vainly seeks to forget.

If Morrison formalizes and thematizes the operation of imaginative construction, she also dramatizes, in the character of "Schoolteacher" (as he is called by the slaves), the consequences of an alternative approach. The scenes with Schoolteacher are paradigmatic for reading the methodology of the white male as scholar and master. Arriving at Sweet Home after the death of its previous owner, Schoolteacher announces himself "with a big hat and spectacles and a coach full of paper" and begins to "watch" his subjects. His methodology—based on numbering, weighing, dividing—suggests the role of the cultural historian (or ethnologist) as one who is concerned with sizes, densities, details, appearances, externalities, and visible properties ("School teacher'd wrap that string all over my head, 'cross my nose, around my behind. Number my teeth").[15]

Schoolteacher possesses the master('s) text, and as a data-collector, cataloguer, classifer, and taxonomist concerned with matters of materiality and empiricism, he divides or dismembers the indivisibility of the slaves' humanity to reconstruct (or perhaps deconstruct) the slave in his text. Reminiscent of Hawthorne's Custom's House Surveyor whose careful and accurate measurements disclose little besides the fact that "each limb [of the letter A] proved to be precisely three inches and a quarter in length," Schoolteacher's precise physical measurements reveal but limited meaning; his putatively scientific techniques are altogether inadequate. Unlike Hawthorne's Surveyor, who discovers himself confronted with a "riddle which . . . [he] sees little hope of resolving," Morrison's historical investigator remains hopelessly unconscious "of his own infirmity."[16] Sethe tells us,

> He was talking to one of his pupils and I heard him say, "Which one are you doing?" And one of the boys said, "Sethe." That's when I stopped because I heard my name, and then I took a few steps to where I could see what they was doing. Schoolteacher was standing over one of them with one hand behind his back. He licked a forefinger a couple of times and turned a few pages. Slow. I was about to turn around and keep on my way . . . when I heard him say, "No, no. That's not the way. I told you to put her human characteristics on the left; her *animal* ones on the right. And don't forget to line them up." (emphasis mine, 193)

Schoolteacher's historiography encodes the notion and forms of "wildness" and "animality." As Hayden White explains, this notion is a "culturally self-authenticating device" intended to "confirm the value of [the] dialectical antithesis between 'civilization' . . . and 'humanity.' "[17] Like Nehemiah Adams, the historical investigator in Sherley Anne Williams's *Dessa Rose,* Morrison's schoolteacher espouses a concept of difference and "otherness" as a form of subhumanity that serves, through a process of negative self-identification, to confirm his own sense of superiority. It is Sethe's "savagery" which confirms Schoolteacher's "civilization," her "bestiality" which confirms his "humanity." Schoolteacher's sense of history is defined by the struggle between culture and nature, and questions of meaning and interpretation turn upon this opposition.[18]

The dismemberment of Schoolteacher's method is the discursive analog to the dismemberment of slavery. Just as his pupils measure and divide Sethe according to Schoolteacher's instructions, so Schoolteacher himself, speaking with the slave catchers, reveals to Paul D "his worth." Overhearing the men talking, Paul D, who "has always known, or believed he did, his value—as a hand, a laborer who could make profit on a farm . . . now [discovers] his worth, which is to say he learns his price. The dollar value of his weight, his strength, his heart, his brain, his penis, and his future" (226). As both slaveholder and scholar, Schoolteacher is involved with the *dis-membering* of slaves from their families, their labor, their selves. It is against these forms of physical, social, and scholarly dismemberment that the act of (re)memory initiates a reconstitutive process in the novel. If dismemberment deconstitutes the whole, fragmenting it into various discrete and heterogeneous parts, then re-memory functions to re-collect, re-assemble, and organize into a meaningful sequential whole through, as we shall see, the process of narrativization.

The scenes of Paul D's figurative dismemberment both refigure the earlier scene of Schoolteacher's anatomical dismemberment of Sethe and prefigure a later scene which Sethe vainly attempts to forget: "I am full God damn it of two boys with mossy teeth, one sucking on my breast the other holding me down, their book-reading teacher watching and writing it up" (70). Like Paul D, who is forced to go around with a horse's "bit" in his mouth, Sethe is forced to submit to the bovine-like humiliation of "being milked." In this grotesque parody of Madonna and child, Sethe's milk, like her labor and the fruits of her womb, is expropriated. But the theft of her "mother's milk" suggests the expropriation of her future—her ability to nurture and ensure the survival of the future embodied in the next generation.

With some irony we learn that Sethe herself has mixed Schoolteacher's ink,

[Schoolteacher liked] how [she] mixed it and it was important to him because at night he sat down to write in his book. It was a book about [the slaves] . . . He commenced to carry round a notebook and write down what we said. (37)

The image of Schoolteacher's ink conflates with the expropriation of Sethe's milk in a symbol that evokes Hélène Cixous's metaphor for "écriture féminine"—namely, women writing a language of the body in the white ink of the mother's milk. It is not only the pages of his notebook, but also the literal inscription of Sethe's back with the markings of Schoolteacher's whip(pen) that constitute the ironically perverse fulfillment of Cixous's call.[19] Appropriating Sethe's "milk" through a process of phallic substitution, Schoolteacher uses the pen—the symbol and instrument of masculine "authority" in the sense that Sandra Gilbert and Susan Gubar use the term—to "re-mark" the slave woman with the signature of his paternity.[20] Sethe must discover some way of regaining control of her story, her body, her progeny, her milk, her ability to nurture the future.

Schoolteacher's association with "the prison-house of language," figured not only in his private ledger, but in the public slave codes as well, refigures the New Testament's personification of the Decalogue. St. Paul tells the churches in Galatia that "the law was our schoolmaster," or (alternatively translated) "we were held prisoners by the law."[21] It is this white/male construction of the law according to the authority of the master discourse that Sethe must first dismantle in order to construct her own story.

For Schoolteacher, history is a confining activity; for Sethe, it must become a liberating activity. She must accomplish precisely what Morrison does in the act of historicizing fiction—namely, "to free retrospectively, certain possibilities that were not actualized in the historical past," and to detect "possibilities buried in the . . . past."[22] As historian, Sethe must liberate her present from the "burden of the past" as constructed in "*hi*story." She must learn to remap the past so that it becomes, for her, a blueprint for the future. Her job is to reconstitute the past through personal narrative, or storytelling. Collingwood has argued that the historian is primarily "a story teller," suggesting that "historical sensibility is manifested in the capacity to make a plausible story out of congeries of 'facts' which, in their unprocessed form, made no sense at all."[23] Like Morrison, Sethe uses the memory of personal experience and what Collingwood calls the "constructive imagination" as a means of re-membering a dis-membered past, and as a means of re-membering a dis-membered family and community.

If Morrison moves "from image to text," Sethe, too, begins with the image and, through a process of narrativization described by Ricoeur as *configuration* and White as *emplotment,* she shapes and animates "rememories" of the past, endowing them with form, drama, and meaning. Narrativization enables Sethe to construct a meaningful life-story from a cluster of images, to transform separate and disparate events into a whole and coherent story.[24]

For Sethe, the past has the power either to make her captive or free. Her feelings, hopes, desires, perceptions—all colored by past incidents and events, culminating in what to her remain unspeakable acts and actions: physical violation and infanticide. Expressing her situation, Sethe thinks, "Freeing yourself was one thing; claiming ownership of that freed self was another" (95). It is her preoccupation with the past that makes it impossible for her to process any new experiences except through the distant lens of the particular events in question. What Gates describes as "this brilliant substructure of the system of slavery"—the dependence of the slave upon her memory—had the potential of making the slave [and later the ex-slave], in some respects, "a slave to [her]self, a prisoner of [her] own power to recall."[25]

If certain events remain unconfigured, others are overly and inappropriately configured. Thus an alternative reading of Sethe's dilemma might be "overemplotment." Using White's model, one might say that she has "overemplotted" the events of her past, that she has "charged them with a meaning so intense that . . . they continue to shape both [her] perceptions and [her] responses to the world long after they should have become 'past history.'" The problem for Sethe, then, is to configure or emplot on the one hand, but to "*re*configure" or "*re*emplot" on the other. She must imaginatively reconstitute, or "re-member," her history "in such a way as to change the *meaning* of those events for [her] and their *significance* for the economy of the whole set of events that make up [her] life."[26] If Gates's assertion that "the act of writing for the slave [narrator] constitute[s] the act of creating a public . . . self," then I propose that the act of re-membering, for the unlettered slave, constitutes the act of constructing a private self.[27] As Ricoeur argues, it is the (re)configuration of the past which enables one to refigure the future—and such is Sethe's task.

If memory is *materialized* in Beloved's reappearance, it is *maternalized* in Sethe's (re)configuration. Sethe gives *birth to her past and to her future:* first to the baby with no name whose angry and sad spirit comes back to haunt 124 Blues-tone Road, and later to the incarnate Beloved, the young woman with "flawless skin and feet and hands soft and new." The return of Beloved, therefore, becomes not only a psychological projection, but also a physical (rather than spiritual) manifestation. Her "rebirth" represents, as it were, the uncanny return of the dead to haunt the living, the return of the past to shadow the present.

Yet it is the notion of "self-distanciation" that intrigues Morrison in this as in other works: "What is it that really compels a good woman to displace the self, her self?," asks Morrison. What interests her is not only the nobility and generosity of these actions, but also the fact that such love ("the best thing that is in us") "is . . . the thing that makes us [as women] sabotage ourselves, sabotage in the sense [of perceiving] that our life ['the best part of ourselves'] is not as worthy." Her method of characterization is intended to suggest this process of displacement—"to project the self not into the way we say 'yourself' but to put a space between those words, as though the self were really a *twin* or a thirst or a friend or something that sits right next to you and watches you. . . ." What Morrison has done is to "[project] the dead out into the earth" in the character of Beloved, so that Beloved becomes the twin self or mirror of Sethe and other women in the novel.[28] Morrison's critical reflections, however, point to another dimension of Sethe's dilemma, a dilemma which combines the private and the public functions of "rememory." If the individual is defined as a conduit of communal consciousness, then (drawing on Teresa de Lauretis) the events of Sethe's life can be emplotted through historiography; conversely, if the community is defined as a conduit of individual consciousness, then the events of Sethe's psychic life can be encoded in psychoanalytic discourse.[29]

It is at the point of this intersection between the personal and the social that we begin to conflate the psychic and the historical. In other words, what I have been describing in terms of a kind of social subjectivity emplotted by historiography can also be figured in terms of psychic subjectivity and represented in the discourse of psychoanalysis. Speaking to the relationship between psychoanalytical and historical consciousness, Norman Brown observes that "the method of psychoanalytical therapy is to deepen the historical consciousness of the individual ('fill up the memory-gaps') till [she] awakens from [her] own history. . . ." Interpreting Freud's notion of "archaic heritage," Brown further develops the link between history and psychoanalysis by reminding us that humankind is a "prisoner of the past in the same sense as [quoting Freud] 'our hysterical patients are suffering from reminiscences' and neurotics 'cannot escape from the past.' " He concludes that not only are all cultures bound to the past, but that individuals are likewise bound to what Freud describes as "the memory-traces of the experiences of former generations."[30]

Linking history and psychoanalysis, then the events in Sethe's life can be encoded in an alternate plot structure. Sethe's past, the sources of her "complex" or dis-ease, manifest themselves in her endless efforts to avoid the past and avert the future. The events in her past—namely, her own violation and the ensuing decision to take her daughter's life—have become sources of both repression and obsession. Sethe must "conjure up" her past—symbolized by Beloved—and confront it as an antagonist. Drawing on Freud's "recommendations on the technique of psychoanalysis," one might say that Sethe must learn to regard her problematic past as an "enemy worthy of [her] mettle, a piece of [her] personality, which has solid ground for its existence and out of which things of value for [her] future life have to be derived." It is her communication with Beloved—and the events of the past which Beloved both symbolizes and evokes—that affords Sethe the opportunity "to become . . . conversant with this resistance over which [she] has now become acquainted, to *work through* it, to overcome it, by continuing, in defiance of it, the analytic work. . . ."[31] Thus, the psychoanalytic process becomes, for Sethe, the means by which she must free herself from the burden of her past and from the burden of *his*tory.

In fact, psychoanalysis, as Michel de Certeau points out, is based on the theme which preoccupies Morrison's novel: the return of the repressed. "This 'mechanism,' " writes de Certeau, "is linked to a certain conception of time and memory, according to which consciousness is both the deceptive *mask* and the operative *trace* of events that organize the present." "If the past . . . is *repressed*," he continues, "it *returns* in the present from which it was excluded. . . ." The figuration of this "detour-return," and its consequences in the lives of individual characters as well as the community as a whole, structures Morrison's novel.[32]

It is in the "poetic" chapters of the novel that the reader senses the full implications of Beloved (as well as the younger daughter, Denver) in relation to Sethe. The retreat of Sethe and her daughters behind the closed doors of 124 Bluestone represents a familial figuration of what Alfred Schutz calls "the succession of generations: contemporaries, predecessors, and successors," associated with the present, past, and future respectively. The connection of Sethe's present with her past is figuratively embodied in her relationship to Beloved while the connection with[33] her future is figuratively embodied in her relationship with Denver. The family thus becomes the site in which to explore notions of "time and being." As a historical field, it represents the complex and intimate interdependence of past, present, and future; as an ontological field, it represents the complexity of the relationship between Self and Other. The family, in other words, becomes a historically constituted social site in which individual subjectivity is constructed.

Further, Beloved symbolizes women in both the contemporaneous and historical black communities. Affiliated with the experiences of various women in the novel, Beloved represents the unsuccessfully repressed "other" of Sethe as well as other women in and associated with the community—including Ella, whose "puberty was spent in a house where she was abused by a father and son"; Vashti (the wife of Stamp Paid, who had ferried Sethe and others across the Ohio River to free land), who was concubined by her young master, and the girl who (as rumor had it) was locked up by a "whiteman" who had used her to his own purpose "since she was a pup." Beyond this, however, Beloved is associated with her maternal and paternal grandmothers and the generation of slave women who failed to survive the "middle passage." As trace of "the disremembered and unaccounted for," Beloved's symbolic function of otherness connects the individual to repressed aspects of the self, as well as to contemporaneous and historical others. It is, in fact, Beloved's implication in the lives of the collectivity of women that makes it necessary that all the women in the community later participate in the ritual to exorcise her.

Central to Morrison's vision, as we have seen, is the reconstitution of self and other through re-memory in the act of storytelling, an act which imposes sequence and meaning on the welter of images and memories which shape and define one's sense of self. Yet, Sethe must not only narrativize her life in White's sense of rendering to her past the formal coherence of story; she must also be able to continue the process of metamorphosis by "metaphorizing" her experiences within narrative.[34] Morrison uses the metaphor of maternity to establish an alternative to the metaphor of paternity common in white/male historical discourse. This recurrent and structuring metaphor complements and amplifies the images of the female body that are encoded in the text. In her remarks in "Site of Memory," Morrison provides a *cognitive* metaphor for representing her reconstructive methods as a novelist. The images of interiority which she privileges suggest specifically female images associated with the "interior" rather than the "exterior" life, with the personal rather than the public representation of experience. Ultimately, such a metaphor suggests that the object of our understanding is *inside* rather than *outside,* and thus can be reached only by what Morrison describes as her method of "literary archeology."[35]

Secondly, Sethe's birthing of the past and future appropriately figures Morrison's use of *depictive* metaphor. If the act of birthing figures Sethe's life-story in a metaphor of maternity, then, the womb functions as an image of corporeal interiority, the counterpart to Sethe's psychic interiority and Morrison's diegetic interiority. As a narrative metaphor, maternity privileges interiority and marks Sethe's entry into subjectivity. Perhaps the best example of this function is found in the scene describing Sethe's reaction upon seeing the incarnate Beloved for the first time:

[F]or some reason she could not immediately account for, the moment she got close enough to see [Beloved's face], Sethe's bladder filled to capacity. . . . She never made the outhouse. Right in front of its door she had to lift her skirts, and the water she voided was endless. Like a horse, she thought, but as it went on and on she thought, No, more like flooding the boat when Denver was born. So much water Amy said, "Hold on . . . You going to sink us you keep that up." But there was no stopping water breaking from a breaking womb and there was no stopping now. (51)

Notably, Sethe rejects, on second thought, the equine metaphor. Further, in a radical reconception of history and culture, her ritual of birthing figures motherhood as a primary metaphor of history and human culture. The postdeluvian connotation of "breaking of the water" historicizes the event and, at the same time, signifies a maternal delivery which becomes a means of "deliverance" from the dominant conception of history as a white/paternal metaphor. Morrison seems to figure here a second immaculate conception, if you will, in which black motherhood becomes self-generative—a process which, in effect, reconstitutes black womanhood. By shifting the dominant metaphor from white to black and from paternity (embodied in the figure of the slavemaster) to maternity (figured and literally embodied in the black female slave), Morrison has shifted meaning and value. It is through this process of destructuring and restructuring, of decoding and recoding, that Morrison redefines notions of genesis and meaning as they have served to constitute black womanhood in the dominant discourse.

To return to the last in our typology of metaphor, the images of motherhood function *heuristically* to explain or "trace" Sethe's history and that of the community along "motherlines." Her past, birthed from a womblike matrix, is read back through motherlines, motherlines tracked through four generations of marked slave women. It is Beloved's "thirst" for these stories that gives her mother "an unexpected pleasure" in *speaking* things which "she and Baby Suggs had agreed without saying so . . . [were] *unspeakable*" (emphasis mine). In speaking, that is, in storytelling, Sethe is able to construct an alternate text of black womanhood. This power to fashion a counternarrative, thereby rejecting the definitions imposed by the dominant other(s) finally provides Sethe with a self—a past, present, and future.

It is Beloved's persistent questions that enable Sethe to re-member long forgotten traces of her own mother, traces carried through memory as well as through the body. Sethe remembers that her own mother bore a mark, "a circle and a cross burnt right in the skin" on her rib. It was the mark of ownership by the master who had as much as written "property" under her breast. Yet like Sethe (as well as Hawthorne's Hester Prynne), her mother had transformed a mark of mutilation, a sign of diminished humanity, into a sign of recognition and identity. Sethe recalls her mother's words: "This is your ma'am. . . . , I am the only one got this mark now. The rest dead. If something happens to me and you can't tell me by my face, you can know me by this mark" (61). Indeed, it is her own markings which help her to decode the meaning of her mother's remarks. Sethe tells her own daughters, Denver and Beloved, "I didn't understand it then. Not till I had a mark of my own."

Constructed and metaphorized along motherlines, Sethe's retelling of her childhood story also enables her to decipher meaning encoded in a long forgotten "mother tongue," meaning which she passes on to her own daughter. Equally important, Sethe's story enables her to reread or reemplot her own experiences in the context of sacrifice, resistance, and motherlove. Although Sethe knows that the "language her ma'am spoke . . . would never come back," she begins to recognize "the message—that was and had been there all along," and she began "picking meaning out of a code she no longer understood." Like the historian confronted with a plethora of documents who seeks to configure a probable story, Sethe seeks to reconfigure events based on "words. Words Sethe understood then but could neither recall nor repeat now" (62). Remembering the story told her by Nan, "the one she knew best, who was around all day, who nursed babies, cooked, had one good arm and half of another"—Nan, who spoke "the same language her ma'am spoke," Sethe is able to reconstruct her own story:

Nighttime. Nan holding her with her good arm, waving the stump of the other in the air. "Telling you. I am telling you, small girl Sethe," and she did that. She told Sethe that her mother and Nan were together from the sea. Both were taken up many times by the crew. "She threw them all away but you. The one from the crew she threw away on the island. The others from more whites she also threw away. Without names, she threw them. You she gave the name of the black man. She put her arms around him. The others she did not put her arms around. Never. Never. Telling you. I am telling you, small girl Sethe." (62)

Interestingly Sethe's name recalls the Old Testament Hebrew name of "Seth," meaning "granted" or "appointed." (Eve named her third born Seth, saying, "God has granted me another child in the place of Abel.")[36] In this instance, it would seem that Sethe signifies the child whose life was spared or "granted" by her mother, who did not keep the offspring of the white men who forced themselves upon her. The story told her as a child about her mother by Nan, another mutilated mother, ironically prefigures Sethe's own actions, but at the same time, challenges her to some accountability. For although Beloved, like Sethe and her mother, bears a mark of mutilation, the scar across Beloved's throat is the mark of Sethe's own hand. And it is the fingerprints on Beloved's forehead as well as the scar under her chin ("the little curved shadow of a smile in the kootchy-koochy-coo place") that enables Sethe to recognize her daughter returned from "the other side."

In light of her recognition Sethe reconstitutes a family story of infanticide, a story of repetition, but repetition with a marked difference. Sethe's story of motherlove would seem to overwrite a story of rejection, and Sethe's task as historian is to find a narrative form that speaks to that difference. But it is her mother's story which refamiliarizes her own story. She receives from her mother that which she had hoped to discover with Paul D: "Her story was bearable"—*not* because it was Paul D's, but *her mother's*—"to tell, to refine and tell again" (99). The maternal discourse becomes a testimonial one for Sethe. What both mother and daughter share is protection of their own children—the one by saving a life and the other by taking a life.

But there are competing configurations as well. The first full representation of the events surrounding the infanticide are figured from a collective white/male perspective, represented by schoolteacher and the sheriff:

Inside [the shed], two boys bled in the sawdust and dirt at the feet of a nigger woman holding a blood-soaked child to her chest with one hand and an infant by the heels in the other. She did not look at them; she simply swung the baby toward the wall planks, missed and tried to connect a second time . . . Right off it was clear, to schoolteacher especially, that there was nothing there to claim. The three (now four—because she'd had the one coming when she cut) pickaninnies they had hoped were alive and well enough to take back to Kentucky, take back and raise properly to do the work Sweet Home desperately needed, were not . . . He could claim the baby struggling in the arms of the mewing old man, but who'd tend her? Because the woman—something was wrong with her. She was looking at him now, and if his other nephew could see that look he would learn the lesson for sure: you just can't mishandle *creatures* and expect success. (emphasis mine, 149-150)

In Schoolteacher's narrative, Sethe is "the woman [who] . . . made fine ink, damn good soup, pressed his collars the way he liked besides having at least ten breeding years left . . ." In his words, "she's gone wild, due to mishandling of the nephew" (149). The white sheriff reads these events as a cautionary tale on "the results of a little so-called freedom imposed on people who needed every care and guidance in the world to keep them from the cannibal life they preferred"(151). Granting authority to the white newspaper's account, Stamp Paid concludes that ". . . while he and Baby Suggs were looking the wrong way, a pretty little slavegirl had recognized [her former master's hat], and split to the woodshed to kill her children" (158). Paul D, who suddenly "saw what Stamp Paid wanted him to see," summarizes events by insisting, "You got two feet, Sethe, not four" (164-165).

Sethe must compete with the dominant metaphors of the master('s) narrative—wildness, cannibalism, animality, destructiveness. In radical opposition to these constructions is Sethe's reconceptualized metaphor of self based on motherhood, motherlines, and motherlove—a love described by Paul D as "too thick." Convinced that "the best thing she was, was her children," Sethe wants simply to stop Schoolteacher:

Because the truth was . . . [s]imple: she was squatting in the garden and when she saw them coming and recognized schoolteacher's hat, she heard wings. Little hummingbirds stuck their needle beaks right through her headcloth into her hair and beat their wings. And if she thought anything, it was No. No. Nono. Nonono. Simple. She just flew. Collected every bit of life she had made, all the parts of her that were precious and fine and beautiful, and carried, pushed, dragged them through the veil, out, away, over there where no one could hurt them (163).

"I took and put my babies where they'd be safe," she tells Paul D (164). And in this way, she explains to Beloved, "[N]o one, nobody on this earth, would list her daughter's characteristics on the animal side of the paper" (251).

Sethe, in effect, creates a counternarrative that reconstitutes her humanity and demonstrates the requirements of motherlove. By shifting the dominant white and male metaphor to a black and maternal metaphor for self and history, Sethe effectively changes the plot and meaning of the story—and finally, the story itself. A story of oppression becomes a story of liberation; a story of inhumanity has been overwritten as a story of higher humanity. It is this process of destructuring and restructuring the dominant discourse and its organizing tropes that enables Sethe (and Morrison) to subvert the master code of the master('s) text. By privileging specifically female tropes in her narrative, Sethe is able to reconstitute her self and her-story within the context of intergenerational black women's experiences as represented in memory and narrative. By placing her life-history within a maternal family history and, by implication, placing her family history within a broader tradition of racial history, Morrison demonstrates not only the strength of motherlines in the slave community, but also how ontogeny followed black and female phylogeny. (It is the absence of Sethe's two runaway sons which, in effect leaves Denver as sole heir and guarantor of the family's future.)

In accordance with Collingwood's notion of "history as reenactment" of past experience, Sethe is able, finally, to "re-enact" a critical moment in her life. Describing this process, in which knowledge of the self is recovered, Collingwood writes the following:

In thus re-thinking my past thought I am not merely remembering it. I am constructing the history of a certain phase of my life: and the difference between memory and history is that whereas in memory the past is a mere spectacle, in history it is re-enacted in present thought. So far as this thought is mere thought, the past is merely re-enacted; so far as it is thought about thought [or the thought underlying an action], this past is thought of as being re-enacted, and my knowledge of myself is historical knowledge.[37]

Like the historian, Sethe is able to "re-act" or "re-think" a critical moment from the past, and is consequently able to perform an action which has the effect of altering her own life-history. In one of the final scenes in the novel, Sethe re-enacts the past, an act which provides an occasion for her to demonstrate her possession *of* rather than *by* the past. Sethe's actions, moreover, demonstrate that the present is bound to the past and the past to the future, and it is precisely the (re)configuration of the past that enables her to refigure the future.[38]

What has in the past been enacted in the psychic field is re-enacted, and dramatically and therapeutically re-worked, in the social field. The "rememory" and repetition of actions which have imprisoned the "patient" in the bonds of the past are broken in a scene of re-enactment in which Sethe rethinks and revises her previous (re)action. In a final and climactic scene of the novel, Sethe is able to "relive" or re-enact the past.

Beloved is, in fact, exorcised during the course of this re-enactment. With the support of "thirty neighborhood women," Sethe is released from possession by the spirit of a now speakable past. Unable to "countenance the possibility of sin moving on in the house," the community performs a ritual of exorcism which "frees" Sethe from the burden of her past:

Instantly the kneelers and the standers joined [Sethe]. They stopped praying and took a step back to the beginning. *In the beginning there were no words. In the beginning was the sound,* and they all knew what that sound sounded like. (emphasis mine, 259)

Evoking "the beginning" in which there were "no words"—only "the sound"—black women's voices revise Scripture ("In the beginning was the word") in such a way that the semiotic (rather than the symbolic) is associated with creation and creativity. In its revision of Scripture, this "key," this "code," this "sound that broke the back of words" represents a challenge to the dominant white and male discourse in which the text of black womanhood is constructed. Sethe is, moreover, "born again" in her reclamation by the community ("[The voices] broke over Sethe and she trembled like baptized in its wash") as much as by the community's exorcism of Beloved. The communal voice of black women, then, possesses the power not only to destroy, but also to create. In fact, Sethe's "re-birth" is predicated upon the rupture of the master('s) discourse. Thus, not only is Sethe "delivered" from the "errors" of her past, but her discourse is "delivered" from the constraints of the master('s) discourse.

It is during the course of the communal exorcism that Sethe espies the "black hat wide-brimmed enough to hide [Schoolteacher's] face but not his purpose. He is coming into her yard and he is coming for her best thing. She hears wings. Little hummingbirds stick needle beaks right through her headcloth into her hair and beat their wings. And if she thinks anything, it is no. No no. Nonono. She flies. The ice pick is not in her hand; it is her hand"(262). Sethe, in effect, re-enacts the original event—remembering, repeating, and working-through the "primal scene" in a process that emblematizes the psychoanalytic process. This time, however, Sethe directs her response to the threatening Other rather than to "her best thing"—her children. But it is not only Sethe who re-enacts the earlier scene; the community itself participates in the re-enactment. Because the community had failed to send warning of the slave captors' approach the first time, its "sin of omission" makes it no less responsible for Beloved's death than Sethe's "sin of commission." In a scene of collective re-enactment, the women of the community intervene at a critical juncture, to save not Beloved, but Sethe. Thus, by revising her actions, Sethe is able to preserve the community, and the community in turn, is able to protect one of its own.

Returning once more to Ricoeur's model, prefiguration denotes the temporality of the world of human action; configuration the world of the narrative emplotment of these events; and refiguration the moment at which these two worlds interact and affect each other. It is Sethe's actions which constitute the prefigurative aspect; her storytelling which constitutes the configurative aspect; and finally, the re-enactment which constitutes the refigurative aspect.[39] Moreover, Morrison enables the reader to connect with the otherness of these past generations—especially as it relates to the experiences of slave women—in a process made possible by "the intersection of the world of the text with the world of the reader." Just as Nan's story of the generational mother enables Sethe to (re)configure her past, so Morrison's story of the historical m(other) enables the reader to do likewise. Moreover, the reader, like Sethe, learns that she must claim and surrender the past in order to refigure the future.[40]

The question of Sethe's accountability, however, must be addressed. Does Morrison, finally, indict or defend Sethe's "too thick" motherlove? Is Sethe truly redeemed from an unspeakable past? If so, by what means? Wherein lies Sethe's "redemption" from the "sins" of the past—both those perpetuated *upon* her and *by* her? Is grace achieved through the spirit of Beloved (the past generations she symbolizes) or by its exorcism? Characteristically, Morrison draws out the paradoxes and ambiguities of this "perfect dilemma." I would suggest that the author, in fact, neither condemns nor condones, but rather "delivers" her protagonist. For Sethe achieves redemption through *possession* by the spirit as well as *exorcism* of the spirit. Significantly, for Morrison, it is not through the Law ("Because the Law worketh wrath"), but the spirit (its reclamation and relinquishment) that the individual achieves "deliverance" from the "sins" of the past.[41] *Beloved,* then, (re)inscribes the conditions of the promise in the New Testament. What is important for Morrison, however, is the mediation between remembering (possession) and forgetting (exorcism). It is the process of "working-through" which the author finally affirms. As in previous novels, Morrison focuses less on "what" and "why," and more on "how." That is, she privileges the journey rather than the destination, the means rather than the end—a process which enables Sethe to achieve redemption through the creation of a cohesive psychoanalytical and historical narrative.

Like Sethe, Morrison herself seeks to achieve some mediation between "resurrecting" the past and "burying" it. Expressing her desire to provide a proper and artistic burial to the historical ancestors figured by Beloved, Morrison says:

There's a lot of danger for me in writing . . . The effort, the responsibility as well as the effort, the effort of being worth it. . . . The responsibility that I feel for . . . all of these people; these unburied, or at least unceremoniously buried, people made literate in art. But the inner tension, the artistic inner tension those people create in me, the fear of not properly, artistically, burying them, is extraordinary.[43]

Intent, it would seem, is to pay the historian's debt to the past, in Ricoeur's sense of rendering to the past its due and, in the process, putting it to rest.

What, then, is Morrison's final legacy to us as readers, and what is her own relationship to the past? Does Sethe become for the reader what Beloved is for Sethe—an embodiment of the past and the experiences of previous generations? What are we to make of the final haunting injunction at the end of the novel that this is NOT a story to "be passed on"—that is, to remember, to be retold? Must Morrison's story, along with Sethe's past, be put behind? Must the reader rid herself of the burden of the past by exorcising from historical consciousness the violence and violation experienced by her ancestresses? If we were to take this injunction seriously, how, then, can we explain Morrison's own commitment to a project of recovery and "rememory"? Clearly, such an injunction would threaten to contradict the motive and sense of the entire novel.

In a 1989 interview, Morrison tells us that *Beloved* is a book "about something that the characters don't want to remember, I don't want to remember, black people don't want to remember, white people don't want to remember."[43] The author's remarks speak to a public desire to repress the personal aspects of the story of slavery. Returning to Morrison's role as historian and analyst, however, we see that her accomplishment in this novel is precisely *not* to allow for the continuation of a "national amnesia" regarding this chapter in America's history. For Morrison, the absent (like the historical) is only the "other" of the present—just as the repressed is only the "other" of the conscious. Read in this context, the narrator's final and thrice-repeated enjoinder resonates with ambivalence and ambiguity. Suggesting that that which is absent is not necessarily "gone" (leaving behind no "name," no "print," no "trace"), the narrator's closing reflections ensure the novel's open-endedness subverting any monologic reading of the final injunction. Is it possible that the narrator means, indeed must she mean, that this is not a story to be PASSED ON—not in the sense of being retold, but in the sense of being forgotten, repressed, or ignored? For if Richard Hofstadter is correct when he says that "Memory is the thread of personal identity, history of public identity," then it would follow that the importance of our private memories becomes, ultimately, the basis for a reconstructed public history.[44]

NOTES

1. Toni Morrison, "Site of Memory" in William Zinsser, ed., *Inventing the Truth: The Art and Craft of Memoir* (Boston: Houghton-Mifflin, 1987), 109-110.
2. See W.E.B. Du Bois, "The Forethought," *The Souls of Black Folk* (Chicago: A.C. McClurg, 1903), viii.
3. See Toni Morrison's "Unspeakable Things Unspoken," *Michigan Quarterly Review* Vol. 28, No. 1 (Winter 1989).
4. "Therefore we conclude that a man is justified by faith without the deeds of the law"

(Romans 3:28); "But that no man is justified by the law in the sight of God, *it is* evident: for, The just shall live by faith" (Galatians 3:11).

5. Contemporary black writers whose work fictionalizes history include, among others, Margaret Walker (*Jubilee*), Ernest Gaines (*The Autobiography of Miss Jane Pittman*), David Bradley (*The Chaneysville Incident*), Alice Walker (*The Color Purple*), Sherley Anne Williams (*Dessa Rose*), and Barbara Chase Riboud (*Sally Hemings* and *The Echo of Lions*).

6. Gloria Naylor and Toni Morrison, "A Conversation," *The Southern Review* 21 (Summer 1985), 583-584.

7. Morrison, "Site of Memory," 111-112.

8. *Ibid.,* 113-114.

9. Like the novelist, the historian, Collingwood argues, "constructs an imaginary picture" consistent with the historical data, testimony, memory, documentation, etc. In an attempt to explain a fragmentary or incomplete record of the historical past, Collingwood further argues that the historian must employ what he calls "the constructive imagination" to create a "coherent and continuous picture" consistent with the available historical data. R. G. Collingwood, *The Idea of History* (London: Oxford University Press, 1946), 245-246.

10. Henry Louis Gates, Jr., "Frederick Douglass and the Language of Self," *The Yale Review*, Vol. 70, No. 4 (July 1981).

11. See Jacques Derrida's *Memoires for Paul de Man* (New York: Columbia University Press, 1986), 102-150 *passim*.

12. Toni Morrison, *Beloved* (New York: Alfred Knopf, 1987). Page references for this work are given in the text.

13. Hayden White, *Tropics of Discourse: Essays in Cultural Criticism* (Baltimore: Johns Hopkins University Press, 1979), 33-34.

14. Paul Ricoeur, *The Reality of the Historical Past* (Milwaukee: Marquette University Press, 1984), 11.

15. See Waldo E. Martin, Jr., *The Mind of Frederick Douglass* (Chapel Hill: University of North Carolina Press, 1984) for a discussion of the relationship between the ethnologist and the cultural historian in the context of nineteenth-century practice: "Practitioners of a broad and allegedly scientific discipline, ethnologists . . . attempted to uncover stages and meanings of human developments primarily in cultural and related physical and secondarily in historical terms" (225).

16. Nathaniel Hawthorne, *The Scarlet Letter* (New York: E.P. Dutton & Co. Inc., 1938), 42, 51.

17. See White, *Tropics of Discourse,* 151. Unlike the notion of historical reconstruction which seeks to account for otherness by questioning the normative model, this method seeks to identify *difference* with *deviance* and/or *diminishment*.

18. Cf. Sherley Anne William's unnamed narrator in "Meditations on History" and Adam Nehemiah in *Dessa Rose*. Both Williams and Morrison share reservations concerning disciplinary behaviors. Their works constitute a critique of certain aspects of both the praxis as well as the practitioners of these activities. Like Williams's characters, Morrison's investigator (who might be as appropriately designated ethnographer-as-historian), represents the author's indictment of the kind of "scholarly" and "scientific" discourse and representation in which the preconceptions and presuppositions of the inquirer subject the results of the inquiry to gross distortions. For critical treatments of Williams's work from this perspective, see my "(W)Riting *The Work* and Working The Rites," in Linda Kauffman, ed., *Feminism and Institutions: Dialogues on Feminist Theory* (London: Basil Blackwell, 1989) and "Speaking in Tongues: Dialogics, Dialectics, the Black Woman Writer's Literary Tradition" in Cheryl Wall, ed., *Changing Our Own Words: Essays on Criticism. Theory and Writing by Black Women* (New Brunswick: Rutgers University Press, 1989).

19. See Hélène Cixous, "The Laugh of the Medusa," eds. Elaine Marks and Isabelle de

Courtivron, *New French Feminisms: An Anthology* (Amherst: The University of Massachusetts Press, 1980) 251.

20. See Sandra Gilbert and Susan Gubar, *Madwoman in the Attic: The Woman Writer and the Nineteenth-Century Literary Imagination* (New Haven: Yale University Press, 1970).

21. The above represent alternative translations of Galatians 3:24.

22. See Paul Ricoeur, *Time and Narrative* (Chicago: University of Chicago Press 1988), Vol. 3, 191-192.

23. See White on Collingwood, *Tropics of Discourse*, 83.

24. According to Ricoeur, emplotment "brings together diverse and heterogeneous story elements . . . agents, goals, means, interactions, [and] circumstances . . . [A]n event must be more than just a singular occurrence. It gets its definition from its contribution to the development of the plot. A story, too, must be more than just an enumeration of events in serial order; it must organize them into an intelligible whole, of a sort such that we can always ask what is the "thought" of this story. In short, emplotment is the operation that draws a configuration out of a simple succession." See Ricoeur, *Time and Narrative*, (1984) Vol. 1, 65.

25. Gates, "Frederick Douglass and the Language of Self," 593.

26. See White, *Tropics of Discourse*, 87.

27. Gates, "Frederick Douglass and the Language of Self," 599.

28. Naylor and Morrison, "A Conversation," 585.

29. Teresa de Lauretis, *Alice Doesn't: Feminism, Semiotics, Cinema* (Bloomington: Indiana University Press, 1984).

30. Freud, according to Brown's reading, extends this to recapitulation theory (ontogeny recapitulates phylogeny) in which "each individual recapitulates the history of the race . . . From this it follows that the theory of neurosis must embrace a theory of history; and conversely a theory of history must embrace a theory of neurosis." See Norman O. Brown, *Life Against Death: The Psychoanalytical Meaning of History* (Middletown: Wesleyan University Press, 1959), 19, 12-13. Robert Guthrie further elaborates on the recapitulation theory: "The recapitulation theory held that an individual organism, in the process of growth and development, passes through a series of stages representing those in the evolutionary development of the species. G. Stanley Hall, for example, believed 'that in its play activity the child exhibits a series of phases corresponding to the cultural of human society, a hunting period, a building period, and so on.' Hall's attempt to mold individual development (ontogeny) with racial characteristics (phylogeny) was supported by many leading behavioral scientists of this time [early twentieth century]. (John Mark Baldwin's *Mental Development in the Child and the Race*, for example, was a frequently quoted source.)" Robert V. Guthrie, *Even the Rat Was White: A Historical View of Psychology* (New York: Harper ¿ Row, 1976), 82.

31. Sigmund Freud, "Remembering, Repeating and Working-Through," *Standard Edition of the Works of Sigmund Freud*, ed. James Strachey (London: Hogarth Press, 1914), Vol. 12, 146-157.

32. Michel de Certeau, *Heterologies: Discourse on the Other*, Theory and History of Literature, Vol. 17 (Minneapolis: University of Minnesota Press, 1986), 3.

33. Alfred Schutz as quoted in Ricoeur, *Time and Narrative*, Vol. 3, 109.

34. Although White's work speaks eloquently to a "classification of discourses based on tropology" (*Tropics*, 22), it is Philip Stambovsky whose work on metaphor and historical writing addresses my concerns more specifically in this instance. Using Maurice Mandelbaum's "three historical forms—explanatory, sequential, and interpretive" as a "context for determining the functioning . . . of . . . metaphor in historical discourse," Stambovsky identifies three functions of metaphor: heuristic, depictive, and cognitive. See Philip

Stambovsky, "Metaphor and Historical Understanding," *History and Theory*, Vol. 27, No. 2 (1988), 125-134.

35. See Kaja Silverman, *The Acoustic Mirror: The Female Voice in Psychoanalysis and Cinema* (Bloomington: Indiana University Press, 1988) for an interesting discussion of the notions of interiority and exteriority.

36. Genesis 5:25. Interestingly, Seth was also the name of the Egyptian god of confusion, described as a trickster-like marginal figure located "beyond or between the boundaries of social definition . . . [who] gleefully breaks taboos and violates the limits that preserve order." See Anna K. Nardo's "Fool and Trickster" in *Mosaic* Vol. 22, (Winter 1989), 2.

37. Continuing, Collingwood writes, "The history of myself is thus not memory as such, but a peculiar case of memory. Certainly a mind which could not remember could not have historical knowledge. But memory as such is only the present thought of past experience as such, be that experience what it may; historical knowledge is that special case of memory where the object of present thought is past thought, the gap between present and past being bridged not only by the power of past thought to think of the past, but also by the power to reawaken itself in the present." R.G. Collingwood, *The Idea of History*, 293-294.

38. We use Collingwood's term advisedly with the admonitions of Ricoeur that although the "re-enactment" of the past in the present operates under the sign of the same, "to re-enact does not consist in reliving what happened," primarily because it involves the notion of "rethinking." And according to Ricoeur, "rethinking already contains the critical moment that requires us to detour by way of the historical imagination." See Ricoeur, *Time and Narrative*, Vol. 3, 144-145. Rather than locate this process under the sign of the same, which implies repetition, I would rather locate it under both the same and the other—repetition with a difference.

39. Ricoeur designates these modes alternatively as mimesis 1, mimesis 2, and mimesis 3 (note that his formulation of mimesis includes what we normally (after Aristotle) call diegesis as well—thus expanding the notion of the imitation of an action to description. Ricoeur makes it clear that refiguration (or mimesis) is a stage which "marks the intersection of the world of the text and the world of the hearer or reader," thereby relating the world configured by the text to the world of "real action." I have modified and extended his model by using the term to describe both the intersection of the inner world of the character and the outer world of her actions as well as the intersection of the world of the text and the world of the reader. See Ricoeur, *Time and Narrative*, Vol. 1, 54-76.

40. "The basic thesis [of refiguration] from which all the others are derived holds that the meaning of a literary work rests upon the dialogical relation established between the work and its public in each age. This thesis, similar to Collingwood's notion that history is but a reenactment of the past in the mind of the historian, amounts to including the effect produced by the work—in other words, the meaning the public attributes to it—within the boundaries of the work itself." Ricoeur, *Time and Narrative*, Vol. 3, 171.

41. See Romans 4:15.

42. Naylor and Morrison, "A Conversation," 585.

43. Toni Morrison, "The Pain of Being Black," *Time* (May 22, 1989). 120.

44. Richard Hofstadter, *The Progressive Historians* (New York: Alfred A. Knopf, 1968), 3.

5.
Re-Weaving the "Ulysses Scene": Enchantment, Post-Oedipal Identity, and the Buried Text of Blackness in Toni Morrison's *Song of Solomon*

KIMBERLY W. BENSTON

Encased within the framing scene of suicidal flight which opens Toni Morrison's *Song of Solomon* is an etiological myth of African-American memory and resistance, a parable of the affirming wit by which the community can circumvent "official" efforts to un-name and dis-locate it. Seeking absolute authorization of the *Main*stream by negating black terms of presence, the city's governors first order all letters addressed to Doctor Street (so named in recognition of the community's sole source of modern healing and earliest instance of bourgeois achievement) to be sent to "the Dead Letter Office"; and then, when blacks persist in employing "Doctor Street" as the legitimate term of their expanding presence there, the "legislators" attempt to impose a silencing map of the name's history by declaring "that the avenue running northerly and southerly from Shore Road fronting the lake . . . had always been and would always be known as Mains Avenue and not Doctor Street."[1]

The community's improvisatory embrace of the city fathers' own discourse cannily evades their monologic violence by refusing the oedipal scenario of surrender or repudiation which the edict seems designed to evoke. "It was a genuinely clarifying public notice," the narrator dryly continues, "because it gave Southside residents a way to keep their memories alive and please the city legislators as well. They called it Not Doctor Street" (4). As an allegory of the self-empowering strategies by which Southsiders protect memory as both continuity and concealment, this parable thematizes the predicament and potential of African-American literary communication. Seeking to "transfer messages" by usurping the legislators' own institutions (the Post Office) and language (Mains Avenue-Not Doctor Street), black expression here would establish a discursive economy in which meaning circulates despite the imposition of a closure directing such interchange to a "Dead" end. The community, in effect, constantly (re)composes itself in the face of the Law's effort to arrest the disseminations of black text and community alike: "other Negroes moved there," and behind them came unabated a flow of letters (4).

The existence of the letters, the continuity of their writing, becomes in itself the sign of the community's will-to-expression. Their force does not depend, for example, on any encrypted meaning or stratagem of circumvention: it is enough that the envelopes be addressed (indeed, the narrator speaks rather more of "envelopes" than of the missives they presumably contain). But for whom, then, is the address written? To whom is the message sent? In moving from the postal and cartographic spaces of official truth to the revisionary "calling" process of communal memory, the text subtly defers these questions, shifting from the distancing technology of writing to the subversive gnosis of speech. Thus if Barthes has asked, in contemplating the abysmal non-origin of "modernity's" referentiality, "Who is Speaking?,"[2] Morrison's question, asked at the margins of this "fading" of Western utterance, might rather be, "To whom, for whom, and, most importantly, with whom is one's *correspondence* intended?" Morrison probes, that is to say, for potential dialogism in the movement of letters between cultural and expressive modes, thereby posing further queries: Is there one representational order that speaks for, of, and to all? Are all efforts to speak otherwise doomed to the specular mimicry of belated opposition? Does listening anew to one mode of long-buried speech necessitate the silencing of still other instances of differing utterance? From what position does one ever dare to speak for another, and what forms of attention, discipline, and care must we practice to establish the kinship such speaking must surely assume?

If the vocal and vocative terms I employ here have a faintly Ellisonian overtone (recall, if you will, *Invisible Man*'s famous interrogative conclusion: "Who knows but that, on the lower frequencies, I speak for you?"),[3] it is because *Invisible Man* provides an especially apt perspective on Morrison's effort in *Song of Solomon* to imagine afresh the conversational idiom of a distinctively African-American voice.[4] We shall return to this Ellisonian perspective, and its intricate revision by Morrison's text, in more detail, but I'd like to begin with a passage from *Song of Solomon* that, in its concentration on the interplay between expression and silence, between distance and intimacy, provides its own perspective on the challenge of performing for and/or with the other.

At the end of the novel's first chapter—a chapter already replete with a stunning array of seriocomic spectacles and images of revelation[5]—we are

SONG OF SOLOMON   89

given a detailed account of Macon Dead's experience of the most wonderful sight of all, his sister Pilate.

Now, nearing her yard, [Macon] trusted that the dark would keep anyone in [Pilate's] house from seeing him. He did not even look to his left as he walked by it. But then he heard the music. They were singing. All of them. Pilate, Reba, and Reba's daughter, Hagar. [. . .] Macon walked on, resisting as best he could the sound of the voices that followed him. He was rapidly approaching a part of the road where the music could not follow, when he saw [. . .] his own home. [. . .] There was no music there, and tonight he wanted just a bit of music—from the person who had been his first caring for. (28)

Having reasserted his worldly authority through a mock-sublime confrontation with a disgruntled tenant, fondling the proprietory keys to patriarchal authority as they jingle in his pockets, Macon finds himself suddenly guided by an unbidden spirit—perhaps of memory, regret, or longing—that leaves him suspended between two radical versions of home: on the one hand, his own domain of endless accumulation and denial, where value is determined by agonistic dramas of force and exchange and affirmed by displays of labor's surplus effects; and, on the other hand, his sister's non-economized sphere of reciprocity, where obligation poses no threat to self-sufficiency and leisure no contradiction to meaningful production.

Surrendering to the sound, Macon moved closer. He wanted no conversation, no witness, only to listen and perhaps to see the three of them, the source of that music that made him think of fields and wild turkey and calico. Treading as lightly as he could, he crept up to the side window where the candlelight flickered lowest, and peeped in. Reba was cutting her toenails [. . .] her long neck bent almost to her knees. The girl, Hagar, was braiding her hair, while Pilate, whose face he could not see because her back was to the window, was stirring something in a pot. (29)

Narrated in a style of exquisite poise and equanimity, a style at once dilatory and directional, laden with narrative information yet almost unconcerned to register significance beyond the rhythms of its own activity, the passage invites us to experience Macon's precarious and transitional position, edging him and us alike toward a threshold of observation and immersion as we approach a scene of literally en-chanting possibilities. For at the heart of the episode is Macon's ambivalent relation to the spectacle of collective (and archetypally feminine) creation, where the repetitive movements of making and unmaking seem to him a salving confutation of his exhausting daytime quests for empowerment. From one perspective, we note that the language of fluidity, conflation, and submission bespeaks the possibility of a metamorphic absorption of and by otherness: the act of listening is trope and substance of renewal through sympathetic identification, an identification which, furthermore, offers satisfaction of long-deferred desire through release of frustrating claims to heroic self-adequacy. Returning to a potentially originary moment of familial plenitude and sensuous fulfillment, and thereby to a forgotten capacity for *caritas,* Macon seems momentarily capable of looking upon Pilate not from within his own fiction of hard-won autonomy but in the increasingly re-familiarized terms of her own selfhood.

Near the window, hidden by the dark, he felt the irritability of the day drain from him and relished the effortless beauty of the women singing in the candlelight. Reba's soft profile, Hagar's hands moving, moving in her heavy hair, and Pilate. [. . .] As Macon felt himself softening under the weight of memory and music, the song died down. The air was quiet and yet Macon Dead could not leave. He liked looking at them freely this way. They didn't move. They simply stopped singing and Reba went on paring her toenails, Hagar threaded and unthreaded her hair, and Pilate swayed like a willow over her stirring. (19–30)

At the same time, however, this incipient dialectic of enchantment and desire is arrested by Macon's inclination to isolated consumption of the scene's enactments. Such a propensity for voyeuristic solitude reduces transfiguring performance to static exhibition, fixing the other by a self-protective gaze which forestalls or even resists movement toward genuine peripety. Remaining at a distance, himself unseen under the protective veil of darkness, Macon indulges the illusory mastery of reified perception (what the passage terms "free looking"). He would occupy the privileged position of a "disembodied divinity,"[6] "relishing" in this moment of repose not the rediscovery of his body's inherent lightness (Morrison evokes here, for reasons elaborated below, the buoyancy of the Homeric hero cleansing in the bath after wearying travel) but the erasure of the body altogether. And with this bodily negation he would eliminate the challenges of being himself a visible (hence vulnerable) figure among mutually affecting others. Balanced between the fear and need of others, between the agonies of estrangement and the enchantments of identification, between the shadows of pure perception and the substance of material acts, between the longing for atemporal return to a supposedly pristine origin and the "responsible" awareness of history's demands—Macon presents to us, in short, an avatar of that in-between figure known in African-American modernism as *the invisible man.*

Sick for home, the invisible man wanders as exile in search for an origin or end that will heal the breach of self and other, where defining divisions of race, family, gender, sexuality, place, and perspective "melt" away. He does so uncertain whether such a site is a privileged ground beyond mediation or an irreducibily shifting terrain of ceaseless mystifications and demystifications—whether, so to speak, the quest is for a pure experience of Pilate's wine and Hagar's hair (which we find later inadequately contained in bottle and box, respectively) or for vision of the wine's stirring and the hair's braiding. But perhaps these terms are not adequate to the passage's own perspective on this unresolved quest for wholeness, for in once again objectifying what we should in fact engage dialectically we run Macon's risk of finally reducing the episode to an all-too-familiar phallic scenario of demand and detour, the *fort/da* of pleasure and reality, accepting the feminine as representation rather than subject of desire. The passage's concluding figure for this conflict in our centering of recognition—its rebuke to our implicit privileging of one experiential and intentional domain over another—is its closural turn from Macon to the vision of Pilate immersed in her unmoving activity of chewing, mixing, and swaying. Such a turn requires of us a new focus: What does *she* think, and feel, and see? What is the story of *her* desire? In his liminal and ultimately self-regarding stance of invisibility, Macon cannot tell us. To know beyond Macon's knowing, we will have to listen to Pilate in greater proximity to her voice and with the fully self-surrendering strength of genuine "care."

But before we do I must hazard another detour, this time to sketch a brief fiction of the narrative terrain stretching between *Invisible Man* and Morrison's text in order to situate the implications of *Song of Solomon*'s revisionary evocation of the modern black wanderer. Throughout *Invisible Man* the hero is impelled by a belief in a foundational design or "plan" whose inner logic, born in the originary "principles" of America's Enlightenment idealism and realized through "responsible" effort of the will, would finally legitimate investment in the template of heroic quest. Yet as old Norton discovers, lost in the underground as he searches for "Centre Street" (564-65), all authoritative structures merely mark a subterranean terrain of detours and supplementary elaborations—though, as the epilogial confrontation of the hero and the old white man itself implies, the specular map of oppositional differences remains in force. And so, trapped between the Scylla of absolute presence and the Charybdis of faceless difference, between desire for a name and scepticism of any namer, the invisible man remains immobilized in his subversively empowered hole, stammering at the brink of an emergence from the oedipal/odyssean struggle to remain unspoken by any paternal voice (be it Norton's or grandfather's, Rine's or Ras's) while still ascending to speech in the frequencies of recovered mastery.[7]

After *Invisible Man,* then—what Robert Stepto hopefully has called the state "after-hibernation"[8]—the wish to transcend this condition of "ambivalence" haunts the African-American writer and protagonist alike. Endeavoring to acquire voice, they sustain through revisionary narratives, by turns prophetic and elegiac, apocalyptic and ironic, the search for a fully epiphanic blackness, seeking a buried name or primal scene of instruction which will generate an unfragmented self. In the post-Ellisonian era, this self-consciously woven double plot takes a variety of forms. In the underground dramas of Amiri Baraka's *Dutchman* and *System of Dante's Hell*, for example, the surface narrative concerns the destructive violence of contemporary black existence, while its subtext is alternately that of a forgotten resistance to servitude or of pre-slavery's suppressed presence of black grandeur. With Ishmael Reed's *Mumbo Jumbo*, on the other hand, the hidden text is precisely a dismembered Book whose sacred inscriptions cannot cohere so as to finally legitimate the continuous presence of an embodied blackness. Both writers, while clearly impatient and mocking in contemplating *Invisible Man's* brooding terror that emergence into structure is an inevitable betrayal of rebellious energy, echo Ellison in their refusal or inability to discover an occluded but transcendent discourse which would suture the wounds opened by *histoire noir*'s deconstructive battle with the shabby logocentrism of mainstream culture.

Seeking to compose a prophetic book from equal parts of jive, Jeremiah, and Jes Grew, Reed's and Baraka's gestures toward what the latter terms a "post-Western" form have the power and limitations of the narrative framework codified by *Invisible Man*. That is to say, the modern black text, from Ellison to Reed, is motivated by an essentially oedipal logic whose conclusion is the illusory evasion or destruction of the father (whiteness, the West, bourgeois ambition—everything captive to the Fanonian dialectic of becoming and overcoming mastery itself), a displacement projected as a redemptive black narrativity either zero-degree or hypostasized. Based on techniques of sly parody and negating refusal, such stagings of "post-Western" discourse provide a trenchant critique of dominant discursive forms, yet paradoxically remain structurally affiliated with the very system it would dismantle. Contestation in this mode may achieve its shock not in dislodging received meaning but in affirming its essential strategies of containment, a final "perverse" turn in the "boomerang" of history so feared by Ellison's hero (cf. 6).

A related but alternative approach to the buried name of blackness, I believe, is suggested in the restructured quest narrative of *Song of Solomon*. Specifically, Morrison's text forges a *communal protagonist, re-imagining the tradition's concern with personal quest-romance in terms which suggest neither a ratification nor a simplistic refusal of inherited paradigms of cultural narrative*. *Song of Solomon* thereby seeks not only to interrogate the dominant scenario which *Invisible Man* and its heirs, in a "double" sense, betray, but further to rethink our sense of that scenario's role in formulating an historical image of African-American expression.

Morrison has specified for us the connection of the oedipal and odyssean topoi to her vision of a "womanist"[9] black fiction in the famous *Chant of Saints* interview, tellingly entitled "Intimate Things in Place" (an interview conducted, notably, while Morrison was at work on *Song of Solomon*). The black woman character, Morrison suggests, often appears as "parent [or] culture-bearer [for] the community"; but, she continues,

> One of the major differences between black men's work and black women's work is that the big scene for black men is the travelling Ulysses scene. They are moving. Trains—you hear those men talk about trains like they were their first lover—the names of the trains, the times of the trains! And boy, you know, they spread their seed all over the world. That going from town to town or place to place or looking out and over and beyond and changing—that's what they do. It is the Ulysses theme, the leaving home. Curiosity, what's around the corner, what's down the track—go find out what that is! And in the process of finding, they are also making themselves.[10]

Read as gender criticism, Morrison's discussion becomes a description of the generically "male" character: defined as thoroughly by mobility as the women in Pilate's house are by a highly charged stillness, the black male hero experiences no rapture or relation that can hold him from pursuit of a beckoning world that is always elsewhere. Legible as a trace in the bodies of those the hero produces and leaves behind, the hero's quest is the quintessential autodidactic journey of self-creation (and noticeably insouciant self-dissemination); it is a quest beyond affiliation (whether familial, sexual, or communal) through which the self is made in distinction to the otherness it finds.

Read as a transparency of a more subversive feminist manifesto, however, Morrison's analysis is, on the one hand, a covert interrogation of the propriety of that male quest—its costs and exclusions—and, on the other hand, of its implicitly enabling denial of female presence and voice. Its vision entails looking beyond and out, not looking out for: as with Odysseus and Oedipus, the possibility of self-generation assumes the privilege of first standing beyond the scene of desire before claiming it in a gesture of inquiry. Like this scene, the scene of a world found if not founded, the odyssean hero is to those he abandons always other and elsewhere, a transformative idea more than a genetic presence. For those he touches and perhaps even for himself, the underside of self-generating restlessness is a loneliness like Macon's, which derives from the distance felt from an other in relation to whom one once defined oneself. For the child or mother, the hero-as-father is not an individual but a function, a privileged floating figure of desire whose primal love is the mechanism of displacement itself—oh those trains! Defined for others by his absence, he is presumably for himself the once-abandoned son who in turn becomes the enigmatic figure whose identity is made not begotten (indeed, earlier in this passage Morrison speaks of writing in *Song of Solomon* about "the feeling of anonymity, the feeling of orphanage"). Identity for him is relational only in a strictly structural sense, an interminable activity of calculating difference and distance from what's down the track.

We must be sure, however, to note that Morrison's account of the Ulysses Scene is less a censure than an encomium, or at least apologia: "Although . . . they do not stay home," she continues, "that has always been to me one of the most attractive features about black male life," then adding in knowing anticipation of the normative feminist response to such a remark (and, proleptically, to *Song of Solomon* itself),[11] "I guess I'm not supposed to say that." And indeed any reading of *Song of Solomon* cannot help entertaining the possibility that the novel is a mimesis rather than an interruption or reversal of the oedipal/odyssean pattern of modern African-American narrative. After all, the novel seems to follow to completion the classic model of a quest for a source, a primal Father whose Name constitutes a philological and psycho-historical riddle of identity, a quest replete with a genealogical imperative that sets in motion the paradigmatic "journey back" of a self-obsessed hero.

Specifically, Milkman's story seems to follow the mythic outline of heroic generation: a birth shrouded in mystery, an expedition into a seemingly pre-cultural wilderness, and, after an uncertain beginning, the willed struggle to assert individuality. Moreover, his story appears to recapitulate the essential pattern and stigmata of oedipal narrative, including such paradigmatic details as the scar of castration (i.e., Milkman's self-nurtured limp), the regressive fantasies of a pre-oedipal nurturance (i.e., the oddly lengthened nursing by Ruth and, in a later displacement/correction into the arena of a mythic progenitrix, the discovery of speech before language in the uncultivated earth of Blue Ridge country), the enjoyment and eventual rejection of incestuous dalliance (i.e., the relationship with "cousin" Hagar), the ironically imitative agon with the father over the keys to the household (i.e., the battle over the mother, taking place, appropriately enough, at the dinner table), and finally the seductive scenario of becoming the father by, as Macon puts it, "working right along side him" (aptly enough, managing the economy and keeping written account of the father's investments). Finally, cannot the valorization of Pilate that surrounds these traditional fictions of goal and closure be itself seen as conforming to the underlying, if silent, assumption of the Ulysses Scene: that is, that Woman must protect, prepare, propel the hero toward his rightful place at the center of an unfolding drama of self-discovery, then vanish once more?

I will suggest, in fact, that Pilate's presence, and the dénouement over which, as active character and genius loci, she presides, make all the difference to the Sameness of the novel's relation to the Ulysses Scene. Through her, the tale of Milkman's attempted recuperation of a fully encoded but lost primal scene becomes instead the (re)discovery of a site of performed meaning. Through her, the old Names, once exhumed, are found to bear not unalterable injunctions but an empowering history of improvisation. And Morrison, like her heroine, does not so much imitate the Ulysses Scene as reweave and perform it,[12] furnishing it forth with a concealed but forgotten mode of being which realizes, rather than rejects, the implications of self-enactment. Concluding as it does with the interpolation and performance of its own embedded double (the discovered "Song of Solomon"), Morrison's epic thematizes its own endeavor to effect what we might regard as a radical, dislocating translation of the quest for a buried Text of blackness, a critical mimesis in which repetition is at once appropriation and revision, at once the inscription of a past forgotten but not erased and the projection toward a future possessed but over-looked.

What I am implying is that *Song of Solomon* does indeed follow the lead of Morrison's celebration of the black male adventure, but only in order to achieve a revolutionary rethinking of that adventure's own suppressed project of self-*surpassing,* not self-begetting, renewal. A pertinent mnemonic of this transactive rewriting is available in the heretical theory concerning the *Odyssey*'s authorship, put forth most memorably by Samuel Butler and Robert Graves.[13] Asserting that this touchstone of the Western phallocentric journey of maturation, initiation, and hardwon sovereign possession was, in fact, composed by a woman, the so-called "authoress of the *Odyssey*" theory holds that while the *Iliad,* as a poem of war, assembly, and political conflict, of physical prowess, public debate, and the common fatality of grieving fathers and vengeful sons was a man's epic written for men, the *Odyssey,* as a poem of feasthall, bath, and bed, of temptation, sexuality, and familial recomposition, was a woman's epic written for women. Calling attention to the confusions and contingencies by which literary values become enmeshed with gender, this impish conjecture has the virtue of redirecting our attention to Homer's text not as a prototypical discourse about the father, but as a polytropic, self-transgressive effort to imagine the feminine—or, perhaps, as a transparently excessive effort to *avoid* imagining the feminine. In particular, the *Odyssey* presents to us, through recurring encounters of Odysseus with the spellbinding enticements of witch-figures, the terror of seduction by female presence and voice. Characterized by an alluring amalgam of scent, song, shuttle, and sexuality, the witch's domain—be it Calypso's cave or Circe's den—threatens the protagonist's redundant movement toward an already-existent identity with the displacing enchantments of alternative ideas of home and self.

> Upon [Kalpyso's] hearthstone a great fire blazing
> scented the farthest shores with cedar smoke [. . .]
> and singing high and low
> in her sweet voice, before her loom a-weaving,
> she passed her golden shuttle to and fro.
> A deep wood grew outside [. . .]
> Ornate birds here rested their stretched wings—[. . .]
> Even a god who found this place
> would gaze [. . .]
> (*Odyssey*, 5.57)
>
> Presently in the hall her maids were busy,
> the nymphs who waited upon Kirkê: [. . .]
> One came with richly colored rugs [. . .]
> a second pulled tables out, all silver [. . .]
> a third mixed wine as tawny-mild as honey [. . .]
> The larder mistress brought her tray of loaves
> with many savory slices, and she gave
> the best, to tempt me. But no pleasure came;
> I huddled with my mind elsewhere, oppressed.
> (*Odyssey*, 10.345)[14]

Odysseus becomes a hero by remaining literally determined; in each encounter, he must experience the voice and body of the feminine without suffering alteration: in particular, listening to the female voice, and yielding to the false center of an alien hearth where "ease" originates from the self-displacing magic of another's power, implies the dreaded snare of ecstasy, a psychic movement without *nostos* to the self-same. And so the feminine-as-witch designates a dangerously liminal space, a margin between bestiality and hyper-acculturation, between abjection and ravishment, where the self is made *into* what it finds. A figure of self-veiling and engulfing metamorphosis, the nymph-witch is in a sense the hero's specular double, an inverted projection of his own impulse to consume the world by holding it at a distance and refusing the drama of mutuality.

We return, then, through our own polytropic weavings of the Ulysses Scene, to the encounter between *Song of Solomon* and *Invisible Man*, which, as the scene of Macon's succumbing to the women's sound implies, is mediated through the odyssean encounter with witchcraft. For at the heart of Morrison's densely woven relation to Ellison is not merely the propriety of male wandering but, further, the status of women within the quest. For the most part, the invisible man, seeking as the vet advises to "be[come his] own father" (154), experiences women as obstacles, as does Odysseus (which, we might note, is no surprise, as the *Odyssey,* with its successful manipulations of sonship and naming, phallic power and maternal nourishment, can be read as an anti-*Oedipus avant la lettre*).[15] In particular, women in *Invisible Man* appear as suffocating nurturers or soporific temptresses. Mary Rambo, like Homer's Kalypso, saves the hero from turbulence, welcoming him, after the miscarriage of Brockway's underbelly and the Hospital's technological baptismal, into her womblike (Ogygian) sphere. Associated, like her Homeric archetype, with water, song, and elaborate preparations of sustenance (she can be heard singing "Blackwater Blues" in the kitchen), Mary seeks to keep her "boy" (as she calls him) chained to her obsessive care. "When [the song] faded I got up and put on my coat. Perhaps it was not too late" (290), the hero says as he leaves Mary's imprisoning, if secure, home in renewed search for publically empowered identity.

Once thrust from the mother, the invisible man experiences women as seductresses and false oracles. One of the most telling of these episodes is the liaison with the woman in red, a sirenic enchantress characterized like Mary by unremitting possessiveness whose potentially lethal domesticity is masked by the enervating display of overrefined *grottesca:*

When she reappeared in the rich red of a hostess gown she was so striking that I had to avert my somewhat startled eyes.
"What a beautiful room you have here," I said, looking across the rich cherry glow of furniture to see a life-sized painting of a nude, a pink Renoir. [. . .] the spacious walls seemed to flash alive with warm, pure color. What does one say to all this?
(*Invisible Man,* 401)

The encounter represents a crisis of vision and voice, as the mock-sublime frenzy of feminine temptation arrests the hero's vital powers of contextual apprehension and critical expression ("I was lost, for the conflict between the ideological and the biological, duty and desire, had become too subtly confused"—406). Modeled on Odysseus's entanglement with Kirkê, the comically debilitating affair anticipates the hero's more threatening ravishment of/by Sybil (named in sly allusion to the prophetess of Petronius's *Satyricon,* whose endless degenerative entrapment suggests the avenging of Kirkê's debasing enticements). In a culminating drama of sexuality suffused with wine,[16] distorting bestiality, a reversion to pre-linguistic primitivism, and dis-spiriting forgetfulness, the affair with Sybil represents the most violently threatening misprision of invisible man's ultimately salvific will-to-representation, a potential "fall." Resisting seduction with difficulty, the hero tears himself loose from enchantment only after scribbling in lipstick a parodic explication of their intercourse on her belly ("She lay aggressively receptive [. . .] I bent to write furiously across her belly in drunken inspiration: SYBIL, YOU WERE RAPED BY SANTA CLAUS SURPRISE"—511). The self-begetting and self-regulating odyssean adventurer (no authoress he) must, it seems, write the feminine before it writes him!

But more than writing the enigma of Woman, the hero's imperative, we soon discover, is to erase its defiling alterity: "I stumbled out and began rubbing out the evidence of my crime. It was as tenacious as sin and it took some time. [. . .] Fortunately she didn't arouse until I was almost finished" (512). What is most notable, indeed, in the novel's depiction of women is their absence in the grand summation of the Epilogue, notwithstanding the hero's general avowal that "in spite of all I find that I love. [. . .] I hate and love" (566–67).[17] This annulment of the feminine (the bitterness of which is screened but the audible "in spite" of the evocation of Emersonian dialectic) is anticipated by the slippage in the hero's experience of women from struggles with embodied subjects to concentration on the empty signifier of the "Woman Question" (his final Brotherhood assignment). One might say that, like Oedipus, the invisible man believes he can solve the question without himself being part of the answer; or, perhaps, again like Oedipus, that he assumes the question must have as its answer, "Man." Inspired by the maternal singer of spirituals in the Prologue to define freedom as "knowing how to say what I got up in my head" (11), invisible man has been in a sense put into discourse by the feminine; through that process identified by Alice Jardine as "gynesis,"[18] this valorization of woman's voice occurs at a strategic moment of beginning, when evasion of the self-destructive agon between hegemonic and nihilistically resisting discourses (the white father and his black sons) without despairing of any master narrative seems otherwise impossible. This momentary staging of female voice has, so to speak, an alterior motive, allowing the hero to posit a "border area" between the unseen and the unsaid, a space of acceptably "criminal" Power which his quest allows him eventually to occupy in hyperbolic self-illumination (cf.7). Preferring to be othered rather than mothered by the inherited discourses of epic tradition and its renegade echoes (be they legacies of Homeric or native sons), the invisible man implicitly addresses a masculine "you" in the novel's final line, freedom remaining deferred and nameless but at least, at last, clearly gendered.[19]

If, as we surmised in surveying Macon at Pilate's window, invisibility can be understood as this refusal to entertain any genuinely unlimited interplay of voices, *Song of Solomon* may be read as an inquiry into the effects, upon *all* participants in an historically charged drama of recognition and peripety, of hazarding this dynamically complementary exchange. For Macon, the kairotic moment offered by his sister's singing remains an inaccessible dream and momentary detour; but this episode is immediately followed by Milkman's first visit to Pilate's house, a scene which in effect becomes the first episode's alternative touchstone, or perhaps we might better say its genuine realization. Macon, describing Pilate as "filthy" and "ignorant," has educated his son in the epic tradition, encouraging him to view his aunt's house as a place of barbaric wildness and engulfing monstrosity that pursues its denial of cultured norms as deliberate taunt to his own toilsome achievement. Seeking to bind Milkman's desire to the accepted burdens of patrilineal law, he forbids the boy to enter Pilate's home—succeeding, however, not in instituting the final authority of the paternal "no," but in mystifying the feminine space with what the narrator terms "unbelievable but entirely possible stories" which left the boy "spellbound" (35). What Milkman finds on Darling Street is indeed a kind of frontier culture, hovering between paradise and chaos, excess and lack, intoxication and instruction, the raw and the cooked (Pilate, remember, "cooks" wine, though she has no need of it herself)—a place so thoroughly embraced by the quotidian and marvelous alike that it cannot be neatly circumscribed by the oscillating language of pollution and miracle which others bring to it. On the one hand, Pilate's family subordinates domestic decorum to somatic need, elevating primary impulses of nurturance to the present-cancelling chronicity of cultural development: as Macon says, "she and her daughters ate like children [. . .] no meal was ever planned or balanced or served" (29). Thus, too, the imperatives of genealogical hierarchy, with its burden of founding cultural taboo, are casually breached: even Macon describes Reba and Hagar equally as Pilate's daughters (just as they both call Pilate "Mama"). On the other hand, this refusal of cultural pattern underscores an uncompromising emphasis on hospitality and concord: "She gave up, apparently, all interest in table manners or hygiene, but acquired a deep concern for and about human relationships" (150). Chastising Reba for attempting to define Milkman's relation to Hagar in the non-contradictory logic of orthodox familial taxonomy ("A brother is a brother if you both got the same mother or if you both—"), Pilate insists on the priority of *caritas* to calculation ("What's the difference in the way you act toward 'em? Don't you have to act the same way to both?"—44).

Taking on masculine dress and bearing, but practicing the female rootmagic that ensures Milkman's birth against the violent interventions of his father,[20] Pilate confounds her world's structures of dominance and difference erected by both oedipal and anti-oedipal narratives (the fictions, we might say, of Macon's empire-building and Guitar's revenge). She asserts instead the will-to-connection against a world insistent upon definition by division and differentiation. In the scene of Milkman's first visit to her house this categorical suspension is abetted by the very imagery of fluidity and interiority which characterizes the horrifyingly absorptive enclosures of epic witches. She offers the boy rapturous performance, simple pleasures made exotic by prohibition, and sustaining concern—materials which, when emanating from the female in the Ellisonian context of the "Ulysses scene," denote sensual surrender to alien voice, but which Morrison transforms into emblems of engendering nurturance, of articulate self-discovery as shared experience. The narrator, evoking the hypnotic enthrallments of epic encounters, tells us that "The pebbly voice, the sun, and the narcotic wine smell weakened [Milkman], and [he] sat in a pleasant semi-stupor, listening to her go on and on. . . ." (40). But Morrison here typically seeks to *write through* the odyssean idiom toward an experience it contains but denies. Thus the signal dimension of Milkman's first meeting with Pilate—and of the subsequent episodes with the women who appear almost as emanations of this healing, teaching, and caring witch—is his learning to *listen* (the word is underscored in each such encounter), to hear anew possibilities of collective consciousness long buried in the old terms of experience as propaedeutic to self-liberating immersion in the other's domain.

If Morrison critiques Ellison by directly refashioning the Ulyssian experience of bewitchment—suggesting thereby that the black woman, far from blocking or distorting the male quest, serves as its enabling agent—she more radically undermines its assumed equation of maleness with mobile self-discovery by subtly presenting the female quest as a parallel, if not prior, version of its male counterpart. For Pilate may appear on the narrative surface to be a consummate revision of the black matriarch (echoing Mary Rambo in many details of setting and speech, both Homeric and Afrocentric). Yet "behind" that role (to employ the text's favorite multiform trope for the past's disacknowledged but always immanent presence),[21] like the names of identity beneath the Song of Solomon, lies a revisionary quest romance of extraordinary dimensions.[22] The crux—if not the center—of this tale is the absence of Pilate's navel, a symptom of post-oedipal freedom from the crisis of origination (and, more generally from inevitable lack and coercive sexual differentiation). Pilate's seamless belly is a visual sign of the blankness, the moral vacuity, of division by sight, a rebuke to the specular logic of non-coincident identity subtending traditional stagings of political, psychoanalytical, and philosophical discourse. "There really was nothing to see. Her defect, frightening and exotic as it was, was also a theatrical failure" (149). Though often categorized with other of Morrison's famous deformities or wounds, Pilate's non-navel is a difference which, in a sense, makes no difference, not a *non*-phallus (nor, for that matter, a deconstructive *anti*-omphalos) but an *a*phallus. For Pilate's belly doesn't imply, like the phallus, that which it is not, its other as lack or totalization, but suggests rather the perversity of oppositional thought *per se*. As Macon himself says, his brotherly intimacy with Pilate precluded any imposition of meaning on this difference between their bodies, just as Pilate—inadvertently mocking the most graphic Freudian trope of masculine mastery—remarks that "He had [a navel]. She did not. He peed standing up. She squatting down. [. . .] She thought it was one more way in which males and females were different" (144). No child, folks reply, you aren't "natural"—by which they really mean that, lacking the mark of castration which supposedly determines, regardless of gender, every person's entrance into symbolic order, you can't be cultural, you can't speak. But, of course, speak she does—Morrison insists that we know Pilate's story only because she tells it. She alone, in a novel saturated with tales, histories, and namings, possesses a legible, verifiable autobiography—for only she, as we'll see, grasps the nature of the bond between knowledge and recognition of otherness implicit in the buried, chiasmal, etymology of narrative.[23]

Though "cut-off" from people at an early age—and, perhaps in consequence, as insouciantly "restless" as any actor on the Ulysses Scene (her "wandering life," indeed, consuming the appropriately odyssean "twenty-some-odd years"—148)—, Pilate manages to forge links to both past and future generations, to a mother she never saw and to descendants she cannot choose. Undefined by existential dramas of banishment, she perspectivizes the theatrical alienation of others (chastising Ruth and Hagar for their proprietary feud over Milkman, she calls attention to the independence of spirit from structure, if not from structurality itself: "Two growed-up women talkin 'bout a man like he was a house or needed one. He ain't a house, he's a man . . ."—138). And so her story becomes an implicit rebuke of the self-protectively hermetic, hibernating impulses of Morrison's modernist predecessors. Divining, as it were, the spirit of her father's ghostly injunction, "You can't just fly on off and leave a body," Pilate refuses to be defined by her exilic condition, and never stops looking for (and looking out for) the other. Similarly, Pilate's performance, self-conscious but not merely theatrical, points not to its own gestures of imposition but beyond itself to its potential constitutive effects in the stories of her audience. Indeed, this is a theory of post-reflexivity that the novel renders "fabulously" thematic: born after her mother's death, Pilate has most reason to declare herself a self-begotten substitute for all genealogical authorities; yet, lugging about the bones of a father who whispers the name of the mother, it is she who carries the burden of parental "inheritance" as a literal calling.

Healing the division between self-finders and culture-bearers traditionally inscribed into African-American literature's "Ulysses scene," Pilate's tale becomes, both structurally and materially, the template for Milkman's reinvention of black modernism's genealogical quest. In the second part of *Song of Solomon,* Milkman renews the tradition's search for the properly named self in a journey which turns upon the choice between two paths leading out of the pivotal cave or underground scene following the death of Macon and Pilate's father: on the one hand, Macon's path for gold, the fetish of paternity, which provides the initial incentive for Milkman's travels south; and, on the other hand, Pilate's passage toward the ghost of one's "first caring," the continual *nostos* of relationships buried under one's name, which leads him ultimately to the "Song of Solomon."

Milkman eventually abandons the father's quest and, as the narrator says, "follows [instead] in [Pilate's] tracks" (261), finding traces of her journey (cf. 146). Even a cursory outline of the effects of this reversal in the adventure's dénouement suggests Morrison's detailed patterning of Milkman's imitation of invisible man in his movement through pre-oedipal and anti-oedipal solutions to paternal authority, key episodes of which include the agon with the men of Shalimone, the negation of cultural identity suffered in the woods (a negation suggested by loss of instruments of civilized calculation and drive, such as watch, pencil, shoes, and car), the communing with the land's pre-lapsarian *Ursprache* (281), the indulgence of guiltless sexuality (288–89), the shedding of his oedipal limp (284). Central to this process, of course, are Milkman's meetings with a series of women who collectively "correct," so to speak, the Ellisonian bevy. Morrison's Circe, for example, is indeed a mythically entrancing woman; yet her gift is not that of a meaningless sexual immortality but rather of a sage, even epiphanic historicity ("birthed just about everybody," she tells Milkman, as she gives him the initial clues to his ancestral name—245). Sweet, like Ellison's Sybil, offers the hero wine, bath, and sexual play— but their effects are both instructive and regenerative, not debilitating. Such moments are crucial to the novel's reconstruction of an animating beginning as both a "looking beyond" and a visceral progress through the oedipal scene. For what Milkman "finds" by entering the scene of feminine instruction—a process which concludes, in recollection of *Invisible Man*'s Epilogue, with his awakening from childish ressentiment in Pilate's basement (336)—what Milkman dis-covers is not a private memoir of disembodied self-authorship but rather an ensemble performance of black historicity enacted by the collective African-American body, itself: *you can't just fly on off and leave a body.*

You can't just fly on off and leave a body. What, then, does this key phrase, and the Song of Solomon which lies beneath it, mean for the post-Ellisonian African-American text? The novel's conclusion approaches this question by way of a dazzling series of transformative moments through which the possibilities of a post-oedipal reality are glimpsed. Encompassing the funeral celebration of Hagar's irreducibly comely blackness ("She was *loved!*"—323), the intertwining of desublimated desire and ethical regret in Milkman's movement from washing Sweet's hair to memorializing Hagar's (289, 338), the epiphany and retrieval of the buried names of blackness (333), the "decision" of Pilate's death (340; cf. 140–41), and the culminating acceptance and suspension of family romance in Milkman's deathly leap (341), these multiple instances of recognition and shock, of realization and reversal, suggest, in their very proliferate excess, the necessary provisionality of any interpretive design. In lieu of a fully nuanced reading of this complex (non)closural drama, I offer a brief précis of *Song of Solomon*'s dénouement which addresses the propriety of re-conceiving the Father, and the possibility of re-calling the Mother, in a womanist reweaving of the Ulysses Scene.

I must begin in some difference from many prior readings of the ending, for I think there is no sense of Milkman's journey having come to a conclusion which encapsulates, from the distance of a retrospective or final perch, the total meaning of his adventure.[24] There is, instead, a continuing process of challenge which forces attention to unseen possibilities beneath imagined origins and desired ends. Thus Milkman reads the names beneath the signs and traces which, heretofore, only bespoke the specular family romances of the father's name dictating the son's (as in the ever-echoing patronymic Macon Dead, Macon Dead, Macon Dead) or the son's subversively repeating the father's (as with the ineradicable gold tracery of *Sonny*'s Shop over Macon's office door):

He read the road signs with interest now, wondering what lay beneath the names. The Algonquins had named the territory he lived in Great Water, *michi gami*. How many dead lives and fading memories were buried in and beneath the names [. . .] Like the street he lived on, recorded as Mains Avenue, but called Not Doctor Street by the Negroes in memory of his grandfather [. . .] He closed his eyes and thought of the black men in Shalimar, Roanoke, Petersburg [. . .] Names that bore witness. Macon Dead, Sing Byrd [. . .] Sweet [. . .] Staggerlee, Jim the Devil, Fuck-Up, and *Dat* Nigger. (333–34)

With the enumeration of Afro-America's "hidden names," unnaming becomes re-collection, a gathering of history as reverberative play and released desire, rather than as monumentalized or forgotten totality. Such discovery distinguishes itself from the odyssean enactment of name as a shift between strategic concealment and rash declaration, and from the oedipal understanding of name as the horrifying uncovering of a self-displacing origin. Beneath the paternal name (Macon Dead) pulses, first, a heretofore occluded collection of postures, which are themselves signs of survival, defiance, joy, celebration; and second, *en abîme*, the activity of naming itself, the ceaseless energy of "bearing witness" which at once links the father to a story he would suppress and dissolves him into that story's endless unnameable self-constitution: *Dat* Nigger. Such discovery suggests the idea of establishing the self as a collective translation or improvisation, as an event which suspends the disabling antinomy of the primary and the belated by repeating with difference the already-enciphered figures of communality.

The Song of Solomon, therefore, is not the telos of Milkman's quest in the sense of offering a final legacy of name or dynastic identity. It is more precisely itself a site of plural preliterate re-weavings, scène, a fabric of languages alluding to a crazy-quilt of cultures, regions, religions, and affiliations:

>Jake the only son of Solomon
>Come booba yalle, come booba tambee
>Whirled about and touched the sun
>Come konka yalle, come konka tambee
>
>Left that baby in a white man's house
>Come booba yalle, come booba tambee
>Heddy took him to a red man's house
>Come konka yalle, come konka tambee
>
>Black lady fell down on the ground
>Come booba yalle, come booba tambee
>Threw her body all around
>Come konka yalle, come konka tambee
>
>Solomon and Ryna Belali Shalut
>Yaruba Medina Muhammet too.
>Nestor Kalina Saraka cake.
>Twenty-one children, the last one Jake!
>
>O Solomon don't leave me here
>Cotton balls to choke me
>O Solomon don't leave me here
>Buckra's arms to yoke me
>
>Solomon done fly, Solomon done gone
>Solomon cut across the sky, Solomon gone home. (306-7)

Encompassing KiKongo and Greek, the Islamic and the Judaic, West Africa and Cuba, priestly exile and burning love within the mother's home, biblical fable and Morrison's own family biography,[25] the Song of Solomon clearly eludes any completed reading, any certain "translation," in its active interweaving of temporal, spatial, and discursive codes. Such partial legibility is not an effect of insufficient data, for no encyclopedia of referents could possibly exhaust the combinatory possibilities of the Song's "cut across" the fabric of discourse. Itself a ceaselessly productive process of translation, it authorizes no relation of original (father) and copy (son): "faithful" translation can legitimate only the act of reinscription *per se*.[26] And, critically, such a movement of retrieval and rearticulation is not the assembling of a static archival mythology,[27] but a profoundly phenomenological and *historical* "repetition," a literal "making present" of the past *as* the call-and-response of self and tradition. Performing the "Song of Solomon" is thus not to rehearse the oedipal scenario but precisely to re-place it by uncovering the story it told but couldn't hear: there is no "home" apart from the other's body; like the deer who "step in their own prints" (85), ever-conflating presence and memory, even the "swollen foot" (cf. 162) makes tracks which the other can follow: *kumbuba yal'e, kumbuba tambi*.[28]

Milkman, then, does not decode the names and the Song; he *rides* them, in keeping with the text's final haunting line—"Now he knew what Shalimar knew: If you surrendered to the air, you could *ride* it" (341). What notion of identity and origins, of performance and history, might this riding portend? The first clue (we have, of course, no ultimate goal in our own improvisatory tracery upon the Song), I think, lies in the word uttered by the Father's Ghost: "Sing." Pilate took this pronouncement, along with the plea not to fly off and leave a body, as a directive to embrace the other through performance, to bind herself to them with the powers of enchantment. Milkman finds that beneath the command lies the name of the mother, supposedly lost both to the past's violence and to the equally violent efforts to forget the past. Understood dialectically, rather than diametrically, these connotations of the word "Sing" imbricate the self's performance and the mother's language, delivering Pilate and Milkman from the father's ghost, allowing *his* burial at last as the singular authoritative voice of desire and law. Singing for Pilate his own riff or "ride" on the Song of Solomon, the extemporized out-chorus "Sugargirl don't leave me here/Cotton balls to choke me," Milkman answers what Morrison has termed the "promise" or gift of Pilate's opening song to the newly born Milkman,[29] revaluing *nostos* as response to the call of the (m)other tongue.

Pilate, in the last words of her mortal tongue, tells Milkman, "I wish I'd a knowed more people. . . . If I'd a knowed more, I would a loved more" (340). If Milkman, riding the Song of Solomon, "knew what Shalimar knew," his riff turns, I think, on this relation of knowing (and thus also of telling) to loving. To accept that the father's law of identity is an illusion of finality, to understand that difference is always already self-difference, that telling or performing one's own story always does more than the tale itself can know; to "surrender," as Macon at Pilate's window finally could not, to the otherness of one's own center, to the discipline of another's speaking; to know that the sight of the other and one's own visibility do not bode fatal enthrallment, that enchantment needn't preclude intimacy, desire satisfaction, or exile a love unmixed with hate—such is the knowledge that carries one into the scene imagined, but buried, in the primal letters addressed from the father's Ulysses Scene.[30] "Now he knew why he loved her so," Milkman thought. "Without leaving the ground, she could fly" (340).

NOTES

I have been the beneficiary, during the course of this paper's preparation, of illuminating conversations with Ruth E. Polk, Gerhard Joseph, and Richard Hardack concerning various aspects of Morrison's art. To them, much thanks, and apologies for continuing insufficiencies.

1. Toni Morrison, *Song of Solomon* New York: New American Library, 1977), p. 4. Further references will be cited in the text.

2. Roland Barthes, *S/Z*, trans. Richard Miller (New York: Hill & Wang, 1974).

3. Ralph Ellison, *Invisible Man* (New York: Vintage Books, 1972 [1952]), p. 568. Further references will be cited in the text.

4. For an excellent discussion of the conversational dynamic in African-American literature in the twentieth century (which, nevertheless, curiously contains no reference to Morrison), see John F. Callahan's *In the American Grain* (Urbana: U of Illinois P, 1988).

5. These include two failed ventures, alternately fatal and comic, of sublime flight (Mr. Smith's "transfixing" leap—7, 9) and rebellion (Porter's drunken rooftop plea for love—25-26), and the theatrical epiphanies of the hero's [Milkman's] quasi-mythical birth ("Did he come with a caul?"-10) and seriocomic naming (14).

6. I borrow the term, by way of Hawthorne, from Edgar A. Dryden's instructive analysis of voyerism and solitude in *Nathaniel Hawthorne: The Poetics of Enchantment* (Ithaca: Cornell UP, 1977). The phrase has obvious pertinence to the final status of Ellison's invisible man, who imagines himself a "disembodied voice" (568) as he writes from the underground. Dryden's explication of "enchantment" in Hawthorne suggestively details a dialectic of communality and withdrawal whose resonance with Morrison, interestingly, depends upon reversal of categories, since for her enchantment denotes not the mechanisms of distantiation but the possibilities of identification. Cf. also Carolyn Porter's *Seeing and Being* (Middletown, Ct.: Wesleyan UP, 1981).

7. The prototype of this moment in the African-American narrative is Frederick Douglass's "rising" to accept the "severe cross" of public speech at the end of the *Narrative* of 1845. Parodied in a succession of "graduation" and political displays throughout *Invisible Man,* this paradigm of self-presentation remains a profound touchstone of the hero's desire at the novel's end (cf. 567).

8. See "After Modernism, After Hibernation: Michael Harper, Robert Hayden, and Jay Wright." In *Chant of Saints: A Gathering of Afro-American Art, Literature, and Scholarship,* eds. Michael S. Harper and Robert B. Stepto (Urbana: U. of Illinois P, 1979), pp. 470-86.

9. The term—which is Alice Walker's [see *In Search of Our Mothers' Gardens* (New York: Harcourt Brace Jovanovich, 1983)], may seem slightly inapt when discussing a work seemingly dedicated to "Daddy," and begun with the epigram, "The fathers may soar/And the children may know their names." I hope to show, however, that Morrison's effort in *Song of Solomon* is, as it were, to locate the "womanism" *within* the apparently monolithic patriarchal tradition *so that* the "Name of the Father" *may* be pronounced without surrender to symbolic violence.

10. Robert Stepto, ' "Intimate Things in Place'—A Conversation with Toni Morrison." In *Chant of Saints,* pp. 213-29.

11 This critique, common in many reviews of the novel, finds eloquent expression in

Cynthia A. Davis's "Self, Society, and Myth in Toni Morrison's Fiction," *Contemporary Literature* 23 (1982), 338-42.

12. A fascinating discussion of such troping of the traditional *textus* in contemporary theoretical discourse is provided by Nancy K. Miller in "Arachnologies: The Woman, The Text, and the Critic." In *The Poetics of Gender*, ed. Nancy K. Miller (New York: Columbia UP, 1986), pp. 270-95.

13. Samuel Butler, *The Authoress of the Odyssey* (Chicago: U of Chicago P, 1967); Robert Graves, *Homer's Daughter* (New York: Doubleday, 1955). While traditional scholars have never been receptive to the Butler/Graves conjecture (which we might assimilate to Virginia Woolf's musings on "Shakespeare's sister" as denoting the occulting of an alternative discourse within the masculine shell of "Western" writing), their dismissive remarks can at times be apt beyond intention: "Mr. Graves [. . .] *est un original* with a compulsive addiction to unusual ideas. His theory and its development are *enchanting* but not convincing" (my emphasis), Andre Michalopoulos, *Homer* (New York: Twayne, 1966), p. 142.

14. *The Odyssey*, trans. Robert Fitzgerald (New York: Doubleday, 1963).

15. Consider, for example, the episode with Polyphemous: with its entwining of savagery and nurturance, intoxication and milk, enclosure and release, the topography of the Oedipus story is here the setting for the *father's* blinding and the *son's* successful declaration of name (in striking at "polyphemous," in fact, Odysseus literally wounds the *"nom-du-père"*). Where Oedipus must cut the womb of his "double sowing," Odysseus emerges with a laugh from the one-eyed parent's cave, extracting recognition and extinguishing the Father's potentially castrating gaze.

16. When the woman-in-red offers the hero "wine or milk instead of coffee," he accepts the wine, "finding the idea of milk strangely repulsive" (402). Anticipating Macon Dead's sense that his son's nickname, Milkman, "was not clean" (15), invisible man here distances himself from the episode's implications of maternal substitution. Much the same can be said of the Sybil encounter. For though overtly an alluring, if aging, enchantress, Sybil is also, as Claudia Tate notes, "like Mary, [. . .] another surrogate mother who comes to deliver the young protagonist from the deception of his false identity with the Brotherhood"—i.e., from the coercive "designs" of the father's false history. See Claudia Tate, "Notes on the Invisible Women in Ralph Ellison's *Invisible Man*." In *Speaking For You: The Vision of Ralph Ellison*, ed. Kimberly W. Benston (Washington, D.C.: Howard UP, 1987), p. 170.

17. This remark reads like a sublimation of his early responses to the feminine, as seen, for example, in the confused reaction to the Battle Royal's white dancer: "I wanted [. . .] to love her and murder her" (19). Indeed, one might say that invisible man appropriates what, in the text's first represented encounter with an exemplary woman, amounts to a *dialogic* connection of love and hate (the feminine, notably, speaking for love): "I said 'Maybe freedom lies in hating.' 'Naw, son, it's in loving,' " replies the old singer of spirituals met in the Prologue's dream sequence (11).

18. Alice Jardine, *Gynesis: Configurations of Woman and Modernity* (Ithaca: Cornell UP, 1985).

19. The urgency of this appropriative silencing of the feminine, and the trace of fascination which it still betrays, can be located in a recurrent motif of the invisible man's experience of women: his capture by the female gaze which signals a latent, if finally disacknowledged, potential for identification. Most memorable in the vision of the blonde dancer at the Battle Royal ("I had a notion," he tells us, "that of all in the room she saw only me with her impersonal eyes"—19), this scopic engagement is felt with Mary "[you] needs a woman to keep an eye on you awhile"—246), Emma (who scans him with "a direct, what-type-of-mere-man-have-we-here kind of look that seemed to go beneath the skin"—295), and the woman-in-red ("She was so striking that I had to avert my somewhat startled eyes"—401). The hero presents these moments defensively as if suffering the castrating gaze of a figure whose

presumed marginality might, if returned, mirror his own disempowerment ("We're kind of alike," Sybil tells him with a smile (509) . . . to which he of course makes no reply).

20. Morrison has spoken of Pilate as "the apogee [. . .] of the best of that which is female and the best of that which is male [. . .] a balance [which] is disturbed if it is not nurtured, and if it is not counted on and if it is not reproduced." "Rootedness: The Ancestor as Foundation." In *Black Women Writers (1950–1980)*, ed. Mari Evans (New York: Anchor, 1984), p. 344.

21. Riding backward in the family "hearse" (31–32), fall[ing] in love with [Hagar's] behind" (43), proceeding against the cultural grain during the time of Emmett Till's death so that "there was nothing to see except their backs" (78), Milkman especially "concentrate[s] on things behind him," and is thus led, by "following behind" Pilate's footsteps, to the concluding scene of excavation and re-covery.

22. For a suggestive outline of the "motif of journey" in black women's writing see Susan Willis's "Black Women Writers: Taking a Critical Perspective." In *Making a Difference: Feminist Literary Criticism*, eds. Gayle Greene and Coppélia Kahn (New York: Methuen, 1985), pp. 219–26.

23. An interweaving of *narrare* and *gnarus*. In recent feminist critiques of phallocentric representation (especially those inspired by Lacan and Barthes), narrative and oedipus have sometimes been seen as hopelessly inextricable (perhaps the most suggestive formulation is to be found in Teresa de Lauretis's *Alice Doesn't: Feminism, Semiotics, Cinema* [Bloomington: Indiana UP, 1984]). We can infer Morrison's contrary effort to forge or re-locate narrative strategies disentangled from the oedipus-as-necessity.

On levels of narration (with especial attention to Pilate's tales) in *Song of Solomon* see Joseph T. Skerrett, Jr.'s "Recitation to the *Griot:* Storytelling and Learning in Toni Morrison's *Song of Solomon*." In *Conjuring: Black Women, Fiction, and Literary Tradition*, eds. Marjorie Pryse and Hortense J. Spillers (Bloomington: Indiana UP, 1985), pp. 192–202.

24. Well-nuanced versions of this reading may be found in Genevieve Fabre's "Geneological Archeology or the Quest for Legacy in Toni Morrison's *Song of Solomon*. In *Critical Essays on Toni Morrison*, ed. Nellie Y. McKay (Boston: G.K. Hall, 1988), pp. 113–14, and Kathleen O'Shaughnessy's " 'Life life life life': The Community as Chorus in *Song of Solomon*." In *Critical Essays*, pp. 131–32. For an utterly contrary reading, rejecting the final moment as anything but bitter catachresis, see Gerry Brenner's "*Song of Solomon*: Rejecting Rank's Monomyth and Feminism." In *Critical Essays*, p. 123.

25. For Morrison's remarks on biographical elements in the song see Bessie W. Jones and Audrey L. Vinson, "An Interview with Toni Morrison," In *The World of Toni Morrison: Explorations in Literary Criticism* (Dubuque: Kendall/Blunt, 1985), p. 130.

26. Cf. Joseph Riddel's account of American literary tradition as a perpetual and self-transgressive act of translation (or, in Riddel's de Manian terms, as the "reading moment" established between the double nodes of arrival and departure, groundless origin and impossible end) in "Reading America/American Readers," *MLN* 99 (1984), 903–27. On the traditional relations of gender to translation, and the consequent anxiety for any feminist intervention, see Suzanne Jill Levine's "Translation As (Sub)Version: On Translating Infante's *Inferno*," *Substance* 42 (1984), 85–94.

27. For a compelling reading of the novel precisely as the overcoming of historical linearity by mythical timelessness, see Valerie Smith's *Self-Discovery and Authority in Afro-American Narrative* (Cambridge, Mass.: Harvard UP, 1987), pp. 151–52.

28. The anthropologist Wyatt MacGaffey conjectures that this KiKongo phrase, typical of a KiKongo children's foot-stamping dance-song, best clarifies the Song's refrain [communication with the author]. The phrase might be translated as follows: "to strike my leg at him/her/it, to strike my footprint at myself," which notably involves the undecidability

of gender and the conflation of possible pronominal referents in KiKongo grammar. (I am grateful to Clinton Johnston for helping me parse the phrase.)

29. "Unspeakable Things Unspoken: The Afro-American Presence in American Literature," *Michigan Quarterly Review* 28 (1989), 27-29.

30. Both the Oedipus and Odysseus stories, arguably, signal a realm *beyond* the agonistic displays of self-authorization where the masculine protagonist can stand free from the endless narration of the phallic scenario. In the eleventh (or middle) book of the *Odyssey,* Tiresias prophesies a final journey for the hero in which, traveling inland rather than on the seas of colonial conquest, he will meet those who, removed from the seemingly universal realm of Greek adventure, take his oar to be a winnowing-fan. Planting this emblem of double-sowing, Odysseus will, according to the prophecy, at last propitiate Poseidon, thereby ending the struggle with authority and its attendant divisions (land/sea, fertility/death, alien/homeboy). Similarly, as Shoshana Felman suggests in "Beyond Oedipus: The Specimen Story of Psychoanalysis" (*MLN* 98 [1983], 1021-53), the final movement of the Sophoclean trilogy, *Oedipus at Colonus,* offers a vision of the hero's birth through a final leap "into the life of his history" which allows him to "assume the Other" and so experience the "radical de-centerment of his own ego."

6.
National Brands/National Body: *Imitation of Life*
LAUREN BERLANT

Advertising ministers to the spiritual side of trade. It is a great power that has been entrusted to your keeping which charges you with the high responsibility of inspiring and ennobling the commercial world. It is all part of the greater work of the regeneration and redemption of mankind.

Calvin Coolidge, 1929[1]

Every normal female yearns to be a luminous person.

Fannie Hurst, *Today is Ladies' Day*[2]

In Nella Larsen's *Passing* (1929), two light-skinned American women of African descent bring each other to mutual crisis. The gaze of one woman virtually embodies the other, calling her back from her absence-to-her-body, an absence politically inscribed by the legal necessity to be non-black while drinking iced tea at the Drayton Hotel in Chicago in 1927. Lost in thought about domestic matters, abstracted from her juridico-racial identity, Irene Redfield senses the gaze of the alluring blond "ivory"-skinned woman who watches her: "Feeling her colour heighten under the continued inspection, she slid her eyes down. What, she wondered, could be the reason for such persistent attention? Had she . . . put her hat on backwards?. . . . Perhaps there was a streak of powder somewhere on her face. She made a quick pass over it with her handkerchief. Something wrong with her dress?"[3]

Something must be wrong with her, she suddenly has a body. She associates this sensation with the colonizing gaze whites wield when trying to detect whether a light-skinned person is white (a white icon) or black (a white hieroglyph): "White people . . . usually asserted that they were able to tell; and by the most ridiculous means, finger-nails, palms of hands, shapes of ears, teeth. . . ."[4] Yet Irene has already similarly catalogued and policed the body of her nemesis, disapproving her explicitly sexual display, her "peculiar caressing smile," "those dark, almost black eyes and that wide mouth like a scarlet flower against the ivory of her skin . . . a shade too provocative."[5] It turns out that the women, Irene Redfield and Clare Kendry, are childhood friends. But they share more than this, in mutually usurping the privilege white Americans have, to assume free passage within any public space they can afford to lease or own—like a taxicab, a table in a restaurant, rooms in a hotel, a private home.

The whiteness of blackness here requires the light-skinned African-American woman to produce some way to ameliorate the violation, the pain, and the ongoing crisis of living fully within two juridically defined, racially polarized bodies—and perhaps, if Hortense Spillers is right that American genders are always racially inflected, two genders as well.[6] Passing for nonblack allows these women to wear their gender according to a particular class style. Irene affects the bourgeois norm of good taste, which means submitting her body to a regime of discipline and concealment; Clare wears the exotic sexuality of the privileged woman as her style of publicity. One style of femininity tends toward the invisible or the "abstract," which involves a wish to cast off the visible body, and the other, toward the erotic, the sensational, which hyper-emphasizes the visual frame.[7] Nonetheless, each of these styles of femininity aims to deflect the racializing scrutiny of white culture, as it abstracts the woman's public identity from the complex juridical, historical, and memorial facts of her "racialized" body. Thus each woman returns the other to her legally "other" body by seeing her, and seeing through her—not to another "real" body, but to other times and spaces where the "other" identity might be inhabited safely. To Clare, who passes racially in her marital, familial, and everyday life relations, it is a relief to leave the specular erotics of the white female body under the gaze of a similarly racialized friend. But for Irene the embodiment resulting from their encounter thwarts her desire—which is not to pass as a white person, but to move unconsciously and unobstructed through the public sphere (which is, in this case, a marketplace where people participate through consumption).

Deborah McDowell has recently argued that these two women desire each other, sexually. *Passing,* in her view, is a classically closeted narrative, half-concealing the erotics between Clare and Irene.[8] But there may be a difference between wanting someone sexually and wanting someone's body: and I wonder whether Irene's xenophilia isn't indeed a desire to occupy, to experience the privileges of Clare's body, not to love or make love to her, but rather to wear her way of wearing her body, like a prosthesis, or a fetish.[9] What Irene wants is relief from the body she has: her intense class identification with the discipline of the bourgeois body is only one tactic for producing the corporeal "fog" in which she walks. "It was, she cried silently, enough to suffer as a woman, an individual, on one's own account, without having to suffer for the race as well."[10] This ideal model of bodily abstraction is understood, by Irene, to be nationally endorsed: despite suffering as a twice-biologized and delegitimated public subject—a "woman," a "Negro"—she displaces her surplus body onto the metaphorical logics of American citizenship, which become the "truth" of her body, her "person." Even though Irene desperately wants to save her rocky marriage, she refuses to emigrate to Brazil with her husband, where national alienation would replace racial: "She belonged in this land of rising towers. She was an American. She grew from this soil, and she would not be uprooted."[11] Married to this constellation of pain, her body the register for brands of race and of gender that specifically refer to the American context from which she has, apparently, parentless sprung, Irene's embrace of the nation seems a pathetic misrecognition. But what kind of body does American national identity give her, and how does the idea of this body solve or salve the pain that the colonized body experiences? And if a desire to be fundamentally American marks one field of fantasy for Irene, how does this intersect her other desire, to be incorporated in another woman's body?

In Irene's case, as often happens in bourgeois-identified "women's literature," this moment of political consciousness takes place in desperation,[12] and rather than think systemically about the state she is in, she reverts to the tendency to faint and fade out that has served her so well, and so analgesically, in the course of her life. But political theory has investigated more extensively the complex relation between local erotics and national identity, between homosociality and political abstraction.[13] So far almost all of this work, for clear historical reasons, has circulated around the construction of the male citizen in the political public sphere. Feminist political theorists, for instance, are reconsidering Enlightenment constitutionality, and how specifically white male privilege has been veiled by the rhetoric of the bodiless citizen, the generic "person" whose political identity is a priori precisely because it is, in theory, non-corporeal. Before moving to *Imitation of Life,* where a narrative of profound female identification is interarticulated with the national public sphere, it is worth spelling out specifically how such a model of political affiliation has figured the American male body, setting up a peculiar dialectic between embodiment and abstraction in the post-Enlightenment body politic.

The Constitution's framers constructed the "person" as the unit of political membership in the American nation; in so doing, they did not simply set up the public standard of abstract legitimation on behalf of an implicit standard of white male embodiment—technically, in the beginning, property ownership was as much a factor in citizenship as any corporeal schema.

Nonetheless, we can see a real attraction of abstract citizenship in the way the citizen conventionally acquires a new body by participation in the political public sphere. The American subject is privileged to suppress the fact of his historical situation in the abstract "person": but then, in return, the nation provides a kind of prophylaxis for the person, as it promises to protect his privileges and his local body in return for loyalty to the state. As Pateman, Landes, MacKinnon, and others have argued, the implicit whiteness and maleness of the original American citizen is thus itself protected by national identity[14]: this is a paradox, because if in practice the liberal political public sphere protects and privileges the "person's" racial and gendered embodiment, one effect of these privileges is to appear to be disembodied or abstract while retaining cultural authority. It is under these conditions that what might be an erotics of political fellowship passes for a meritocracy or an order defined by objective mutual interests.[15] The white, male body is the relay to legitimation, but even more than that, the power to suppress that body, to cover its tracks and its traces, is the sign of real authority, according to constitutional fashion.

Needless to say, American women and African-Americans have never had the privilege to suppress the body: and thus the "subject-who-wants-to-pass" is the fiercest of juridical self-parodies as yet authored by the American system. While this system prides itself liberally on the universal justice it distributes to its disembodied or "artificial" citizen, the mulatta figure is the most abstract and artificial of *embodied* citizens. She gives the lie to the dominant code of juridical representation by repressing the "evidence" the law would seek—a parent, usually a mother—to determine whether the light-skinned body claimed a fraudulent relation to the privileges of whiteness. By occupying the gap between official codes of racial naming and scopic norms of bodily framing conventional to the law and to general cultural practices, the American mulatta's textual and juridical representation after 1865 always designates her as a national subject, the paradigm problem citizen—but not only because she is indeterminate, and therefore an asterisk in the ledger of racial and gendered binarism that seems to organize American culture, as some critics have argued.[16] Irene Redfield's case suggests another way of looking at the national reference of the juridically problematic body: her will-to-not-know, to misrecognize, and to flee her body by embracing the Liberty Tree suggests that she experiences herself as precisely not abstract, but as imprisoned in the surplus embodiment of a culture that values abstraction; and that her affinity for the bourgeois, the individual, the subjective, and the unconscious symptomatize her desire to shed her two racially marked gendered bodies in fantasies of disembodiment, self-abstraction, invisibility. The very vulnerability she feels in her body would be solved by the state's prophylaxis: identification with state disembodiment might suppress or deflect what Spillers calls the "pornotroping" of racist patriarchy.[17] I do not mean to say that embodied subjects in the culture of abstraction always seek invisibility; following Elaine Scarry and Spillers we see that abstraction from the body's dignity and the subject's autonomy has been a crucial strategy of political oppression.[18] Moreover, we see in "camp," in youth, in sexual, and in ethnic subcultures strategies of corporeal parody and performance that recast and resist the public denigration of the non-hegemonic "other" body. But sometimes a person doesn't want to seek the dignity of an always-already-violated body, and wants to cast hers off, either for nothingness, or in a trade for some other, better model.

In *Passing,* when women drink iced tea, shop, and have parties, and in *Imitation of Life,* when women make pancakes, picnics, and movies, the colonized female body is not abstract, but hyper-embodied, an obstacle and not a vehicle to public pleasure and power. At the same time, the erotic sensation released in the conjunction of women with each other affirms and reasserts the body, in a way more in line with the oft-used feminist and colonial studies interest in the transition from invisibility to presence, and margin to center. It is the logic of this dialectic between abstraction in the national public sphere and the surplus corporeality of racialized and gendered subjects—its discursive expressions, its erotic effects, its implications for a nationalist politics of the body—that I want to engage in this paper. What would it take to produce the political dignity of corporeal difference in American culture, where public embodiment is in itself a sign of inadequacy to proper citizenship?

Imitation of Life —which exists in three versions, the Fannie Hurst novel and the films of John Stahl and Douglas Sirk—addresses these questions by linking the struggles of an Anglo- and an African-American woman, both single with a daughter, to a tale of economic success: in this complex text the women fight for dignity and pleasure by mutually exploiting the structures of commodity capitalism and American mass culture. As we trace the various embodiments of *Imitation of Life,* we will see its "stars" transformed into trademarks and corporate logos, prosthetic bodies that ideally replace the body of pain with the projected image of safety and satisfaction commodities represent. From some angles these commercial hieroglyphs look like vehicles of corporeal enfranchisement; but we will also see the failure of the erotic utopia of the female commodity, as the success montage of one American generation can not reframe the bodies of the next.

Specifically, in every version of the text the white woman struggles to achieve economic success and national fame, while living in a quasi-companionate couple with the black woman, who does the domestic labor; the black woman, who is also instrumental in the white woman's mastery of commodity culture, remains a loyal domestic employee, even in the wealthy days. But once the women have leisure and security, their bodies reemerge as obstacles, sites of pain and signs of hierarchy: the white daughter falls in love with her mother's love object; the light-skinned African-American daughter wants to pass for white, and so disowns her dark-skinned mother, whose death from heartbreak effectively and melodramatically signals the end of this experiment in a female refunctioning of the national public sphere.[19]

For purposes of economy, my discussion of these narratives will be organized around the form of commodity aesthetics through which they trace the American female body: the trademark. Hurst's 1933 novel represents the business and life history of a white person named Bea Pullman, who assumes professionally her husband's name and gender after his death, and, "passing" for male, opens a hugely successful pancake franchise named "B. Pullman." The visual logo that accompanies her masculine signature, however, represents not the pseudo-body of its white, male producer (whose race and gender are deceptively presumed by the concealment of "his" given name), but is displaced onto yet another corporeal other, her African-American housemate, Delilah Johnson. As a visual icon, Johnson is known, not surprisingly, as "Aunt Delilah." In contrast to Hurst, Stahl's 1934 film associates the pancake business only with the trademark and brand name "Aunt Delilah." Miming the passing from novel to film, he honors her with both a logo and a huge, hieroglyphic neon sign; finally, Sirk's 1959 film isolates the white woman in the neon sign and the public body. Sirk renames the trademark characters, and some of their professions: Bea Pullman, "the pancake queen," turns into Lora Meredith, actress, with her name up in lights on Broadway. Delilah turns into Annie Johnson, and remains a domestic laborer, but with no cachet in popular culture. Thus more than names change in these interpretations of *Imitation of Life:* I will not attempt to do full readings of these texts, but to see how they collectively imagine the American body politic from the points of view of the overembodied women who serve it.[20]

II. "B. PULLMAN" AND "H. PRYNNE": THE FEMININE USES OF CAMOUFLAGE

Fannie Hurst's *Imitation of Life* occurs in the midst of carnival. It opens in summertime, in Atlantic City, in 1911. But the crisis of the body we witness there has, at first, nothing to do with leisure culture, nor the service industry that lives on the cycles of its pleasure. Instead, in the novel's first scene we witness a paradigm moment of sentimental fiction, a daughter's private response to her mother's death. But the content of this moment is remarkable in its grotesque embodiment of the feminine:

"It struck Bea, and for the moment diverted her from grief, that quite the most physical thing she had ever connected with her mother was the fact of her having died. She found herself, crying there beside the bier, thinking of her mother's legs. . . . her arms and legs and breasts and her loins there, under the bengaline dress . . . stiff and dead."[21]

"There had been so little evidence, during her lifetime," she thinks, "of any aspect of her [mother's] physical life": and yet "the physical fact of [Bea's own] coming of menstrual age" (1) revealed to her the repulsive and upsetting fact that her mother had "committed the act of sex" with "that crumpled figure over there in the corner of the darkened parlor, his back retching as he cried" (4). This primal scene, of sex after death, is unbearable to Bea: her response is mentally to dismember her mother, to protect her after the fact from the embodiment that had made her whole, and therefore penetrable. This style of mourning, and of preserving the memory of the maternal form by breaking it apart in a kind of catalogue, is not only Bea's awakening to her mother's body.[22] It is also her initiation into sexual self-consciousness: mourning "had felt like wine" to Bea, "fizzing down into, and exciting and hurting her" (5).

The erotics of female identification, then, are here tied up with a sublime amalgam of pleasure, pain, and physical defamiliarization that comes from Bea's mother's death. Bea's attraction to this mix of sensations is reinforced by her father's subsequent domination of her life: not only is she, at 17, forced to replace her mother functionally in the household, but she is pressured into marriage to Mr. Pullman, a man her father chooses. This idea in itself does not upset Bea, who is rightly accused of "marrying marriage" rather than a man, for love (42). Marriage, with its usual transformations of a woman's name and sexual practice, is the conventional mode of female self-abstraction, and in marriage, Bea experiences abstraction doubly. While sex with Benjamin Pullman is simply a "clinical sort of something, apparently, that a girl had to give a man," "[i]t was amazing what feeling secure did to the front one put up in the world" (55, 57). Being fit with the false front and the mental prophylaxis of marriage also admits Bea into the world of "girl-talk," as she and the neighborhood women now speak frankly about deviously managing men and faking orgasms (58). This is to say that her entry into marriage provides Bea with a prosthetic identity, estranges her from her body in both an alienating and a pleasing way, and consolidates her relations to other women. Bea wishes that marriage weren't physically self-alienating, but this, she learns, is a fact about marriage. Her intuition is further confirmed by her father's tyranny: debilitated by a stroke soon after her marriage, his physical brutality to Bea throughout her entire life makes him an ever-present "symbol of littleness from which she needed emancipation" (177).

But there is something good about her association with men, and this is in their connection to the national public sphere: specifically the activity of national politics and of capitalist enterprise. Men sit around the bourgeois home speaking their political opinions, which Bea registers but has no interest in; but Hurst's narrator provides a counter-consciousness to Bea's mental limits. She repeatedly analogizes the personal choices Bea makes to the political agency of the American citizen: for example, "Thus in the year when men were debating whether a college professor was of sufficient stamina for Presidency of the United States, Bea lifted her face, which intimated yes, for the betrothal kiss of Mr. Pullman" (33). They marry two days before the election, in midst of a raucous political parade; the house in which she marries is bedecked with the double symbology of a wedding bell and the American Flag. Since these events take place before women had the national franchise, Bea's private acts are the only "votes" she has; and insofar as her later successes mark her *for other women* as a proto-feminist, this self-abstracting private event becomes, in retrospect, the first of a set of steps she takes into national existence.[23] It should be said that the historical and ideological pressure of feminism on American women's public self-presence explicitly follows Bea everywhere throughout this book; but, like Irene Redfield, Bea needs to see herself as acting without agency under the pressure of necessity, and has no affective relation to collective life, to politics, or history. Hurst stages this isolate sentimentality as a problem Bea has, a mental blockage symptomatic of her sex class.

Along with gaining closer proximity to the political life of the nation, Bea's affiliation with Pullman brings her closer to the capitalist public sphere.[24] Hurst's representations of the capitalist presence in American everyday life are quite institutionally specific, as if she had contracted to advertise commodities in her narrative the way Hollywood films do now.[25] But the status of brand names and well-known corporations in *Imitation of Life* isn't simply referential or commercial: by the turn of the century, product consciousness had become so crucial a part of national history and popular self-identity that the public's relation to business took on a patriotic value. As political parties became less powerful, and as capitalism became less local and more national, the imagined co-presence of a consuming public in the emerging and transforming mass culture became a central figure of America, and crucial for its intelligibility[26]; indeed, Robert Westbrook writes that around this time political parties began using the strategies of advertising to vitalize American citizenship in the political public sphere by characterizing it as consumption behavior.[27]

Like Bea's father, Mr. Pullman works for the great "Pickle and Relish Company." Daily he stands on "Amusement Pier" lecturing on "the life history of the tomato from the vine to the ketchup bottle," while handing out pickle stickpins and samples (13). His authorized biography of the tomato, which exists in an ironic linkage to a plagiarized biography of Abraham Lincoln's life he also delivers (14–15), discloses a corporate strategy to posit the commodity form and the brand name as the last stage of natural and national growth. By 1911, this form of suturing nation and nature was also associated with the sexual and commodity desire traversing Atlantic City, an interpenetration that makes Bea feel uncomfortably sexualized: pictures of Heinz Pier, to which Hurst clearly refers here, reveal scantily clad advertising beauties in the space of national/commodity history and distribution, linking up food and women in a public erotics of consumption, leisure, and knowledge.[28]

This conjunction of leisure culture and its servants subverts the discriminations of the bourgeois domestic economy. The capitalist public sphere absorbs the erotic investments of bodies in proximity, of contact through public exchange, and even of information culture, which emerges here as the new history of the nation, seen through its commodities. Meanwhile, the conventional topographical distinction between the home and the work spaces of the bourgeoisie does not hold: when the family travels, it travels to company functions; when the family moves, it is passively "transferred"; and a side business Mr. Pullman runs, selling maple syrup to local hotels, takes place within the home's instrumental space. In addition, Bea attends to the little "economies" of domestic labor with the zeal of an entrepreneur: but she is a formalist, and needs to see the home she runs as a sentimental nexus of consolation and escape. Bea does not live a split between domestic ideology and practical social relations, but she sees it as her job to maintain and intensify its reality at the level of theory. Then tragedy strikes. Soon after her marriage, Mr. Pullman dies in a train wreck. Bea is pregnant, then, and gives premature birth to a girl, Jessie; she is also thrown into poverty, burdened by a child and an invalid father.

Simultaneously Bea is imbricated more deeply into separate spheres: the domestic/maternal and the public/capitalist. For her this is an impossible subject position, mapped out according to two mutually reified gender logics. Hurst stages Bea's mutation serially: first, her ether-inspired corporeal dissolution in the pain of childbirth evokes the sublimity of mortality the specter of her mother raised—". . . and when they started to try and amputate her legs by pulling them out from the sockets, she screamed, and there was the upper half of her separating from the something going from her . . ." (72). She emerges from this event reconstructed and regendered, in a new, maternal body. In the next chapter, Bea is startled out of sleep, as if the sleep of childbirth, inspired to look at her husband's business cards. They reveal graphically that she can assume Pullman's business and gender identity because they share a first initial, B (73). This initial solves a problem she's been having on the job market, where her bourgeois female body has been exposed to the indignity of being all wrong for all the public positions she seeks. But the maple syrup business (run, suggestively, by H. Prynne of Vermont) is mail order, and so her female body would be suppressed, non-knowledge: Bea thinks of her paper transvestitism as simply a wedge into the capitalist public sphere, but it's an identity she never fully relinquishes.[29] Bea emerges, then, from the first stage of female abstraction, marriage, to the second stage, where identity is marked by labor and self-alienation. Maternal and masculine work works the same way on Bea's body, however—she is exhausted, anesthetized. Both labor in the family and labor for money absorb her libidinal energy, or, as Hurst puts it, "Countless little budding impulses seemed to have been nipped in the frozen garden of her expectations" (88). She nonetheless retains her theoretical commitment to producing an unalienated domestic scene: but her need to earn wages disrupts the separate spheres on which her theory was based, and she displaces her need onto the capitalist public sphere, where she goes from serving her husband's leisure to serving as her husband, in the leisure industry. The contradictions of Bea's position threaten to disembody her permanently, an outcome she both wants, and doesn't want.

For the next fifteen years, Bea "buckles herself" into the worker's body like a suit of "armor" (186). At first, she lives "on a minus sign" (93), selling maple syrup in the back alleys of Atlantic City. At the height of Bea's exhaustion, she walks up to an "enormously buxom figure of a woman with a round black moon face that shone above an Alps of bosom, privately hoping that the scrubbed, starchy-looking negress would offer herself" as a sleep-in-maid (91): this woman, Delilah Johnson, tenders the offer and comes not only to run the house, but to provide Bea with the candy and pancake recipes she soon turns into commodities, in search of a franchise and a fortune. Later, selling "Delilah Delights" brand pancakes and candies in hotels, and then in her own restaurants, Bea becomes more like a classic capitalist, increasingly distant from the public scene of consumption. As the brains and the name behind the business, Bea remains almost entirely behind the veil of the male moniker. In addition, Bea uses "Aunt Delilah's" body to stand in for her own. When she imagines Delilah as a mammy-like trademark, Delilah protests, and says she wants to dress beautifully, to create a stylish image inheritance for her daughter to remember her by (105). But Bea forces Delilah to play the mammy, and in this coerced guise she becomes the prosthetic public body of "B. Pullman," the store, and Bea Pullman, the woman.

Bea relies on Delilah to do much more than to protect Bea's body: the "social hieroglyphic" or trademark representing Delilah serves to create consumer desire for the products of the "B. Pullman" restaurants. As Stahl's film displays, when Delilah stands framed in the store's plate glass window making her authentic pancakes, the *mise en scène* of capitalist aesthetics merges with actual production. Bea relies on Delilah's double embodiment as icon and laborer to engender public "need" for her commodity. Delilah can do this because she is a professor in the true religious sense, who trains "imitations" or "replicas" of herself in the "University of Delilah" (184): there, she teaches "Jemimesis," or, how to commodify the "mammy's" domestic aura, which each waffle, pancake, and candy she makes is supposed to install in the consumer, like a communion wafer. In Delilah the religious aura of the commodity and the everyday imitation of God merge, in an uncanny repetition of Marx's analysis of how commodities become invested with soul and pseudo-agency: to Bea, this is imitation in the good, the best sense.[30] But Bea displaces onto Delilah more than her need to manage the public sphere. Delilah is also Bea's private maternal supplement, raising Jessie and caring for her father. And finally, she is Bea's wife and mother, the only person who touches her body during the 1920s, massaging her back and feet after the long day at the office. In short, Delilah solves for Bea "the corporeal problem of being two places simultaneously," both in everyday life and in the capitalist public sphere (140). Because Delilah can "be" both places, Bea has to "be" in neither. In Delilah, Bea achieves the condition of prophylaxis she has sought since her mother's death.

Never for a moment does Bea question her structural relation to Delilah: to Bea, their cohabitation is as a priori and untheorized as are their different places in the racial and class hierarchies of the dominant culture. Because Bea herself is so desperately liminal, masquerading as the difference between the white man's name and the black woman's body, she has no consciousness of her privilege. Rather, like Delilah's mulatta daughter, Peola, Bea uses her perverse opportunity to capitalize on racist patriarchal culture, by creating a compensatory "body" to distract from the one already marked by the colonial digit. Peola "passing" creates a juridically fraudulent white body, while Bea incorporates public "persons"—companies and copyrighted trademarks—who sublate history, and the violence of the colonized body.

Then one day Bea awakens to the distance she has traveled from the sensational body in which she might live. This is, in part, because fame and money eroticize her in the public eye, which is curious about how she pleasures her body under the stress of success. Second, she discovers the body as a site of potential pleasure because it is "sex o'clock in America," and the New Woman of the 1920s reveals to Bea another way to negotiate the public female body: in an armor not of bodiless abstraction, but of cosmetic masquerade. And finally, because capitalist practice carries its own erotic charge, its processes of abstraction are homoeroticized by Bea: she is openly attracted to other women who engage in what she calls "the racy ingredient of competition" (244) within the national public sphere. These feelings are congealed when Bea meets Virginia Eden—a beauty magnate, her own name a hieroglyph (a means of passing) that condenses the erotics of "sex solidarity," the American/Jeffersonian *locus amoenus,* and a Jewish background (she was born Sadie Kress). Eden opens the erotic floodgates in Bea: dates her, makes her a business "proposition," and seduces her into a contractual collaboration. "You and me ought to work together, Pullman. You make women fat and comfortable. My job is to undo all that and make them beautiful. You're grist to my mill. I want to be grist to yours" (193).

Awakened in the garden of Eden, Bea then becomes an erotic object for her female employees (she opens a gym so that they might also turn their bodies into erotic armor, and they fall so in love with Bea, that her male secretary starts intercepting their "obnoxious" gifts and love letters [189]. But when their business deal falls through, Bea experiences the erotic pain of female alliance once again: for "Virginia Eden's teeth were as pointed and polished and incisive as a terrier's, and with them, when she sank, she drew blood" (201). Then, the feeling of being embodied and excited by Eden scares Bea. She begins immediately to hyper-heterosexualize herself and falls in love with an unattainable man, Frank Flake.[31] After this embodied interlude, she returns to the life of abstraction. For Bea has not finally attained her national position by identifying with women, or with anything sensual. She has achieved success, within the auto-containment of the commodity form, by reinforcing the very apparatus whose practices she flees: in hiding behind the colonial simulacrum of a "male" employer who owns the copyrighted image and labor of an African-American woman.

A trademark is supposed to be a consensual mechanism. It triangulates with the customer and the commodity, providing what W. F. Haug calls a "second skin" that enables the commodity to appear to address, to recognize, and thereby to "love" the consumer.[32] Bea repeatedly turns to this abstract erotics for love and protection. This is what Delilah is, and represents. And in this sense, Delilah's fractured public identity—as herself, as an autonomous iconic image, as a servant of "B. Pullman"—foregrounds the irregular operations of national capitalism on the bodies of racially and sexually gendered subjects. In other words, at the same time as Delilah brings dispersed fields of exchange into proximity and intimacy, she also shows their non-analogousness. While Bea is protected by hiding behind Delilah's tremendous public body, Delilah's status as a living trademark takes over her own meaning and history: she married a bigamist and gave birth to a daughter cursed with Ham's opposite—light skin in a racist culture; she escaped the South to protect her daughter from the most brutal forms of racism. But when Delilah dies, the press reports that "her people" love her because the popularity of her facsimile legitimated blackness in public white culture. She is also, the press says, a constant reminder to white "national consciousness" of the dignity of her race; during World War I she becomes a domestic icon of the doughboys, who dream of a safe domestic political space after the most horrible of wars. It matters not to the public that she dies a most humiliating, lonely, and grotesque death, "in her huddle on the floor, a heterogeneous twist of pain, her back in an arch, her torso writhing" (319–320): for "Delilah" has become the trademark who lives on, interminably. Through her forced abstraction, and not her biographical person, Delilah reconfigures the capitalist and the national public spheres to include, even to foreground, the American class of overembodied, colonized subjects. In this she provides an alternative image to the logics of liberal culture. At least this is someone's liberal fantasy projection of what such a trademark might do.

III. AUNT JEMIMA AND UNCLE SAM

It is, for sure, the fantasy condensed in the face and history of Aunt Jemima, whose aura in American culture Hurst borrows for "Aunt Delilah." in *Imitation of Life*. Aunt Jemima was introduced to America at the Columbian Exposition in 1893. This links her up with the origin of American progressive modernism, the alliance between industry and the state to produce new "frontiers" of production and invention, and the induction of advertising itself as an arm of American sovereignty: it was to promote this event, after all, that the Pledge of Allegiance was written.[33] A huge success, Aunt Jemima became associated with a line of new products that included the "skyscraper, the long-distance telephone, the X-ray, the motion picture, the wireless telegraph, the automobile, the airplane, and radium."[34] She herself was an example of state-of-the-art technologies: the invention of the "half-tone" printing process at the turn of the century that enabled advertisers to install a new realism in the human trademark; the emergence of a new "logocentric" style, which encouraged consumers to link products with personalities[35]; the invention of ready-mix convenience foods, of which her pancake mix is the first to "emancipate" the housewife.[36] She did not, however, contain the promise of further racial emancipation. As Hazel Carby's recent discussion of the Fair's contempt for African-Americans shows, the exoticization of Aunt Jemima would surely mark the limit of what the consuming public could bear, in the linkage of African and American.[37]

The "promise" of Aunt Jemima thus went much farther than household convenience: her condensation of racial nostalgia, national memory, and progressive history was a symptomatic, if not important, vehicle for post–Civil War national consolidation. At the fair she was embodied by a woman, Nancy Green, who lived in an enormous flour barrel. Periodically she would come out to sing and tell tales. "Some of her script was drawn from the words of the old vaudeville Aunt Jemima song, some from [pseudo-]memories of her own plantation days in the Deep South," and some from her own invention.³⁸ The association of exotic, primitive women with pancakes and domestic consolation was reinforced by popular fantasy, as the renown of *Little Black Sambo* suggests. One other context is relevant to Aunt Jemima's phantom presence in *Imitation of Life:* the analogy embedded in the trademark's address to the notion of the bourgeois housewife's domestic "slavery." In one 1919 advertisement, for example, the copy is explicit: Jemima's pancakes were the last hope this side of Abraham Lincoln to maintain the union of the North and the South; housewives who buy Aunt Jemima will not only be emancipated from labor, but will keep the family together by keeping politics out.³⁹ In this way the trademark itself bridges the nuclear household and national history, along with helping to produce the kinds of historical amnesia necessary for confidence in the American future.

Something like this amnesiac activity is narrated in Hurst's *Imitation of Life*. The accumulated "pancake wealth" of the nation does not transform the injurious conditions of the national/capitalist public sphere. But since the commodity is the modern embodiment of the legitimate "artificial person," Americans in the text equate personal emancipation through it with shedding the collectively shared body of pain to gain a solitary protected self. This is Bea's strategy, which works so well that she ends up alone, enfranchised, but not empowered. But John Stahl's 1934 *Imitation of Life* reads the text's utopian potential. Without looking away from the culture of abuse that saturates even American leisure, Stahl imagines *Imitation of Life* within an affirmative female economy. This utopia is not the abstract "paradise" of heterosexual, natural bliss Steven Archer offers Bea (Claudette Colbert), on an island "elsewhere," outside of the frame; nor is it in sentimental womanhood, where differences dissolve through maternal identification—as in Delilah's (Louise Beavers) cry to Peola (Fredi Washington), "I'm your Mammy, child! I ain't no white mother!" Instead, Stahl derives from Hurst's text the positivity of difference: of female households and workplaces that protect the hyper-embodied frame; of an unalienated capitalist public sphere; and an identity in labor that eases the psychic burdens of gender and race. These "spaces," however, are really temporalities, moments in time when certain possibilities coalesce. This means that the film's "solution" is also framed as failure: in Delilah's commercial and Peola's racial hieroglyphic, and the impossibility of their suture, in American culture.

Delilah enters Stahl's *Imitation of Life* by accident, misreading the address of an advertisement, and ending up at Bea Pullman's (Claudette Colbert) door. To convince Bea that Bea has indeed asked for her, Delilah (Louise Beavers) reads her the ad's text, which describes her own subject position in the marketplace: she's a "girl," "a housemaid, colored, not afraid of hard work." She says that she has been looking for jobs, answering ads like this, but no one will take her, because she has a child, and the ads don't call for a child . Then she advertises her child: she's been "brung up right, not drug up, like most of 'em is." Peola comes in and performs for Bea: she says "Good Morning" in patrician diction, an act she has clearly practiced. While at first Bea protests that she cannot afford financially to succumb to Delilah's hard sell, seeing Peola induces her to revise the terms of the ad and to fold this female family into her own equally impoverished unit. No longer a "girl," Delilah becomes to Bea "200 pounds of mother fighting to keep her baby."

This scene is extraordinary in the way it shows Delilah textualizing, characterizing herself, in little sound-bites: it is apparently the lot of the marginal subject to self-commodify verbally, to objectify and promote her own qualities, in a culture that, corporealizing, presumes her insufficiency. Advertising rhetoric, then, starts to look like a mode of colonized discourse. Delilah's insertion of Bea into the generic slot of the white housewife who consumes "colored" domestic labor is misguided, however. To rent the abandoned Boardwalk pool-hall that turns into "Aunt Delilah's," Bea is forced to sell herself in roughly the same way. Without capital, as she later says, "All I had was talk."

These two contradictory structures mark the relations of Bea and Delilah in Stahl's film: in one mode, the traditional nomenclature and spatialization of the domestic worker in the private home still obtains, especially as the women achieve leisure. Delilah is always "Delilah," while the other is "Miss Bea"; when they can afford a spacious house, the "domestic" lives beneath, and the employer, above. In addition, as they gain leisure, their bodies diverge, becoming more socially proper to the public iconography of race, class, and gender in early 20th-century America. The African-American woman grows larger, and darker, and her clothes get slightly better; the Anglo-American woman becomes a vital "new woman," wearing corsets and bobbed hair and slinky things.[40] But during the first ten years of struggle to gain financial stability and public dignity, the women live in the closest of quarters. In physical style they are equivalent, dressing in uniforms appropriate to their work; then, they inhabit their bodies in much the same way—exhausted; and they are shot at the same respectful distance by Stahl. But the film occasionally violates its accent on their shared class and maternal difficulties. The recurrent success montage that traces Delilah's transformation into a trademark emits the same odor of racist expropriation that permeates Hurst's novel.

For Bea takes Delilah's pancake recipe, her maternal inheritance, and turns it into a business; she takes Delilah's face, and turns it into a cartoon. Stahl stages Delilah in this scene as a buffoon, a position which provides her an opportunity for ironic commentary. On hearing Bea manipulate the rhetoric of credit to bilk businessmen into advancing their wares, so that she might transform a boardwalk pool room into a feminine domestic business space ("Aunt Delilah's Pancakes"), Delilah acts as a comic soundtrack, singing in a worried tone "I puts my trust in Jesus," as she washes the windows. But her disbelief in the efficacy of the capitalist logic she hears Bea using is turned back on Delilah too, as Bea aggressively frames and interpellates her within that logic.

When Bea asks Delilah to smile for the trademark sign, Delilah smiles a small and hesitant smile. But Bea forces her to assume and to freeze in a "blackface" pose, which she dutifully maintains long after Bea needs her, to Bea's great delight. Stahl shoots the huge face of smiling Delilah in extreme close-up, and uses shot-reverse-shot cutting back to her frozen, smiling, saucer-eyed face as if to underscore how mentally insufficient Delilah is to her situation in the white patriarchal capitalist public sphere. But the grotesque hyper-embodiment of Delilah in this sequence violates her own and the film's aesthetic codes: I feel certain that her graphic decontextualization is specially designed to allude to and to ironize Aunt Jemima, in her role as a site of American collective identification.

The film's interference with the Aunt Jemima in Delilah is reinforced elsewhere. After Delilah's visual degradation, we see her making pancakes in the store, dressed as her trademark likeness; then, the film depicts a mass of imitation Delilahs, originating in her human face and fulfilled in her neon sign. But these women, who are shown packaging and mass producing Aunt Delilah's Original Pancake Mix, are explicitly industrialized, associated frame by frame with the disembodied human labor that generates their "product"; bodies without heads, they are filmed in an expressionist and not a cartoonish mode. They are surrounded by history: they are produced in history.[41] And when Delilah's product finally makes it into boxes, which are shown repetitiously moving along the production line, the soundtrack refers to the humanity abstracted by and condensed into the commodity, playing a sharply escalating series of the musical phrase "Nobody Knows the Trouble I've Seen," which is also featured in the very opening moments of the film, over the credits.

In Delilah, Stahl gives Aunt Jemima a body dignified by labor and inscribed by struggle; but, distorted by racist magnification, she is "very deceivin' as to proportion." Indeed, in this seemingly stereotypical guise, Delilah utters the film's most political sentences. In that sense too she is decommodified, an anti-Aunt Jemima. She ironizes the tradition of grotesque African-American representations in American consumer culture, which includes the distortions of the Hurst novel itself; and, most important, Delilah talks back to the nation from within her fictive frame, in the mammy's costume. No tales of the sunny south from her, or sweet memories of the plantation: when she steps out of her flour barrel she speaks of the political brutality of the national public sphere. When Peola explodes in rage at being called "black" by Jessie, Delilah, on screen in uniform, tells Peola to "submit" to the cross her light-skinned father bore: and in an intense close-up that reflexively undermines the comic quality of the earlier caricature of her "trademarked" face, she faces the question of who is to blame for the pain of racist embodiment.

It ain't her fault, Miss Bea. It ain't yourn, and it ain't mine. I don't know rightly where the blame lies. It can't be our Lord's. Got me puzzled.

At the moment Delilah settles on her perplexity, she looks away from the people on the screen, and turns her face toward the camera. Thus the unspoken word in this speech is national, as she looks directly out at the audience: here, in her white, fluted chef's cap, she addresses her audience specifically as Americans. Delilah is generally read as an apologist for the discriminations of racist culture, because she argues that Peola must reconcile herself to the pain of her embodiment. Despite the manifest power of religious belief that ameliorates her own experience of racial violation, Delilah also engages in political analysis; in fact, this entire scene reveals, in brief asides, the rage at the other side of her resignation. Two comments in particular frame both Delilah's reading of her own history, and her desire to protect Peola from repeating it by way of spiritual and financial support. Just prior to Peola's first public outburst against identification with her mother's blackness, Bea and Delilah work in the store and fantasize about what they want for their lives, and the lives of their daughters. Bea comments that Peola is smarter than Jessie; Delilah replies, "Yesm. We all starts out that way. We don't gets dumb till later on." What is "dumbness" here, if not Delilah's name for the mental blockages to rage and pain—what I earlier called "the-will-to-not-know"—that distinguish the colonized subject? Delilah's personal wish is just to get off her feet; but before then she will make certain that Peola is prepared, financially and educationally, to become a teacher, never to do housework for anyone. Teachers are "smart": not dumb, not full of sublimated rage, not sentenced to the life of the body as Delilah is, although she says she accepts the burden of her frame as part of the Lord's work.

The irony, of course, is that Delilah can pass through American culture because she has given her body over to its representation of what her subject position is. Her very darkness, which over-embodies her in the national public sphere, also domesticates her, because she is entirely intelligible to the juridical satisfaction of the white mind. The film's pictographic move from her surplus body to her gigantic neon luminosity emphasizes her objectification: it always seems to be night in the sky behind her luminous body. In contrast, Peola's resistance to the official and popular rule of racial classification makes her body a different kind of obstacle. Peola would have to choose to be "black," to submit to a colonial corporeal regime, according to her own agency. But to choose to be visible in a culture of abstraction, to be a racial hieroglyph in everyday life, would be to choose a form of slavery. She simply can't inherit her mother's strategies of passing, because she doesn't have her mother's body—as juridically defined, and culturally staged. She looks, and dresses, much more like Bea.

Thus one way of reading the racialized sign in this film is to see the contradictions, within its regime of visual representation, between the commercial and the personal racial hieroglyph: the cultural capital of the mother's public hyper-embodiment versus the juridically constructed enigma of the daughter's, which can and cannot be registered in the mirror and the film. Each racialized corporeality requires a special kind of self-licensing: thus Delilah looks forward to leaving her body completely, as it is so saturated by unrequited cultural fantasy; while Peola wants to be "white," which means she wants to relinquish one of her bodies, to become less meaningful, more American. Since Bea and Jessie share the same frame, the same color, the same class style, they will not have this problem, and can affirm themselves while choosing each other.

But the contradictory and fracturing logics of race here produce another form of homosocial fantasy, which requires relinquishing the individual body as the primary unit of social meaning. When Delilah asks Peola to be a good girl, and go to a high-toned college, we might think, as many critics do, that the film endorses the racial assimilation of African-Americans. But she is also asking Peola to understand and to live her class interests, as a member of a contested collectivity. Delilah herself did not have the privilege to do this in the 1920s; like many of her race class, she was dependent on the national market for "colored" domestic work. But for a film that takes place on the New Jersey boardwalk and then in New York City, *Imitation of Life* records almost nothing of American leisure culture, or the political public sphere; for a film that takes place during the Depression, we hear only fleeting references to unemployment. In contrast to the novel, which is manifestly national and institutional in its scope, Stahl's film doesn't seem to believe in the value of an abstract, coherent national or capitalist space. He finds America directly on the body, its surfaces; but the surfaces of the body are marked almost solely with collective signs, which map out the subject's vulnerabilities, the routes her pain travels. This kind of pain is not the individuating, isolating kind; it is the source of a political confederation, the public world women might make. But female alliance across race is not the film's solution to the fragmenting effects of American hierarchy. Rather, the film offers it as a first step, in effecting a shift away from the centrality of national identity as such. Delilah's funeral reveals on screen a concealed but vital and ongoing public sphere, within the black community. In contrast to the novel, where all of America melts into the public space of mourning for Delilah, this funeral is run by the black churches and lodges that specialize, among other things, in ritualizing the passing of an individual person from a world where pain is a collective burden. The emergence of this suppressed locus of costume and ceremony isn't merely a species of colonialist "artefacting" on Stahl's part[42]: it deconstructs the simulacrum of "one" American public sphere, and reveals that the notion of one dominant culture is one of the culture's most powerful myths. What if *Imitation of Life* were told from Delilah's point of view? The film approaches this by excluding the elements of cultural life to which she has no access. And by having her speak from within the trademark, it creates a space for political agency that exists elsewhere, and here, in her death as well. As Bea's final embrace of Jessie under the neon gaze of Delilah confirms, one must recognize that the body wrought by pain, memory, history, and ritual is collective. It is not aberrant or objectively in excess. In so shifting the public meaning of the "overembodied" body, the Stahl text imagines a crucial victory over the abstract and individualizing lure of Paradise, whether in America or elsewhere. This anti-nationalist message is, paradoxically, brought to us by a national trademark. Perhaps this was the only voice to which the audience would listen.

IV. WHITE NEON, BLACK GOLD: THE SIRKEAN SYSTEM[43]

In the thirties versions of *Imitation of Life,* national nostalgia for a safe domestic space was played out in commodity culture through the production and transcendence of a black trademark. The idea was that public investment in a commodity form, with its humanoid skin and soul, would consolidate a nation shaken by a monstrous war and debilitating depression: and so Aunt Jemima, who had served so well after the Civil War, was "modernized" in "Aunt Delilah," displacing Uncle Sam. In the novel, this trademark is appropriated callously from the body of a black domestic worker as part of a white woman's emancipatory strategy. In Stahl's film this trademark is given public speech, and speaks from the political place of surplus embodiment and the personal rage of collective suffering. Twenty-five years later, Douglas Sirk pulls back the black trademark's curtain, and reveals the white woman hovering there: in one of the great *tu quoque* sequels of our time, his *Imitation of Life* exposes the form of the white woman to the commodification she has for so long displaced onto the black woman's body.

As in Stahl's film, Sirk's narrative of female commodification hinges on a woman's relation to publicity. Advertisements do much of the critical work of this film: the opening shot of Lora Meredith's (Lana Turner) face, which is repeated later for emphasis, shows her bending over a sign that announces the "1947 Coney-Island Mardi-Gras." This frame reasserts the film's situation in Carnival, on the "fat Tuesday" of public culture that portends Lent's impending melodrama. But this film occupies the very public spaces excluded in Stahl's rendition—as if in a shot/reverse shot relation, Sirk shoots the boardwalk from the beach that Stahl never represents. Sirk puts "the masses" back in mass culture and condenses the national identity of their taste and their desire in the surplus corporeality of Lora Meredith. While in the thirties texts of *Imitation of Life* an ethic of bourgeois propriety motivated light-skinned women to escape the hyper-determination of the public body, in the fifties the culture so embraces spectacular things that to be American means to want more body, more presence. But since presence, in mass culture, is signified by the image, Lora Meredith's stardom merges her embodiment and abstraction—in a way peculiar to women but symptomatic of the gaudy culture at large. And so Lora Meredith becomes her own prosthesis, projecting herself into simulacral public spaces where the commodity, representation, and the body meet. That her fraudulence is America's has been widely discussed, by Sirk himself, and by every critic who writes on this film: my interest here is to show specifically how Sirk determines the female trademark, transforming its public iconicity, its stereotypicality, into a national problem.

The transformation of Lora Meredith into "Lora Meredith" involves a self-instrumentalizing contract with her director, David Edwards. The montage sequence in which he proposes to make her sexually and professionally generic involves photographically removing her body from his apartment, moving the shot across the public space he calls her "empire" and scattering her across the nation. In the ten years that this sequence covers, Lora's body becomes progressively reified: her name replaces Edwards's name in the lights, and increases in prominence; her face floats, separated from her body, amidst overlapping marquees; her image is delaminated from her face, and splayed on national magazine covers; and, toward the end, women in the audience mime her look, so that projection of her visual image is no longer necessary to transmit to us her dominion in the national/capitalist space of fantasy consumption.

Although the montage transmits a ridiculous brightness, and although all the evidence is that Lora is a shallow actress—since Broadway and Hollywood apparently seek only a "girl with a certain *Je ne sais quoi* . . . that something [she] managed to get with the dog"—the humiliation to which Lora is exposed is mainly not professional, but domestic. The film establishes its disciplinary home economy in its very first scene, when Lora loses her daughter—now named Susie—on the beach. This loss introduces Lora both to Steve Archer (John Gavin), her soon-to-be-suffering lover, and Annie (rather than Delilah) Johnson (Juanita Moore), her soon-to-be-suffering "maid": they themselves are linked by their spatial proximity to a policeman, whose job is also to find the mother who has lost her young blond child. Everyone in her household polices Lora, including the children; each pronounces a monologue that catalogues explicitly Lora's inadequacy as a lover, mother, employer—in part because she really does lie and self-deceive to further her career, but mainly because public life is "imitation" and private life is "real," where women are concerned.

Yet there is something odd and ambivalent and even masochistic about the family's compulsion to repeat the argument for domesticity. More than anyone, Steve Archer brings this message to Lora. When they meet, he aspires to hang his photos in the Museum of Modern Art—for example, the picture he takes of Lora on the Mardi Gras sign titled "Mother in Distress." But falling in love with Lora compels him to give up his dream, and to ask her to give up hers. He tells her: "What you're after isn't real." What's "real" to him is "the nicest looking green folding money," and sex, besides. When she says, "What about me? What about the way I feel?" in defense of her life-long dream to act, he replies, "Stop acting." (In a later scene, when she offers to give up Steve for her daughter's sake, as Claudette Colbert does, Susie repeats this: "Stop acting, Mother.") Yet Steve returns repeatedly to the scenes of her acting: twice we see him in loving audience, both on the stage and off. He is addicted to consuming her product: he says, "You know, I still have you in my blood . . ."

This dynamic of attraction, rejection, discipline, and performance has its uncanny "blood" repetition in the maternal relation of Annie to her daughter, now named Sarah Jane. Sarah Jane is light-skinned, an inheritance from her father, who "was practically white" (as is Susan Kohner the actress in fact, white). Throughout her youth Sarah Jane blames her mother (rather than, say, the state of the law) for her condition, and chooses a style of racial passing that negates her mother's "servile" mentality and manner, featuring instead libidinous, assertive physicality. Sarah Jane's racial passing is simultaneously sexual and theatrical: but in this she is typical of women. For in this film a woman who lives with difference—either gendered or racial—enjoys no prophylactic private sphere, no space safe from performance or imitation. This internal estrangement is as real for Annie as it is for her daughter. Annie comments that Lora's home has got to be better than the racist brutality of the South, but this is the closest she comes to saying that she feels at home where she lives. In any case, Sarah Jane mimes Lora in understanding that physical allure is the capital a woman must use to gain a public body. But this capital turns out to be as counterfeit for Sarah Jane as it is for Lora.

The writing on the wall in the scene where Frankie (Troy Donahue) beats up Sarah Jane for camouflaging the "trouble" with her mother (she tells Frankie that she's the daughter of rich, conservative parents; but the trouble she has is maternal shame) stages Sirk's negative homage to Stahl's *Imitation of Life*. The empty store in front of which the young lovers meet sports a prominent FOR RENT sign, but this empty store will not provide a secure space for a female affective and economic unit. Rather, it reflects the brutality that takes place outside that unit—in the public space. Moreover the plate glass window that had contained the authentic embodiment of Delilah's icon now reflects the public truth of American culture: the word "liberty," reflected backwards off a marquee from across the street meets up with the word BAR. In conjunction—or in "disjunction"—they condense the story and the conclusion of both of the narratives Sarah Jane lives, in her Anglo- and her African-American frames.

After Frankie rejects Sarah Jane, she takes to the life of the white showgirl. She is not good enough to achieve the self-iconicity of mass culture: she earns no success montage. Instead, Sarah Jane's mode of self-instrumentality is to hyper-emphasize her body in the present tense of performance, in the mode of the naked gold figurine that is trademark of the Moulin Rouge, where she works. By making herself a thing, she takes over her own cultural objectification as a racialized subject, relying on male narcissism to separate her sexual "value" from her juridical body. Both of her performance scenes are extremely carnal, although opposite in their mode of allure: in the first, she dresses and sings raunchily about her need to embody herself sexually, so that she might avoid the fate of passive, feminine women who have "empty, empty arms"[44]; in the second, at the Moulin Rouge, she is one of a chain of indistinguishable mute showgirls in a chain on a conveyor belt. They mime *en masse* a scene of seduction, drinking, and intercourse. You might even say they mime a success montage, in its mix of seriality and repetition; however the success referred to in this sequence belongs not to the persons who embody it, but to the audience, whose mastery is one with the privilege of consuming. In contrast, the audience of Sirk's film is not exactly positioned like the public consumer of the female sexual fetish. When the film shows these scenes, it routes them through Annie's maternal eyes. Twice we and Annie see Sarah Jane in a sexual and racial performance: we watch Annie have an inverted primal scene, transfixed and sickened as her daughter does a "number." As with Steve and Lora, Sarah Jane is in Annie's "blood": it is as if the light-skinned female body in performance is irresistible to its consumers, even when it produces pain, and not arousal of the theater's Aristotelian emotions or the girlie show's carnal sensations.

If Lora and Sarah Jane produce the "unreal" simulations, what does Sirk hold out for authenticity? I have already suggested that Annie and Steve, who police imitation with an unwavering moral passion, become implicated in female fraudulence by their addiction to it. Steve and Annie assume pain the way Lora and Sarah Jane want pleasure: and if the star-crossed women overinvest in the ecstasy and value of being public objects, the star-crossed blood lovers turn their pain into its own kind of spectacle. In short, if the film spends its most explicit time on the "problem" of the prosthetic public female body, it also shows how the problem of the female body itself becomes a commodity.

The paradoxes involved in this double commodification come together at Annie's opulent funeral. As the final scene in the film, the funeral might look like a privileged site of authentic public display, as I have argued that it does in the Stahl version. For like Delilah, Annie has a secret non-diegetic life in the black community. Annie says plainly that this life has not made it on screen because, "Miss Lora, you never asked." The funeral scene at the church brims with pomp and costume: but the ornate procession seems to reclaim the potential for public spectacle to produce dignity within American life. And the song Mahalia Jackson sings, "Trouble of the World," describes the weary one's relief at leaving for the Lord's house, where presumably there is no back room or basement. Finally, the ornate procession itself seems to reclaim the potential for public spectacle to produce dignity within American social life. Compared to the rest of the film it is unfrenetic, measured, subdued. It is also the only time we see men in costume, as if perhaps signaling a patriarchal reclaiming of public spectacle. But as the procession rolls down the street, the camera pulls back behind a frosted window: the window reads "costume rentals."

This ironizing text is authentic, like graffiti. On the walls of consumer America, as in this film of *Imitation of Life,* public advertising seems to be the only "agent" of truth. Sirk himself has said that he intended to undercut the funeral, by making it bizarre and embarrassing; he also shot Mahalia Jackson deliberately to look grotesque. He couldn't understand why Jackson moved the audience, in her luminous cry for relief from her body; and, suspicious of public culture and popular expression, Sirk could not imagine that a representation of public female dignity might seem emancipating, after all the corporeal humiliation his characters endure.[45] Sirk preserves in his *Imitation of Life* the American loathing of the public body; he plays out, even in his own . . . irony, how the ethic of universal and abstract dignity embodies the citizens it wants to humiliate.

I have argued that in American culture legitimacy derives from the privilege to suppress and protect the body; the fetishization of the abstract or artificial "person" is Constitutional law, and is also the means by which whiteness and maleness were established simultaneously as "nothing" and "everything."[46] In *Passing* and in *Imitation of Life* Anglo- and African-American women live the effects of their national identity directly on the body, which registers the subject's legitimacy according to the degree to which she can suppress the "evidence." One of the main ways a woman mimes the prophylaxis of citizenship is to do what we might call "codecrossing." This involves borrowing the corporeal logic of an other, or a fantasy of that logic, and adopting, it as a prosthesis. The way women have usually tried this is heterosexual: but marriage turns out to embody and violate the woman more than it's worth. Thus other forms of bodily suppression have been devised. This is how racial passing, religion, bourgeois style, capitalism, and sexual camp have served the woman; indeed, in *Imitation of Life* this ameliorative strategy has become the "trademark" of female existence, across race and class and sexual preference.

What does this tell us about the potential national identity holds for the subjects it has historically burdened with bodies? We have seen that in modern America, the artificial legitimacy of the citizen has merged with the commodity form: its autonomy, its phantasmatic freedom from its own history, seem to invest it with the power to transmit its aura, its "body," to consumers. We have seen, in *Imitation of Life,* light-skinned women embracing the commodity's promise, although this embrace itself results in many different forms of embodiment. Sometimes the commodity becomes a prosthetic body, an apotropaic shield against penetration and further delegitimation; sometimes the body itself becomes the object of public consumption, protected by the distance between the image, performance, and actual form. But the films and the novel give the lie to the American promise that participation in the national/capitalist public sphere has emancipatory potential for the historically overembodied. First, the strategy of abstraction that distinguishes white bourgeois style "solves" the problem by disciplining and shedding the public body, which forces the woman to live with the torture of its perennial return. Second, the body of the dark-skinned African-American woman is apparently unabstractable on her own behalf. Even Aunt Delilah's nostalgic public form represents a history of violence that is simultaneously personal and national in scope. This is why the amelioration of religion is so crucial to the black mothers of these texts, for there is no imaginable space in America, not even in the most benign white woman's house, where she will see relief from the body's burden. In Stahl's version, Bea and Delilah do escape into the sisterhood of the laboring body, but once leisure is achieved they revert to the default forms of their culture. For light-skinned African-American women, then, the choice of public identity comes to be between two bodies of pain, not two possible modes of relief from indeterminacy.

There is a moment in Hurst's *Imitation of Life* that crystallizes the distances between the nation's promise of prophylaxis to the "person" and the variety of female genders it creates. At the moment before Bea has her first experience of intercourse with her husband, she goes upstairs to put on the nighttime garb of the virginal bride, on her way to the hymenal altar.

She has never before entered their "master bedroom": the "darkies" put it together, during the wedding day. Bea, frightened, thinking of her mother, catalogues the objects on Mr. Pullman's mantle.

Framed photographs of an exceedingly narrow-faced pair of parents, deceased. One of quite an aged aunt, deceased. A framed program of the Pleiades Club, the one on which Mr. Pullman was announced to read his paper on Abraham Lincoln. And of all things! Dear knows from where, the black girl had unearthed a picture which must, in some way, have got mixed up with his other belongings. A horrid cabinet-sized thing of a woman, which Bea turned face down, in stockings and no clothes, trying on a man's high hat before a mirror. With what seemed like actual malice, that picture had been propped up against one of the china pugs. Those darkies . . . (50)

At the moment when Bea is to leave her ignorant girlish body behind for the sexual knowledge of womanhood, she finds her husband's pornography. The "thing" of a woman represented there violates everything she knows about her proper New England husband; and Bea understands that this woman has preceded her in his fantasy life. Bea turns the picture face down because she doesn't want to face it. She wants instead to blame it on the "black girl" who set up the room; she wants to displace her disgust at the masculine embodiment of women onto the black women who serve her. I have suggested that Hurst's version of Bea habitually relies on black women to be embodied: but along with revealing her own racial and class instrumentality, the picture suggests a politically "malicious" correspondence between Anglo- and Afro-American women.

The "thing" of a woman the picture depicts is having a wonderful time. She is fantasizing in a mirror, which itself frames the genitaled trunk of her body for the husband's pornographic gaze. However, the text does not consider what the man wanted from the picture. Let us imagine,then, for a moment, what this woman might be thinking. Surely, her costumed appendages signify a fantasy of agency: I might assume a male body, or masquerade as another kind of woman. But the hat this "thing" of a woman wears is not just any hat: it is Lincoln's hat. The text clues us into this by referring to Mr. Pullman's speech about Lincoln: the one he plagiarized from the *Encyclopaedia Britannica*. This 1911 article about Lincoln reminds us that he was for white woman suffrage, as well as reluctantly for the emergence of black slaves from property to personhood; the article also characterizes Lincoln as the most feminine of Presidents, because of his sensitive heart.[47] In conjunction with the prop of the hat, the woman wears most likely a pair of dark stockings. Perhaps she is enjoying imagining how an amalgam of races and genders might look, if legitimately embodied as citizens, or even as President, within the national frame. Bea is certainly not thinking this: she is too busy blaming the "darkies." Or maybe the "thing" of a woman parodies Lincoln's promise, revealing the bodies of light and dark women to be "things" his proclamation did not liberate. Thus Lincoln's hat reminds us that the nation holds out a promise of emancipation and a pornographic culture both. And that, as Delilah says of Peola's picture, "It never done her justice."[48]

NOTES

My special thanks to Andy Parker for conceiving of this panel, and to Corey Creekmur, Laura Kipnis, Michael Warner, Tom Stillinger, and many members of the audience, for their inspiring and challenging conversation.

1. Frank Presbrey, *The History and Development of Advertising* (New York: Doubleday, Doran and Company, 1929), 625.
2. Fannie Hurst, *Today is Ladies' Day* (Rochester: Home Institute, 1939), 3.
3. Nella Larsen, *Passing,* in *Quicksand and Passing,* ed. Deborah E. McDowell (New Brunswick, NJ: Rutgers University Press, 1986), 149.
4. Larsen, *Passing,* 150.
5. Larsen, *Passing,* 148–149.
6. Hortense J. Spillers, "Mama's Baby, Papa's Maybe: An American Grammar Book," *Diacritics* 17, no. 2 (Summer 1987):77–80.
7. For an elaboration on the regimes of discipline (as concealment, as grotesque or carnivalesque display) that have expressed the bourgeois body, see Peter Stallybrass and Allon White, *The Politics and Poetics of Transgression* (Ithaca, NY: Cornell University Press, 1986).
8. Deborah E. McDowell, "Introduction," *Quicksand and Passing,* xxvi–xxxi.
9. I take the notion of xenophilia (and much inspiration, besides) from Cameron Bailey, "Nigger/Lover: The Thin Sheen of Race in *Something Wild*," *Screen* 29, no. 4 (Autumn 1988):30.
10. Larsen, *Passing,* 225.
11. Larsen, *Passing,* 235.
12. Elsewhere I elaborate on how American "women's culture" constructs literary "modes of containment"—notably in sentimental and melodramatic narrative—that both testify to women's colonization within a racist/patriarchal/capitalist culture and mark the self-construed obstacles to specifically political thought and action toward social change by bourgeois-identified women. See "The Female Complaint," *Social Text* 19/20 (Fall 1988), 237–259.
13. See, for example, Paula Baker, "The Domestication of Politics: Women and American Political Society, 1780–1920," *American Historical Review* 89, no. 3 (June 1984):620–647.
14. Some major attempts to dissect masculine/Enlightenment citizenship are: Ruth H. Bloch, "The Gendered Meanings of Virtue in Revolutionary America," *Signs* 13, no. 1 (1987):37–58; Mary G. Dietz, "Citizenship with a Feminist Face: The Problem with Maternal Thinking," *Political Theory* 13, no. 1 (February 1985): 19–37; Jean Bethke Elshtain, *Public Man, Private Woman* (Princeton: Princeton University Press, 1981); Moira Gatens, "Towards a Feminist Theory of the Body," in *Crossing Boundaries: Feminisms and the Critique of Knowledges,* eds. Barbara Caine, E.A. Grosz, Marie de Lepervanche (Winchester, MA: Allen and Unwin, 1988), 59–70; Joan B. Landes, *Women and the Public Sphere in the Age of the French Revolution* (Ithaca, NY: Cornell University Press, 1988); Catherine A. MacKinnon, *Toward a Feminist Theory of the State* (Cambridge, MA: Harvard University Press, 1989); Anne Norton, *Reflections on Political Identity* (Baltimore: Johns Hopkins University Press, 1988);

Carole Pateman, *The Sexual Contract* (Stanford: Stanford University Press, 1988); Hanna Fenichel Pitkin, *Fortune is a Woman: Gender and Politics in the Thought of Niccolò Machiavelli* (Berkeley: University of California Press, 1984); Iris Marion Young, "Polity and Group Difference: A Critique of the Ideal of Universal Citizenship," *Ethics* 99, no. 2 (January 1989): 250–274.

15. Powerful arguments against these quasi-objective appearances of masculine American political culture can be found in: Iris Marion Young, "Impartiality and the Civic Public: Some Implications of Feminist Critique of Moral and Political Theory," *Feminism as Critique,* ed. and introduced by Selya Benhabib and Drucilla Cornell (Minneapolis: University of Minnesota Press, 1987), 57–76, and Nancy Fraser, "What's Critical about Critical Theory? The Case of Habermas and Gender," *Feminism as Critique,* 31–56.

16. Casting the mulatta as an ur-figure of political and rhetorical indeterminacy is the perspective of: Jane Gaines, "White Privilege and Looking Relations: Race and Gender in Feminist Film Theory," *Screen* 8, no. 4 (Autumn 1988): 12–27, and Hortense J. Spillers, "Notes on an alternative model—neither/nor," in *The Difference Within: Feminism and Critical Theory,* ed. by Elizabeth Meese and Alice Parker (Philadelphia: John Benjamins Publishing Company, 1989), 165–187.

17. Spillers, "Mama's Baby, Papa's Maybe: An American Grammar Book," 67.

18. Elaine Scarry, *The Body in Pain: The Making and Unmaking of the World* (New York: Oxford University Press, 1985), 108–109; Spillers, *Ibid.*

19. The vast majority of critical work on *Imitation of Life,* which almost always reads the Stahl and Hurst versions through the lens of the vastly successful Sirk narrative, focuses on maternal and familial relations (to the exclusion of specifically political ones) as the central "problem" for which the narrative provides an answer. This is, in part, because of the generic (over)emphasis of film criticism, which marks this complex text as melodrama and therefore as generated by social contradictions within the family. This criticism tends to denigrate Hurst's and Stahl's texts, for "giving in" to sentimentality, and to elevate Sirk's more explicitly critical stance toward American culture. I think each side of these valuations is extremely limited. See Christine Gledhill's (otherwise excellent) "The Melodramatic Field: An Investigation," in *Home is Where the Heart Is: Studies in Melodrama and the Woman's Film,* ed. by Christine Gledhill (London: BFI Publishing, 1987), 5–39; E. Ann Kaplan, "Mothering, Feminism and Representation: The Maternal in Melodrama and the Woman's Film, 1910–40," in *Home is Where the Heart Is,* 113–137; and Marina Heung, " 'What's the Matter With Sara Jane?': Daughters and Mothers in Douglas Sirk's *Imitation of Life,*" *Cinema Journal* 26, no. 3 (Spring 1987): 21–43. Lucy Fischer's forthcoming introduction to her critical edition of Sirk's screenplay gathers the most comprehensive bibliography available on this complex text and moves beyond the auteurist and generic impasses of the criticism. See "Three Way Mirror: *Imitation of Life,*" in *Imitation of Life,* ed. Lucy Fischer (New Brunswick, NJ: Rutgers University Press, 1991).

20. Other crucial transformations within this "complex text" (the "work" in its three versions) also take place over time. For example, the domestic plot about the rivalry between the white daughter and the white mother finds three different resolutions: in the novel, the daughter marries the mother's love interest; in Stahl's film, there is no marriage and the two women "choose" each other; in Sirk's film, the love plot works, with the older woman settling in with the man. Also, the mulatta daughter becomes progressively pathetic, insufficient, and submissive to the dominant order over the course of the complex text. The aggregate narrative fate of both daughters, unable to benefit directly from their mothers' successes, suggests some obstacles to thinking/effecting a post-patriarchal female mode of inheritance in American culture, and constitutes a counter-narrative to the mothers' confidence in labor and capital's liberatory possibilities. I bracket these concerns here, focusing instead on the adult women, who are already living the overembodiment into which their daughters are only emerging.

21. Fannie Hurst, *Imitation of Life* (New York: Harper and Brothers, 1933), 1, 5. The bodily cataloguing to which I refer occurs throughout the chapter: this hybrid passage from its first and last sentences is its most economic formulation. Future references to the novel will be contained in the text.

22. The relation between cataloguing the woman's body and national identity has been beautifully worked out, from the point of view of its service to patriarchal national cultures, by Patricia Parker, "Rhetorics of Property: Exploration, Inventory, Blazon," in *Literary Fat Ladies: Rhetoric, Gender, Property* (New York: Methuen, 1987), 126–154. Bea's strategies of female identification are ambiguously related to the patriarchal strategies of control Parker sees, because her will-to-disembodiment and abstraction proleptically subverts the procedures she mimes.

23. The social history of women's movement into the American political public sphere follows the half-conscious Bea through the novel: Hurst not only taps the history of suffrage, of women's emergence as citizen-consumers, and of women's increased participation in the work force during the World War I, but also the fear women in the Depression had that their ideological and material gains would be lost them. The bibliography on these coterminous movements is enormous: for general histories, see Martha Banta, *Imaging American Women: Idea and Ideals in Cultural History* (New York: Columbia University Press, 1987); Nancy F. Cott, *The Grounding of Modern Feminism* (New Haven: Yale University Press, 1987); Robert L. Daniel, *American Women in the 20th Century* (New York: Harcourt Brace Jovanovich, 1987); Sara M. Evans, *Born for Liberty: A History of Women in America* (New York: The Free Press, 1989). For Hurst's reading of the complex movement toward female "personhood," economic, and sexual legitimacy during this period see Fannie Hurst, "Are We Coming or Going?," *Vital Speeches of the Day* (December 3, 1934):82–83; *Today is Ladies' Day;* "A Crisis in the History of Women: Let us have action instead of lip-service," *Vital Speeches of the Day* (May 15, 1943): 479–80.

24. I describe the national public space as fundamentally "capitalist" following Simon Frith, who argues that the notion of "capitalist culture" addresses the "ideological experience" of capitalism not fully accounted for by traditional formulations of economic practice. Simon Frith, "Hearing Secret Harmonies," in *High Theory/Low Culture: Analyzing Popular Television and Film*, ed. Colin MacCabe (New York: St. Martin's Press, 1986), 53–70.

25. There is a story yet to be told about the way advertising appears differentially in novels and films of the 1920s and 1930s. Film historians show that very early on the frame of the movie screen, the shop window, and the product package borrowed each other's function in the circuit of production and consumption, and of creating social value. On the early history of cinematic and commodity coordination, see Jeanne Allen, "The Film Viewer as Consumer," *Quarterly Review of Film Studies* 5, no. 4 (Fall 1980):481–499; Charles Eckert, "The Carole Lombard in Macy's Window," *Quarterly Review of Film Studies* 3, no. 1 (Winter 1978):1–21; Elizabeth Ewen, "City Lights: Immigrant Women and the Rise of the Movies," *Signs* 5, no. 3, Supplement (Spring 1980): S45–S65; Mary Ann Doane, "The Economy of Desire: The Commodity Form in/of the Cinema," in "Female Representation and Consumer Culture," eds. Jane Gaines and Michael Renov, *Quarterly Review of Film and Video* 11, no. 1 (1989): 23–33; and Jane Gaines, "The Queen Christina Tie-Ups: Convergence of Show Window and Screen," in "Female Representation and Consumer Culture," 35–60. Jennifer Wicke argues that literature and advertising carried on a similar (although less capital-intensive) mutual dependency earlier, at the turn of the century. See *Advertising Fictions: Literature, Advertisement, and Social Reading* (New York: Columbia University Press, 1988).

26. Peter Dobkin Hall, *The Organization of American Culture, 1700–1900: Private Institutions, Elites, and the Origins of American Nationality* (New York: New York University Press, 1984), 209–281; T. J. Jackson Lears, "From Salvation to Self-Realization: Advertising and the Therapeutic Roots of the Consumer Culture, 1880–1930," in *The Culture of*

Consumption: Critical Essays in American History, 1880–1980, eds. Richard Wightman Fox and T. J. Jackson Lears (New York: Pantheon Books, 1983), 1–38; Garth S. Jowett, "The Emergence of the Mass Society: The Standardization of American Culture, 1830–1920," *Prospects* 7 (1982):207–228.

27. Robert B. Westbrook, "Politics as Consumption: Managing the Modern American Election," in Fox and Lears, *The Culture of Consumption,* 1–38.

28. Vicki Gold Levi, ed., *Atlantic City: 125 Years of Ocean Madness,* text by Lee Eisenberg (New York: Clarkson N. Potter, Inc., 1979), 28–31.

29. "H. Prynne" is really "Hiram Prynne," a Vermont businessman who uses his initial in his business dealings for " Prynne and Company." I gather that the text posits a genetic relation between Hawthorne's Hester and Hurst's Bea: Bea "inherits" from Hester the tactic of giving herself over to the name of the father (the A, the "B.") in order to "pass" through public culture in a relatively dignified way.

30. Karl Marx, *Capital,* in *The Marx-Engels Reader,* ed. Robert C. Tucker (New York: W. W. Norton and Co., 1978), 320–321.

31. Earlier I linked Bea's tendency to link sexual desire with women (her mother), pain, and bodily abstraction: but the scary return of this form of desire in her bond with Virginia Eden may also respond to the "heterosexual revolution" that accompanied the emergence of modern consumer culture and the modern female consuming body. While capitalism made it possible to live outside of economic dependence on the nuclear family, the twenties witnessed strong ideological pressure on women to choose heterosociality as a component of the new consumer narcissism. "Beauty culture" (and here Eden surely suggests Helena Rubenstein) was administered by women to women: but *for* men. See Mike Featherstone, "The Body in Consumer Culture, "*Theory, Culture and Society* 1, no. 2 (September 1982):18–33; Rayna Rapp and Ellen Ross, "The Twenties' Backlash: Compulsory Heterosexuality, the Consumer Family, and the Waning of Feminism," in *Class, Race, and Sex: The Dynamics of Control,* eds. Amy Swerdlow and Hanna Lesinger (Boston: G. K. Hall, 1983), 93–107; John D'Emilio, "Capitalism and Gay Identity," in *Powers of Desire: The Politics of Sexuality,* eds. Ann Snitow, Christine Stansell, and Sharon Thompson (New York: Monthly Review Press, 1983), 100–113).

32. W. F. Haug, *Critique of Commodity Aesthetics: Appearance, Sexuality and Advertising in Capitalist Society,* trans. Robert Bock, Introduction by Stuart Hall (Minneapolis: University of Minnesota Press, 1986), 50.

33. Robert W. Rydell, *All the World's A Fair: Visions of Empire at American International Expositions, 1876-1916* (Chicago: University of Chicago Press, 1984), 46.

34. Presbrey, *The History and Development of Advertising,* 360.

35. Presbrey, *Ibid.,* 356; 382–384.

36. Arthur F. Marquette, *Brands, Trademarks and Good Will: The Story of the Quaker Oats Company* (New York: McGraw-Hill Book Company, 1967), 137–141; Joseph Boskin, *Sambo: The Rise and Demise of An American Jester* (New York: Oxford University Press, 1986), 139.

37. Hazel V. Carby, *Reconstructing Womanhood: The Emergence of the Afro-American Woman Novelist* (New York: Oxford University Press, 1987), 3–6. See also Robert W. Rydell, "The World's Columbian Exposition of 1893: Racist Underpinnings of a Utopian Artifact," *Journal of American Culture* 1, no. 2 (Summer 1978): 253–275; Ann Massa, "Black Women in the 'White City'," *Journal of American Studies* 8, no. 3 (December 1974): 319–337; Elliott M. Rudwick and August Meier, "Black Man in the 'White City': Negroes and the Columbia Exposition (1893), *Phylon* 26, no. 4 (Winter 1965):354–361. For a discussion of how African-American women's particular marginality at the fair linked up to its production of the modern/American/woman, see Banta, *Imaging American Women,* 499–550.

38. Marquette, *Brands, Trademarks and Good Will,* 146.

39. This ad is taken from Robert Atwan, Donald McQuade, and John W. Wright, *Edsels, Luckies, and Frigidaires: Advertising the American Way* (New York: Delta, 1979), 92.

40. While Stahl's *Imitation of Life* was vastly popular in African-American communities (Cripps, 303), its depiction of the reproduction of American racist and class hegemonies in the household of Bea and Delilah has provoked a long tradition of negative criticism. The paradigm text is Sterling Brown, "*Imitation of Life:* Once a Pancake," *Opportunity* 13 (March 1935): 87-88. Following Brown's example, William Harrison, "The Negro and the Cinema," *Sight and Sound* 8, no. 29 (Spring 1939): 17; Peter Noble, *The Negro in Films* (London: Skelton Robinson, 1948), 61-63; Donald Bogle, *Toms, Coons, Mullatoes, Mammies and Bucks: An Interpretive History of Blacks in American Film* (New York: Viking, 1973), 57-60; Thomas Cripps, *Slow Fade to Black: The Negro in American Film, 1900-1942* (New York: Oxford University Press, 1977), 301-303; Jeremy G. Butler, "*Imitation of Life:* Style and the Domestic Melodrama," *Jump Cut* 32 (1987): 25-28; Donald Bogle, *Blacks in American Films and Television: An Encyclopedia* (New York: Garland, 1988), 113-115. For a brief history of the film's production and reception, see Thomas Schatz, *The Genius of the System: Hollywood Filmmaking in the Studio Era* (New York: Pantheon Books, 1988), 231-232.

41. Another facet of the film's cultural work in this scene is the metonymic linkage of Delilah to the body of white ethnic American immigrants. The man for whom Delilah produces her cartoon image is an Italian actor who engages in his own grotesque comic physical performance, complete with thick accent: Stahl shoots him as a direct parallel to Delilah, with Bea in the spatial center. Since Delilah is explicitly an "immigrant" from the South, her juxtaposition with him, and their equivalent service functions (helping Bea produce a business, performing slapstick comedy) signifies yet another relay the film makes among social marginalities in non-melting pot America.

42. Bailey, "Nigger/Lover," 40.

43. This is Paul Willemen's phrase and idea, founding *Screen*'s revival of Sirk's reputation in the 1970s. Following this line, many cinema theorists and historians valorize Sirk's avant-garde exploitation of Hollywood's laws of genre: he is said to have worked so excessively within the melodrama as to have saturated it with irony (along with the American culture that requires its consoling release). While I don't disagree with this general reading of Sirk's political position, this section of the essay explores the limits of his irony, as it circulates around the female body. Paul Willemen, "Towards an Analysis of the Sirkean System." *Screen* 13, no. 4 (Winter 1972/3): 128-134; See Fischer, *Imitation of Life,* for the extensive Sirk bibliography. My reading of Sirk's irony is more in line with that of Michael E. Selig, "Contradiction and Reading: Social Class and Sex Class in *Imitation of Life*," *Wide Angle* 10, no. 4 (1988): 14-23.

44. The lyrics to this song signify that the discursive, erotic, and political space between Sarah Jane and Annie is entirely an effect of Sarah Jane's "white" skin, which can approximate for her a fantasy of racial invisibility. "The loneliest word I heard of is 'empty,' and anything empty is sad. An empty purse can make a good girl bad, you hear me Dad? The loneliest word I heard of is 'empty,' empty things make me so mad. So fill me up with what I formerly had. Now Venus, you know, was loaded with charms, and look at what happened to her. Waitin' around, she's minus two arms—could happen to me, no sir! Now is the time to fill what is empty, fill my life brim full of charms. Help me refill these empty, empty, empty arms." The first time we see Sarah Jane dance erotically to its score is in her bedroom—where, during the dance, she not only kicks a stuffed animal (a lamb) but steps threateningly near a record of *Porgy and Bess* strewn across her floor.

45. James Harvey, "Sirkumstantial Evidence," *Film Comment* 14, no. 4 (July-August 1978): 55. Here is the entire passage:

HARVEY: Or the funeral scene.

SIRK: The Funeral itself is an irony. All that pomp.
HARVEY: But surely there is no irony when Mahalia Jackson signs. The emotion is large and simply and straightforward.
SIRK: It's strange. Before shooting those scenes, I went to hear Mahalia Jackson at UCLA, where she was giving a recital. I knew nothing about her. But here on the stage was this large, homely, ungainly woman—and all those shining, beautiful young faces turned up to her, and absolutely smitten with her. It was strange and funny, and very impressive. I tried to get some of that experience into the picture. We photographed her with a three-inch lens, so that every unevenness in the face stood out.
HARVEY: You don't think the funeral scene is highly emotional?
SIRK: I know, I know but I was surprised at that effect.

46. Richard Dyer, "White," *Screen* 29, no. 4 (Autumn 1988): 49.
47. *Encyclopedia Britannica,* 11th ed., 703–710.
48. This is from the Stahl 1934 version.

7.
A Small Boy and Others: Sexual Disorientation in Henry James, Kenneth Anger, and David Lynch

MICHAEL MOON

In this essay I am concerned with a group of texts that have been produced over the past century: chiefly, Henry James's "The Pupil" (1891), Kenneth Anger's film *Scorpio Rising* (1964), and David Lynch's *Blue Velvet* (1986). I shall be analyzing the ways in which each of these texts draws much of its considerable uncanny energies from representing heavily ritualized performances of some substantial part of the whole round of "perverse" desires and fantasies, autoerotic, homoerotic, voyeuristic exhibitionistic, incestuous, fetishistic, and sadomasochistic. Particularly striking are the ways in which all these texts foreground the mimed and ventriloquized qualities of the performances of ritual induction and initiation into "perverse circles" which they represent, rather than attempting to de-emphasize the mimetic secondariness of these representations, as realist texts and ordinary pornography both commonly do. Since René Girard launched his influential critique of the object-theory of desire twenty-five years ago, his argument that it is not the putative object of desire but mimesis that is primary in the formation of desire has been usefully elaborated by a number of theorists.[1] Of these, Mikkel Borch-Jacobsen's recent rereading of Girard's hypothesis "against" some similarly fundamental hypotheses of Freud's has been highly suggestive for my own current project. " . . . [D]esire is mimetic before it is anything else," Borch-Jacobsen writes.[2] Rather than focusing on simple triangulations of desire among persons, as he criticizes Girard for doing, he attempts to theorize the thoroughly *dis*orienting effects mimesis has on desire (" . . . [D]esire is not oriented by pleasure, it is (dis)oriented by mimesis. . . . "; p. 34).

In the texts I am looking at, I want to consider some of the ways in which sexuality is not so much oriented by its object, by the perceived gender or age, race, social class, body type, style of dress, etc., of its object, as it is *disoriented* by mimesis. There are many more people who respond strongly (whether or not they recognize or acknowledge any positive component to their response) to images of male-male sadomasochism, for example, than there are people who identify themselves as gay-male sadomasochists—this at least became clear in the aftermath of the controversy about the Corcoran Gallery's cancellation of its projected exhibition of Robert Mapplethorpe's photographs. The reason for this strong response is not simply because these images induce the viewer at least momentarily to violate (painfully and/or pleasurably, depending on one's point of view) the general interdiction of sadomasochistic object-choice among males in our society, for just such object-choices flourish in many institutional settings; relations of inflicting and receiving psychological and physical pain, with the sexual element of this interchange suppressed or not, are considered not shocking aberrations but ordinary and even necessary practice in the military, in prisons, in many corporate organizations, athletic teams, and schools of all levels. It is the domestication of many of these procedures into "discipline," the daily practice of institutional "law and order," with only those interchanges that are most flagrantly sexually enacted isolated and stigmatized as "sexual perversion," that conduces most of us to disavow our insiders' knowledge of sadomasochistic pleasures most of the time.

As with other kinds of largely disavowed knowledges, the knowledge of ostensibly minority pleasures like sadomasochism plays constantly around the margins of perception of the "normal" majority—that most audacious of theoretical fictions. If in an important sense *no* desire is our own—i.e., originates with us; if desire is indeed primarily induced by imitation, mimed and ventriloquized, then it is impossible to maintain our ordinary "orienting" notions of which desires we are at home with and which ones we are not. Powerful images of ostensibly perverse desires and fantasies disorient our currently prevailing assumptions—symmetrical and pluralistic—about our own and other people's sexual orientations by bringing home to us the shapes of desires and fantasies that we ordinarily disavow as our own. In forcing us to recognize at least liminally our own familiarity or "at-homeness" with these desires these images produce *unheimlich*—uncanny—effects. In the texts I am discussing, the process of inducing uncanny effects is inseparable from the related process of inducing effects of what I am calling sexual disorientation to denote the position of reader- or viewer-subjects at least temporarily dislocated from what they consider their "home" sexual orientation and "disorientingly" circulated through a number of different positions on the wheel of "perversions," positions which render moot or irrelevant our current basic "orienting" distinction, homo/heterosexual. I am interested in doing this not in order to try to efface this distinction, which on the gay side has been so murderously enforced over the past century, never more so than it is today, but, to the contrary, to extend our thinking about the dependence of both so-called high and popular culture during the same period on the sexually "perverse" for their energies and often for their representational programs.

Roy Orbison's 1963 song "In Dreams" figures importantly in *Blue Velvet*. It begins, "A candy-colored clown they call the sandman tiptoes to my room every night, / Just to sprinkle stardust and to whisper, 'Go to sleep, everything is all right.' " Orbison's "candy-colored clown they call the sandman" has commonly been taken to mean—as so much figurative writing in pop music of the sixties and after has been—to mean simply "drugs," in this case "downs" or "sleepers." Without discounting this entirely, I want to press on the intertextual relation of the "sandman" of Orbison's and Lynch's texts with that of E.T.A. Hoffmann's 1816 story "The Sandman" and Freud's 1919 essay "The Uncanny," which takes Hoffmann's story as its model literary text.

In Hoffmann's story, a young student named Nathanael believes that an old instrument-peddler who calls himself "Coppola" is the same man who, as the lawyer Coppelius, used to pay mysterious nocturnal visits to Nathanael's father, until the night the boy's father was killed by an explosion and fire in his study, from the scene of which Coppelius supposedly fled. During this time the child Nathanael had developed the fixed notion that old Coppelius was the nursery-fable figure "the Sandman" in the flesh—rather repellent flesh, little Nathanael thinks.

Freud interprets the story's uncanny effects as proceeding from castration anxieties, which it registers around the figure of Nathanael who displaces his fear of castration by his father onto his father's evil and uncanny double, Coppelius.[3] As is the case with so many of Freud's key formulations, we get only the "heterosexual plot" of the "sandman" narrative in his reading of it. Neither Freud nor any of the other readers who have published interpretations of the story has, to my knowledge, made anything of the narrative's continuous engagement with a thematics of male-male sadomasochism and pedophilia, as when Nathanael says that Coppelius had "mishandled" or "manhandled" him once when he caught the boy spying on him and his father, violently twisting his hands and feet and moving as if to pluck out his eyes.[4] Later in the story Nathanael claims Coppelius "had entered him and possessed him" at the time he caught him spying (p. 292). Nathanael's "madness" takes the form of a series of hysterical outbursts in which he keeps crying, "Whirl round, circle of fire! Merrily, merrily! Aha lovely wooden doll, whirl round!" (pp. 303, 308). It is possible to see how the hallucinatory contents of his delirium may derive from a premature and precocious induction into the "perverse" "circle of fire" he enters when as a child he spies on the mysterious nocturnal activities of his father with Coppelius. He keeps hysterically mistaking his relation to the "lovely wooden doll"; in the second half of the story he falls in love with the girl-automaton Olympia, a figure which is on one level of his confused thoughts an image of his physically invaded child self and on another an image of his infantile perception of the phallus of the father and/or Coppelius as a terrifying and powerful machine (". . . wooden doll, whirl round!"). Lacan speaks of one of the primary significations of the phallus as being its character as the visible sign of the sexual link, or what he calls the "*copula*,"[5] and Nathanael's belief that Coppelius renamed himself "Coppola" after his attack on him and his alleged murder of his father underscores Coppelius's position as phallic terrorist in Nathanael's story.

Part of the uncanny power of Hoffmann's "The Sandman" no doubt derives from the undecidable relation of this "perverse" narrative to the familiar oedipal one about Nathanael's relation to his father and his female sweethearts which psychoanalytic theory has privileged. Hoffman's text reveals with stunning force how thoroughly any given reader, including Freud and subsequent critics of "The Sandman," may be both "at home" and "not at home," simultaneously and in undecidable combination, with these powerful and "perverse" undercurrents. The film *Blue Velvet,* too, oscillates between a conventional, linear, oedipal plot and a "perverse," circular, and ritualistic one. The trajectory of the oedipal plot of *Blue Velvet* is also racist, sexist, ageist, and homophobic in the ways to which the oedipal so readily lends itself: a young man must negotiate what is represented as being the treacherous path between an older, ostensibly exotic, sexually "perverse" woman and a younger, racially "whiter," sexually "normal" one, and he must at the same time and as part of the same process negotiate an even more perilous series of interactions with the older woman's violent and murderous criminal lover and the younger woman's protective police-detective father. This heterosexual plot resolves itself in classic oedipal fashion: the young man, Jeffrey, destroys the demonic criminal "father" and rival, Frank; rescues the older woman, Dorothy, from Frank's sadistic clutches; and then relinquishes her to her fate and marries the perky young daughter of the good cop.[6]

But that is not the whole story of the film: there is an anarchic second plot that emerges intermittently but unmistakably in which subject positions and transferrals of identities and desires are highly volatile. Young Jeffrey arrives at the film's end at the object of his oedipal destination, the high-school student Sandy (notice how the name of even this character, the only principal one in the film supposedly located well outside the "perverse" circuits it traverses, links her with Orbison's and Hoffmann's uncanny "sandmen"), but he is frequently swept off course from this oedipal trajectory, not only by his attraction to and involvement with Dorothy, "the Blue Velvet Lady," but by his only marginally less intense "involvement" with her lover Frank and the other men who surround him. There are two moments in the film which I shall discuss at some length in which the supercharged valencies of male-male desire are represented with particular graphic power. In these scenes, characters enact a whole series of uncanny relationships between males of different ages, social classes, and supposed sexual orientations—orientations which get thoroughly disoriented when they get swept near the flame of "perverse" desire that flows around the figures of the chief sadomasochistic pair, Frank and Dorothy.

Anyone who watches *Blue Velvet* with "The Sandman" in mind may well be struck by how densely intertextual the film is with the story, not only in its repeated evocations of the figure of "the sandman," but also in its "perverse" plot: as in Hoffmann's "The Sandman," a young male gets unexpectedly initiated into a circle of sadomasochistic and fetishistic desires. Lynch's characters, like Hoffmann's, indulge in a round of spying and retributive and eroticized beating on each other, and of mimed and ventriloquized desire. Early in the film Jeffrey hides in Dorothy's closet and spies on her. When she catches him, she forces him to strip at knifepoint and subsequently introduces him to sadomasochistic sex, as both direct participant and voyeur. When on one occasion later in the film Frank catches Jeffrey leaving Dorothy's apartment, he forces both of them to come with him for what he calls a "joyride," the first stop of which is at Ben's, where Jeffrey is preliminarily punched a time or two (by Frank and Ben) and Ben, looking heavily made-up, lip-synchs Roy Orbison's song about "the candy-colored clown they call the sandman," until he is interrupted by a grimacing Frank, who manically orders everyone present to get on with the "joyride."

The initiation ritual to which Frank is subjecting Jeffrey at this point in the film is extremely ambiguous: the younger man is being intimidated and frightened away from Frank and his circle of perversions at the same time that he is being forced and welcomed into it. The contradictions do not stop at the figure of Jeffrey; they extend to everyone present at the scene of initiation: in Frank's obvious pleasure *and* pain during Ben's lip-synching; in Ben's "suave" behavior toward Frank, as Frank calls it, and Ben's sadistic behavior toward Jeffrey (he hits him in the stomach), as well as in Ben's being both male and "made up," i.e., wearing cosmetics; in Dorothy's being brought to Ben's both to be terrorized and punished and to be allowed to see her small child, who is being held hostage there; in the mixed atmosphere of Ben's place, which appears to be a whorehouse with a staff of mostly grandmotherly-looking whores, several of whom are sitting around a coffeetable, suburban-homestyle, chatting with Ben when Frank and his party arrive. Ben's lip-synching of "In Dreams" functions as both a kind of "tribute" to Frank and also as a kind of threat to Jeffrey that some uncanny figure called "the candy-colored clown" or "sandman" is going to "get him"—but, as one sees in the pain Frank registers in his face during the latter part of the lip-synch, this figure "gets" Frank, too; he seems almost on the verge of breaking down before he yanks the tape from the player and orders everyone to "hit the fuckin' road."

When Frank, Dorothy, Jeffrey, and the others make their next stop it is at a deserted spot far out in the country. Here Frank starts hyperventilating and playing sadistically with Dorothy's breasts. Unable to remain in the voyeuristic position in which he has been placed for the moment, Jeffrey first orders Frank to "leave [Dorothy] alone" and then leaps forward from the backseat of the car and punches Frank in the face. Frank orders Raymond and his other henchmen to pull the boy out of the car and to put the song "Candy-Colored Clown" ("In Dreams") on the car's tapeplayer. The action between Frank and Jeffrey becomes most densely ritualistic at this point. Frank smears lipstick on his mouth and kisses it onto Jeffrey's lips, pleading with him to leave Dorothy alone (the same thing Jeffrey had ordered him to do a minute before), and threatening to send him "a love letter" if he does not, explaining to him that by "a love letter" he means "a bullet from a fuckin' gun." "If you get a love letter from me, you're fucked *forever*," Frank tells Jeffrey. He then starts speaking to Jeffrey the words of the song playing on the tapeplayer: "In dreams I walk with you, / In dreams I talk to you; / In dreams you're mine, all of the time, / We're together in dreams." Frank then wipes the lipstick from the boy's lips with a swatch of blue velvet, instructs the other men to "hold him tight for me," and, to the crescendo of the song's chorus ("It's too bad that these things / Can only happen in my dreams"), begins to beat Jeffrey mercilessly. As Jeffrey presumably loses consciousness, the music and the scene fade out.

When Lynch has Frank mouth the words of the song a second time, this time directly to a Jeffrey whom he has ritually prepared for a beating by "kissing" lipstick onto his mouth and wiping it off with a piece of blue velvet, it is as though Lynch is both daring the viewer to recognize the two men's desire for each other that the newly discovered sadomasochistic bond that unites them induces them to feel *and* at the same time to recognize the perhaps more fearful knowledge that what most of us consider our deepest and strongest desires are not our own, that our dreams and fantasies are only copies, audio- and videotapes, of the desires of others and our utterances of them lip-synchings of these circulating, endlessly reproduced and reproducible desires. Lip-synching is the ideal form of enunciation for the ritualized and serious game of "playing with fire"—i.e., with the game of inducing male homosexual panic and of recognizing, at least in flashes, the strong S-M component of male-male violence—that Frank, Ben, and Jeffrey play: lip-synching a pop song allows Ben to "come on" to Frank, and Frank in turn to "come on" to Jeffrey, singing about how "In Dreams" they possess the man to whom they're singing—without doing so in any way that "counts" for more than the phantasmatic and mimicked moments the two pairs of men share.

The lip-synch/lipstick initiation to which Frank subjects Jeffrey ritualistically enacts the rupture between the sayable and the unsayable about the intense sadomasochistic bond between them, both as they transact this bond through their shared involvement with Dorothy, and as it threatens, just at this point in the film, to bypass mediation through her—i.e., to become simply a male-male S-M relationship. It also marks the point of lack on the part of both men of an "original" voice or "original" utterance and the consequently ventriloquistic character of their—and our—desires. The fascination with other men's lips, with men kissing each other, especially in the context of a sadomasochistic relationship, and with the look of smeared lipstick on men's lips—all these bespeak the generally enforced misrecognition of many men most of the time of the relation between their own ostensibly "normal" male heterosexuality and their relation to the penetrable orifices of their own and other males' bodies; it is a sign of the "scandal" of the liminal gendering—one might say the minimal gendering—of the mouth and anus, the repression of which "scandal" so much energy and anxiety in straight-male relations are invested in concealing and revealing, as is evident in the most basic buzzwords of male-male abuse, "cocksucker" and "asshole" and "faggot," a set of terms and relationships of male-male power into which almost every small boy in our culture is interpellated as a crucial part of his elementary education. The "candy-colored clown they call the sandman" whom Ben and Frank mimic (the "made-up" and intensely flashlit look of both their faces as they lip-synch is a sign that they are "clowning") is a figure for the circulation through the men in these scenes of a mostly disavowed familiarity with, and in varying degrees, adeptness at, sadomasochistic desire and practices between males.

It would be a significant oversight to ignore the roles of the women in these scenes—Dorothy especially and the other woman who joins the "joyride" at Ben's—in the initiation ritual carried out on Jeffrey. Dorothy moves over to the driver's seat when Frank and the other men drag Jeffrey out of the car to beat him, but her real position remains abject: she shouts, "Frank, stop! Frank, stop!"—to no avail—then lays her arms and her head on the steering wheel and weeps, as Frank carries on with the ritual violence in which she is relegated to the position of a Stabat Mater who can't bear to look. The other woman who has joined the group is unphased, is perfectly "at home," with the scene of male-male sadomasochism she has been transported to witness: she climbs out of the car onto its roof, where she dances to the strains of "In Dreams," combined with the rhythmic sound (the "beat") of Frank's fists falling on Jeffrey's body, with the mechanical imperturbability of Olympia, Nathanael's automaton-sweetheart in Hoffmann's "The Sandman."

It is surely relevant to the way women in this scene are relegated to positions of either abjection or affectlessness to mention that, as Lynch had it in the original script for *Blue Velvet,* Frank was, at this point in the film, supposed to rape Jeffrey, to enact literally his telling Dorothy, in response to her fearful question when they leave Ben's, "Where are we going?," "We're takin' your neighbor [Jeffrey] out to the country to fuck."[7] Lynch's decision to film the scene "otherwise," to transmute Frank's violation of Jeffrey and his body from a literal rape to a symbolic ritual, raises questions about the way males and male bodies are privileged in this film and the way women—again, Dorothy especially—are abjected in it. It is important in this connection, for example, that the representational economy of nakedness in the film is initially presented as a gender-symmetrical one: Jeffrey spies on Dorothy undressing as he hides in her closet, and when Dorothy discovers him she forces him to undress while she watches. But there is no scene performed by a male that corresponds to the climactic one late in the film performed by Rossellini, when, as Dorothy, she comes staggering, naked and incoherent, out into the street where Sandy's drunken ex-boyfriend and his buddies are picking a fight with Jeffrey. Dorothy's punctual arrival, nude, at a second scene of male-male violence has the effect of rescuing Jeffrey from a second beating; catching sight of her, the drunken ex-boyfriend first asks Jeffrey mockingly, "Is that your mother?" (thereby voicing for Jeffrey and the viewer the oedipal anxieties the film frequently both engages and mocks), but even the drunken teenage boy seems to lose interest in baiting Jeffrey when he sees how badly off Dorothy really is. There is a dynamic relation between Jeffrey's being let off the hook—not only from the violence being immediately threatened at this point in the narrative but from any real threat of violence for the rest of the film—and Dorothy's being reduced at this climactic moment to a literal vision of staggering naked abjection. The excessive and appalling degree to which Dorothy and her body are exposed to the general gaze at this point serves the other characters and their director-author to underwrite the "happy ending" which subsumes Jeffrey and Sandy and, supposedly, Dorothy and her little son (her lover Frank and her captive husband both die in the violence at the end of the film). We should also recognize how it serves retroactively to underwrite Lynch's sublimation of male-male rape in the scene between Frank and Jeffrey into a beating that leaves sexual violation enacted only on a symbolic plane.

One of the most pervasive of the fantasies informing the "perverse" initiation rituals I'm discussing and the uncanny, sexually disorienting effects they produce is that of a person's being able to ravish and hold captive another person by the unaided agency of a powerful gaze, and the attendant danger of this gaze's making its director more rather than less highly susceptible to other people's gazes (in *Blue Velvet,* for example, Frank tries repeatedly to control Dorothy's and Jeffrey's gazing behavior toward him). The fantasy of the pupil of the eye as the focal point of visual and erotic capture is at the core of Henry James's tale "The Pupil," which treats of a series of visual and erotic captures and struggles to escape both into and away from a "perverse" circle constituted by a brilliant little boy, his loving and beloved tutor, and the boy's mother, who is attractive and socially ambitious but perpetually financially embarrassed. The precincts of James's fiction may seem remote from those of a recent and flagrantly "perverse" film like *Blue Velvet,* but they are not as far apart as they may at first appear. Despite James's own announced distaste for the project of some of his contemporaries of representing "perversion" relatively openly and sensationally—Wilde's *Dorian Grey,* for example—James's own literary explorations of the circulation of "perverse" desires are elaborate and searching, and remarkably unconstrained by contemporary standards of gentility and prudery. "The Pupil" was summarily rejected by the editor of the *Atlantic Monthly,* one of the very few times one of James's fictions was declined by the journals to which he regularly contributed. James professed to be unable to understand why, but it may well have been because it produced the same kinds of discomfort in the editor that an anonymous critic writing in the *Independent* expressed a few years later in response to *The Turn of the Screw.* "How Mr. James could . . . choose to make such a study of infernal human debauchery . . . is unaccountable," the reviewer writes, going on to say, "The study . . . affects the reader with a disgust that is not to be expressed. The feeling after perusal of the horrible story is that one has been assisting in an outrage upon . . . human innocence, and helping to debauch—at least by standing helplessly by—the pure and trusting nature of children. Human imagination can go no further into infamy, literary art could not be used with more refined subtlety of spiritual defilement."[8] In other words, James's work looked to some of his contemporaries—and may look to us, if we allow it to—the way *Blue Velvet* looks to us: shocking and disturbing. Or to put it another way, if James were writing today, his work would look more like *Blue Velvet* than it would like Merchant and Ivory's ponderously reverent period "recreations" of his novels.

One thing James's work registers continuously that Merchant and Ivory's betrays little feeling for is the investment of "sexiness" in, the fetish-character of, a given epoch's favored fashions in dress and styles of interior decoration. The Paris of the Second Empire was the most formative setting of James's childhood according to his own testimony, and it is a principal setting of "The Pupil." The bourgeois culture of this period may be said to have had its own intense velvet fetish. According to Walter Benjamin in his study of Baudelaire, bourgeois domestic interiors at the latter end of the period had become velvet- and plush-lined carapaces for a social class that seemed to want to insulate itself from the world from which it derived its wealth and power behind a grotesque barrier of such luxury fabrics—in clothing for ordinary and ceremonial occasions, in upholstery and wallcoverings, and, perhaps most significantly, in linings for instrument cases, jewelry boxes, and coffins.[7]

"Velvet" is everywhere in James, once one becomes aware of it, and it is there unsurprisingly, given the characteristic settings and concerns of his fiction—freedom and domination, glamor and stigma, during what he calls in the preface to "The Pupil" "the classic years of the great Americano-European legend." When the tutor Pemberton in "The Pupil" wonders resentfully how his penurious employers can manage to keep installing themselves in what the narrator calls the "velvety *entresols*" of the best hotels in Paris, "the most expensive city in Europe," "velvet" still bears the unambiguously positive charge it had carried forty years before in Thackeray's *Vanity Fair*, the repository of so many of James's basic props for signaling fine degrees of upward and downward social mobility, as when Becky Sharp finds herself at one of the peaks of her success being waited on by a "velvetfooted butler."[10] There is a striking detail in the opening lines of "The Pupil," however, that suggests the more ambiguous charge a luxury fabric could bear as sign late in the nineteenth century. When the characters of Pemberton the tutor and Mrs. Moreen are first introduced, he is called simply "[t]he poor young man" and his new employer, Mrs. Moreen, is "the large, affable lady who sat there drawing a pair of soiled *gants de Suède* through a fat, jewelled hand. . . ."[11] This description occurs in the second sentence of the story and it is easy enough for one to overlook it as a gratuitous "realistic" detail, but on reflection one can see in what rich detail these images signify "trouble ahead" for Pemberton and even the ambiguous nature of that "trouble." Mrs. Moreen's gesture of drawing her soiled suede gloves through her "fat, jewelled hand" mimes an unspoken desire—not necessarily her own—for her son, who is both the only other person present at this conversation and the most mixed quantity in the story, the figure in it who is neither entirely innocent of the shabbiness or willful moral abjectness of the rest of the Moreen family, nor entirely guilty of it, but rather only tainted or "soiled" with it by unavoidable association. Pemberton squirms with discomfort during this initial (and initiatory) interview because Mrs. Moreen is performing this curious mime of displaying a bit of her dirty laundry to him instead of settling the matter of his salary, which the narrator refers to as "the question of terms." What Pemberton does not see at the beginning of the story is that while his salary is not being discussed, his real compensation for his work—an invitation to desire Morgan—is being repeatedly issued in mime by Mrs. Moreen. His intense but unnamed relationship to her little son—here is the real "question of terms" that is in contest in the story and beyond it—will partake of the mixed character of her "soiled" gloves. Rather than being something that sets them apart from the rest of the Moreen household, the "scandal" of the intimacy between tutor and pupil is perfectly "at home" with the more inclusive "scandal" of the kind of mixed clean-and-dirty surface Mrs. Moreen and the rest of the family show to the world. I shall return to the detail of the soiled gloves a little later on.

When Morgan dies at the story's climax, his body doesn't end up simply in his tutor's arms, as it might if the story were just a pederastic idyll, as I would argue it is not, nor does his body end up in his mother's arms, in the kind of vignette that would anticipate the similar death of little Miles in the arms of his governess at the climax of *The Turn of the Screw*. Rather, the body of the dead boy ends up suspended between his tutor and his mother. When Pemberton sees that Morgan is dead, the narrator says, "[h]e pulled him half out of his mother's hands, and for a moment, while they held him together, they looked, in their dismay, into each other's eyes." The resemblance of this last image in the tale to its first one is striking: young Morgan's dead body occupies precisely the place of the dirty suede gloves, but this time instead of merely noticing them unreflectively while Mrs. Moreen pulls them through her hands, Pemberton actively intervenes to draw Morgan's body "half out of [her] hands." Suspended between childhood and manhood (he has grown from age eleven to fifteen in the course of the story) and between mother and tutor, Morgan's body at the moment of death becomes a kind of uncanny puppet, a "soiled" handpuppet like a "soiled" glove. Although Pemberton and Mrs. Moreen have repeatedly quarreled over which of them has made the greater "sacrifice" for Morgan, the boy himself ends up, perhaps not entirely unwillingly, the sacrificial victim of the rituals the three practice, leaving tutor and mother in the utterly abject position of members of a collapsed cult.

I want to consider a little further the possible significance of "soiled" suede as a figure for relations in "The Pupil." Like those of "velvet," the erotic and class associations of "suede" have shifted and mutated considerably over the past century and more. The possible erotic association that makes soiled "suede" rather than velvet the appropriate figure for whatever unnameable bond unites Mrs. Moreen and her little son at the beginning of the story, a bond into which they admit, and with which they secure Pemberton, is primarily a verbal one: English-language guides to proper dress from mid-century forward inform the reader that the newly fashionable fabric "*Suède*" is "undressed kid." Those who would argue that "undressed kid" could not have meant, even subliminally, "undressed child" to James and his readers because "kid" did not then in that place and time commonly mean "child," need only look in the OED to see that it was precisely in the decade or two before "The Pupil" was written that "kid" as a term for "child" ceased to be "low slang" as it long had been and entered into common use among the English upper class as a term of familiar affection for a child or children of one's own: William Morris writes of the health of his "kid'in a personal letter of the 1860s, and Lord Shaftesbury makes a notation of several happy days spent with his "wife and kids" in a passage from his journal published in the 1880s. If my translations of the phrase "drawing a pair of soiled *gants de Suède* through a fat, jewelled hand" into "handling dirty undressed-kid gloves" and, possibly, into other permutations of that phrase, including "handling a dirty undressed kid," seem farfetched, it is only because the erotic wish encrypted, mimed but unspoken, in the text of "The Pupil" is precisely the kind of meaning that requires just such high-intensity translation or decoding—not only because James may have been to some degree unconscious of this meaning but also because of our own resistance to recognizing the access to "perverse" energies that his writing frequently affords us.

Rather than assenting to the notion that texts like "The Pupil" and *Blue Velvet* are historically, politically, and stylistically remote from each other and consequently not susceptible to the same modes of interpretation, I want to argue that the successful obfuscation of these kinds of connections by several successive generations of literary critics has done a deep disservice not only to James's writing, but also to the historical and political configuration in which it was produced and to the culture of our own day, which has, for all its differences, by no means resolved the kinds of political and sexual-political conflicts James anatomizes so unsparingly. To indulge an invidious comparison for a moment, I think James's practice in Pupil" is, if anything, more rather than less radical than Lynch's in *Blue Velvet*. The film's marginalization of Ben, the only character in the film explicitly marked as gay, is a sign of this. In effect quarantined from the rest of the film, his appearance is restricted to only one scene, although what he fleetingly represents—ties between men *not* mediated through a captive woman—is not. Lynch's raising the age of his boy-initiate Jeffrey into his early twenties is another significant normalizing gesture on his part; if *Blue Velvet* has been a controversial film, imagine how much moreso it would have been if Lynch had followed James's practice in "The Pupil" of making his boy-initiate a *boy*—i.e., not over fifteen.[12] Discarding the "heterosexual plot" on which narratives of "perverse initiation," from Hoffmann's "The Sandman" to *Blue Velvet,* have traditionally depended, James in "The Pupil" produces his "perverse" plot almost undiluted by normalizing or heterosexualizing measures.

One must look beyond the example of Lynch to someone like Kenneth Anger, I think, to find work that explores the dynamics of "perverse" desire as uncompromisingly as James does. Anger is one of the figures who represents something closest to a "direct route" between figures like James and Lynch. In thirteen segments of complex montage, each set to a different pop tune of the two-or-three-year period before the film was made—the ancestors of today's ubiquitous rock videos—Anger's film shows the members of a motorcycle gang preparing for a race by tinkering with their bikes, dressing up in elaborate fetish gear, snorting cocaine, and performing a series of rituals including a mock orgy-and-torture session. These fetishistic and largely mock-sadomasochistic preparations culminate in a motorcycle rally in which the bikers race their 'cycles around a track to the tune of such pop songs as "Point of No Return" and "Wipe-Out"—terms that may well remind us of what the group of texts I've been discussing represent as the traumatic and irreversibly shattering qualities of precocious initiation into "perverse circles."

One way of reading *Blue Velvet* is as a text that Lynch unfolded out of the "Blue Velvet" segment of Anger's 1964 film *Scorpio Rising*. In this segment, as Bobby Vinton croons, "She wore blue velvet," the film represents not a woman in blue velvet but a bike boy (three of them, in fact) in blue *denim* donning black leather and chains. While the song invites its auditor to fantasize a specularized and fetishized girl or woman—a figure like Lynch's Dorothy, "the Blue Velvet Lady"—Anger's film presents specularized and fetishized boys. Rather than the kind of undisrupted miming or lip-synching that characterizes male behavior and serves as a vehicle for a limited range of male-male desires in Lynch's film, Anger's film at moments like the one I am considering drives a wedge between the aural effects and the visual ones it is producing. By representing leather boys "dressing up" to the tune of the song "Blue Velvet," Anger produces the disorienting shock effect—quite successfully, judging from the outraged reception and censorship of the film during the early years of its reception—of placing males in the position of the specularized and fetishized "supposed-to-be-female" figure of sexist—and heterosexist—representational regimes.

The kinds of erotic and erotically disorienting substitutions in which *Scorpio Rising* deals, of which the blue-velvet bike-boys episode is a chief example, are certainly an important aspect of the pleasures of Anger's text. Another aspect of this pleasure I would not overlook is the one common to this as well as to all of the other texts I have been discussing of representing the fetish—whether it be velvet or suede, denim or leather—as a primary focus of the various "perverse" desires that all these texts mime; in them, the fetish is an exemplarily disoriented marker of desire, not itself either the object of desire, nor simply the kind of substitute phallus it is in classical Freudian theory but something—at least as much a practice as it is an object—that locates itself undecidably between mimetic desire and the indefinitely wide range of objects on which that desire may fasten. *Scorpio*

Rising literalizes more thoroughly than any other text of which I am aware not only the priority of mimetic desire over object-desire, but also the priority of the fetish over other "perverse" investments.

One further link from Anger back to James's milieu passes through the figure of Aleister Crowley, someone whose work and career have been perhaps even more important for Anger than those of the two gay film directors whose influence is most obvious in his work, Eisenstein and Cocteau. A generation younger than James and exactly the kind of cultivator of a "perverse" public image that James strenuously avoided associating himself with, Crowley began his career as a member, along with Yeats and others, of the occult society of the Order of the Golden Dawn. Crowley spent most of his career performing and writing about forms of ritual magic based on "perverse" sexual practices, and Anger has been an avowed disciple of his since boyhood. Anger's precocity was the first very notable fact of his own career; the story of its beginning reads like one of the tales of always-premature, "perverse" initiation I have been considering. Left on his own one weekend by his parents when he was seventeen, Anger, no doubt fulfilling many suburban parents' worst nightmare about their offspring, made a film—*Fireworks*—starring himself about a seventeen-year-old boy who is "picked up" by a gang of sailors and raped and disemboweled by them. That the atmosphere of the film is lyrical and witty rather than horrific suggests that Jean Genet might have had little to teach this boy-filmmaker about "perverse" desires and their representation. As the narrator of "The Pupil" says of Pemberton the tutor's efforts to fathom the remarkable resourcefulness and resilience of his little charge, "When he tried to figure to himself the morning twilight of childhood, so as to deal with it safely, he perceived that it was never fixed, never arrested, that ignorance, at the instant one touched it, was already flushing faintly into knowledge, that there was nothing that at a given moment you could say a clever child didn't know. It seemed to him that *he* both knew too much to imagine Morgan's simplicity and too little to disembroil his tangle." Like little Morgan and his tutor and the other "small boys" and young men that figure in these texts, we all often find ourselves possessing what seems to be both more knowledge than we can use and less than we need when we try to think about such difficult issues as our own relations to children and young people, including our students, and our no less complicated relations to our own child selves. Those uncanny figures, as James writes, sometimes seemed to know their most painful lessons almost before they learned them. As I think the examples I have been discussing suggest, we have much to learn from these child-figures when they return to haunt us with their uncommon knowledge of the "perverse" energies that impel desire.

NOTES

1. For Girard's major formulations of his theory, see "Triangular Desire," the first chapter of *Deceit, Desire, and the Novel: Self and Other in Literary Structure*, trans. Yvonne Freccero (Baltimore: Johns Hopkins Univ. Press, 1965), pp. 1-52; "From Mimetic Desire to the Monstrous Double," in *Violence and the Sacred*, trans. Patrick Gregory (Baltimore: Johns Hopkins Univ. Press, 1977), pp. 143-168; "Mimetic Desire," in *Things Hidden Since the Foundation of the World*, trans. Stephen Bann and Michael Metteer (Stanford: Stanford Univ. Press, 1987), pp. 283-347; and Walter Burkert, René Girard, and Jonathan Z. Smith, *Violent Origins: Ritual Killing and Cultural Formation*, Roger G. Hamerton Kelly, ed. (Stanford: Stanford Univ. Press, 1987), esp. pp. 7-20 and 121-129. Eve Kosofsky Sedgwick's reformulation of Girard in the opening pages of *Between Men: English Literature and Male Homosocial Desire* (New York: Columbia Univ. Press, 1985), esp. pp. 21-25, has had a formative effect on my thinking about the relation between gender and sexuality and the circuits of desire, in this project as in previous ones. I am very grateful to Eve for her generous and challenging conversation during the time I was planning this essay—as I am to Jonathan Goldberg for his characteristically unstinting attention to several early drafts of it. I also wish to thank Marcie Frank and Stephen Orgel for several extremely helpful suggestions for improving it.

2. *The Freudian Subject,* trans. Catherine Porter (Stanford: Stanford Univ. Press, 1988), p. 26. Hereafter cited in the text by page number.

3. "The 'Uncanny'," in Philip Rieff, ed., *Studies in Parapsychology* (New York: Collier, 1963), pp. 19-60.

4. "The Sandman," in E.T.A. Hoffmann, *Tales of Hoffmann* (Hammondsworth: Penguin, 1982), p. 282. Hereafter cited in the text by page number.

5. Lacan equates the phallus with the "*copula*" in "The signification of the phallus," *Écrits: A Selection,* trans. Alan Sheridan (New York: Norton, 1977), p. 287.

6. Kyle Maclachlan plays Jeffrey in *Blue Velvet;* Laura Dern, Sandy; Dennis Hopper, Frank; Isabella Rossellini, Dorothy; and Dean Stockwell, Ben.

7. Andy Warhol's diary entry for December 15, 1986, reads in part: " . . . Dennis [Hopper] told me the other night that they cut the scene out of *Blue Velvet* where he rapes Dean Stockwell or Dean Stockwell rapes him and there's lipstick on somebody's ass." (*The Andy Warhol Diaries,* ed. Pat Hackett [New York: Warner, 1989], p. 784). Warhol's account of this is obviously somewhat garbled, but it does suggest that Lynch had planned (and he and his actors had perhaps filmed) a more literal male-male rape scene than the "symbolic" one that appears in the film.

8. *The Independent* (January 5, 1899), 73; rpt. in Robert Kimbrough, ed., *Henry James: The Turn of the Screw* (New York: Norton, 1966), p. 175. Shoshana Felman discusses this review in *Writing and Madness: Literature/Philosophy/Psychoanalysis,* trans. Martha Noel Evans and the author with the assistance of Brian Massumi (Ithaca, N.Y.: Cornell Univ. Press, 1985), pp. 143-144.

9. Benjamin, *Charles Baudelaire: A Lyric Poet in the Era of High Capitalism,* trans. Harry Zohn (London: Verso, 1983), pp. 46-47.

10. *Vanity Fair* (New York: New American Library, 1962), p. 257.

11. Citations to the text of "The Pupil" are to Leon Edel's edition of the tale in *The Complete Tales of Henry James,* Vol. 7, 1888-1891 (Philadelphia: Lippincott, 1963).

12. Joshua Wilner has urged me to consider that it may be more proper to think of the

young man Pemberton as the initiate in James's story, rather than the boy Morgan. Yet even if one grants this, James's practice remains radical: if we take Pemberton to be James's initiate, and he is roughly as old as Lynch's Jeffrey (i.e., no longer a boy, definitely a young man), it is nevertheless true of James's two "initiators" (Morgan and his mother) that one of them is hardly more than a child. Frank and Dorothy, the primary initiators in Lynch's film, are by contrast represented as being emphatically no longer young, while Jeffrey's young girlfriend Sandy is conventionally represented as someone who is just outgrowing the role of being an innocent child.

8.
Walden's Erotic Economy
MICHAEL WARNER

> *No longer used as a full-time instrument of labor, the body would be resexualized. The regression involved in this spread of the libido would first manifest itself in a reactivation of all erotogenic zones and, consequently, in a resurgence of pregenital polymorphous sexuality and in a decline of genital supremacy. The body in its entirety would become an object of cathexis, a thing to be enjoyed—an instrument of pleasure. This change in the value and scope of libidinal relations would lead to a disintegration of the institutions in which the private interpersonal relations have been organized, particularly the monogamic and patriarchal family.*
>
> *These prospects seem to confirm the expectation that instinctual liberation can lead only to a society of sex maniacs—that is, to no society. However, the process just outlined involves not simply a release but a transformation of the libido: from sexuality constrained under genital supremacy to erotization of the entire personality.*
>
> —Marcuse, Eros and Civilization.[1]

How did sexuality come to be understood as a need for liberation? I want to take up this question with the unlikely example of Thoreau, examining the utopian strand within the distinctly male erotics of his writing. Why Thoreau? After all, it may seem counter-intuitive to read *Walden* for its utopian sexual politics. Perry Miller, for one, points out the discrepancy between Thoreau's longing for erotic relations and his inability to imagine actual relations of sexuality. Miller calls him "perverse," "prudish," "positively absurd," "simply monstrous," and just "queer."[2]

I do not disagree. But Thoreau's writings circle around conspicuously unsatisfied desires—for a new sensuality, a new body, and for as yet unimaginable libidinous relations with others, especially other men. "In the presence of my friend," he writes an early journal entry, "I am ashamed of my fingers and toes. I have no feature so fair as my love for him. There is a more than maiden modesty between us. I find myself more simple and sincere than in my most private moment to myself. I am literally true *with a witness.*"³ Or a few months later, "I seek a man who will appeal to me when I am in fault . . . In his intercourse I shall be always a god today, who was a man yesterday. He will never confound me with my guilt—but let me be immaculate, and hold up my skirts" (February 8, 1841; 1:258). I want to stress that Thoreau's desire to hold up his skirts before a male witness does not simply function as an index of existing libidinous relations. It is not clear that what is called sodomy or any other available practice exactly corresponds to the wish expressed here. Thoreau wants what Marcuse would call a transformed libido.

This is not a simple claim. At a time when the politics of sexuality is contested more than ever, in struggles over such issues as pornography, reproductive freedoms, arts funding, and AIDS, the political history of sexuality has become both more important to understand and more difficult to theorize. In each of these contexts people advocate one view or another of what sexuality is, where it comes from, what's good about it, and what's bad about it. The proliferation of conflicts over these issues makes it necessary to think now of sexualities in the plural, intersections of different and overdetermined histories. The most obvious consequence has been that a consensual, normal sexuality can no longer be taken for granted. Another consequence, however, may pose a deeper theoretical challenge. Although multiple sexualities and their multiple histories resist the regime of the normal, they equally resist any other notion of what is intrinsic to sexuality, including the notion that sexuality naturally resists power and repression. Sweeping and synthetic histories of sexual repression and liberation, represented most famously by Marcuse's *Eros and Civilization,* have been criticized by Foucault and others for implying an intrinsically liberating sexuality, a pure culture of the polymorphous, an ahistorical political meaning for sexuality. Erotic life has not always seemed to be essentially a wish for liberation. Where Marcuse declared that "the fight for Eros is the *political* fight" (xxv), the question remains open as to whose erotics will count as Eros, what context makes an erotics utopian, and how struggles over erotics can be linked to different political fights.

In the very monstrousness of Thoreau's difficult expressions of desire, we can see the appearance of a whole set of themes that would have been incomprehensible to an earlier generation of, say Washington Irving, and that find their full theorization in writers like Marcuse: that eros threatens any integrated image of the self; that the self needs remaking in response to this threat; that the self is threatened by eros because the conditions of market society produce a false self-relation; that eros calls for a transformed individuality; and that a change in social conditions would require a change in the sexuality of the individual. All of these themes are utopian in the rather strict sense that Thoreau cannot concretely imagine their realization. That is why they appear only in his queerness, his monstrous recoilings and perversely absurd demands. Hence I speak of something more than an organized discipline of sexuality when I refer to these articulated wishes as an erotics.

The utopian impulse of his erotics is what countless normalizing apologies for Thoreau have tried to eliminate, assimilating his expressions of desire to putatively realizable forms of romance. From the earliest memoirs of Thoreau to a recent popular biography, one appealing strategy has been to imagine a thwarted heterosexual romance that would explain and compensate for Thoreau's aloofness.[4] But even this fanciful literature cannot conceal his resistance to all the rhetorics of romance and sexuality that were available to him. I find Thoreau instructive in the history of sexuality partly because of just how difficult it is to normalize his erotics. Again, however, this need not mean that his is a purely polymorphous sexuality. It means first that Thoreau understands eros to threaten a self-dissolution— the distinctive theme of the post-Enlightenment discourse of sexuality in the West. Second, it means that his erotics runs counter to the organization of normal and officially abnormal sexuality. To imagine sexual practice is for him to imagine a different society. This is not always the case with people's erotics, and although Thoreau may be an unusual example in some ways, the erotic disposition of his writings is historically significant in the way it combines the theme of self-dissolution with its frustration by existing sexualities, thus linking subjective experience to an unrealized promise of freedom.

When Marcuse describes how difficult it is to imagine a new and improved libido, he claims that the Western literary tradition already has images of such freedom: Narcissus and Orpheus. Like Thoreau, they are queer and monstrous images of sexual freedom. Most of the West's cultural heroes, such as Prometheus, embody for Marcuse the very themes of productivity and progress through toil and repression that have created the need for erotic liberation. Narcissus and Orpheus, however, stand "at the opposite pole" (161). The homoerotics of both figures represents a rejection of a procreative order of sex. Eros, in them, turns against reproduction. In doing so, eros turns against production, since Narcissus and Orpheus relate to nature through the aesthetic attitudes of contemplation and play, respectively. Marcuse finds in their "perverse" erotics the desire to have done with any uses of the body—even sexual uses—defined by gain and mastery of the body.

In *Walden* Henry Thoreau strikes the posture of Narcissus. A young man turns his back on the beckoning voices of the world, goes to a pond in the woods, and there surrenders to the appeal of a self-relation in nature. Although the mythic analogy is never explicit, Thoreau courts the comparison repeatedly—I would say obsessively—in thematics of echoes and reflections. He describes the pond as "earth's eye; looking into which the beholder measures the depth of his own nature."[5] Later in the same chapter, he stages his longing to address the reflective surface:

Why, here is Walden, the same woodland lake that I discovered so many years ago . . . The same thought is welling up to its surface that was then . . . It is the work of a brave man surely, in whom there was no guile! He rounded this water with his hand, deepened and clarified it in his thought, and in his will bequeathed it to Concord. I see by its face that it is visited by the same reflection; and I can almost say, Walden, is it you? (93).

Passages like these only imply an erotic potential, whether "normal" or "perverse." It would be another half-century and more before Narcissus would become the eponym of a pathology, and Thoreau treats the posture as exactly the most normal thing in the world, making common sense look pathological by contrast. His stance of contemplative reflection appears to bear out Marcuse's remarks on Narcissus, since he uses it to reject an orientation toward production for its own sake, or profit reinvested through deferred gratification. The context of the last passage, in fact, is the approach of woodchoppers, the railroad, the icemen, and Irish laborers' shanties to the pond. In contrasting himself to them Thoreau, like Narcissus, adopts an attitude of contemplative enjoyment, though it is difficult to say whether he is contemplating himself or the world.

These passages are about self-reflection rather than eros, even though both have overtones of longing. They make puns about thinking: thoughts "welling up," thoughts "deepened and clarified," thoughts "visited by the same reflection." In a colloquial but accurate way we could say that these passages are too self-conscious to be very erotic. At the same time, the passages in question turn on a sense of longing. "I can *almost* say, Walden, is it you?" The question is not quite askable, at least if addressed to Walden. And an answer is not likely to be forthcoming. The "brave" and guileless man whom Thoreau imagines here, possibly addressed as Walden, is admired but unavailable. And the viewer of the ponds' reflections is just as admirably unavailable, measuring the depth of his own nature in Nature's surface. Thoreau's contemplative enjoyment cannot quite be realized. The scene he depicts, moreover, has an erotic subtext both in the classical legend and in Thoreau's journal. When Thoreau talks of measuring the depth of his own nature in the eye of the lake, we might remember that the loving male friend makes him feel true with a witness. And when he addresses the reflection with an appeal for recognition, we might remember his desire to be immaculately naked before the friend's look.

The passages from *Walden* draw together a great number of similar passages from the journal, including this one, a singular condensation of *Walden's* thematics:

The lake is a mirror in the breast of nature, as if there were there nothing to be concealed. All the sins of the wood are washed out in it . . . In the night it is my more than forty feet reflector . . . I love to consider the silent economy and tidiness of nature, how after all the filth [sic] of the wood, and the accumulated impurities of the winter have been rinsed herein, this liquid transparency appears in the spring.

I should wither and dry up if it were not for lakes and rivers. I am conscious that my body derives its juices from their waters, as much as the muskrat or the herbage on their brink. The thought of Walden in the woods yonder makes me supple jointed and limber for the duties of the day. Sometimes I thirst for it. (Dec 2, 1840; 1:198–99).

This is a scene of thirsting and longing because of the disparity between the body Thoreau has and the body he wants. As in *Walden,* he wants a fuller self-awareness in the mirror of the lake, nothing concealed—as if there were nothing to be concealed, he says. Here, he thinks a more naked self-contemplation will make his body more juicy, more supple. But he inhabits a present condition of filth and impurity. He wants to purge that filth through self-awareness in a natural scene, an ascetic imperative that motivates the entirety of *Walden.* But Thoreau's is not just any asceticism. He does not aim to mortify the flesh. Paradoxically, his ascetic wish for purification is also a wish to reenable a sensual self-relation. It leads him to the body as much as from the body.

Thoreau appears to turn away from the sensual body when he imagines a contemplation of himself in nature's mirror. That self-regard is ascetic insofar as he understands it in terms of purity and impurity. In "The Ponds," having said that "Walden is a perfect forest mirror," he goes on to say that it is "a mirror in which all impurity presented to it sinks" (188). And in the conclusion of that chapter, he claims that the reflective ponds "are too pure to have a market value; they contain no muck. How much more beautiful than our characters, are they!" (199). On the other hand, because the self-regard he longs for will be contemplative rather than instrumental, he imagines that he will no longer need to fear the violation and dissolution that sensuality brings. In the coming flood, he will not need to purge his reflection of impurity; he will not need to eliminate the muck from the purity of the pond. Always accompanying Thoreau's self-integrating asceticism, which dominates the opening chapters of *Walden,* is a second, resensualizing and self-dissolving movement.

The latter gathers strength only toward the end of the book, especially in "Spring." In that chapter, purgative language more extreme even than that of the journal entry culminates in a picture of self-dissolution. Then, muck is all, and not even the muskrat is safe. In the journal entry, the muskrat draws juices from the lake just as Thoreau does. But in the penultimate paragraph of *Walden*, Thoreau writes, "The life in us is like the water in the river. It may rise this year higher than man has ever known it, and flood the parched uplands; even this may be the eventful year, which will drown out all our muskrats" (333). The anticipated flooding of spring represents a surge of unwilled sensuality that can dissolve selves and drown muskrats. The journal entry foreshadows this seasonal movement of *Walden* from "the accumulated impurities of the winter" to the "liquid transparency" predicted in the general enema of the spring. This scene of dissolution, however, has not always been a self-evident description of our desires. Under what conditions does it make sense?

As a transformation of ascesis, Thoreau's self-relation marks a partial break in the history of capitalist culture. Capitalism's first premise is an ascetic one. Weber's arguments to this effect remain powerful: capitalism presupposes that labor will be oriented by the economic conditions of scarcity and accumulation, and that it will be conducted beyond the point of subsistence. Labor has to be thought of as worth doing even when no necessity or gratification is in sight. Most of the world's cultures, even some recalcitrant subcultures in the West, reject these premises. They are not self-evidently reasonable premises, but capitalism could not have come about in the form we know without a culture in which they held. Weber argues that they were established through a secular extension of Protestant asceticism as an understanding of labor and profit. The essential point, leaving room for a good deal of historical variation, is that capitalism does not just produce a cultural rhetoric of self-relation; it *is* a cultural rhetoric of self-relation. But it is a problematic one. Where the value structure of Protestantism initially enabled an economic ascesis to be vocational and redemptive, by the middle of the nineteenth century that same ascetic self-relation, now secularized, had become, in Weber's famous phrase, an iron cage. "Men labor," as Thoreau puts it, "under a mistake" (5).

Given the context of liberal market culture, Thoreau's remodeled ascesis necessarily addresses economic questions because the economy presupposes ascesis. He frequently makes the connection in the most explicit way possible; the project of defining the "necessaries" that might give purpose to labor is less a blind essentialism than an attempt to insert labor into another economy, one that would no longer presuppose self-renunciation. Even when the context is not explicitly economic, Thoreau's wish for a resensualizing purification engages the ascetic self-relation of capitalism. In "Higher Laws," the chapter that more than any other gives expression to Christian asceticism, Thoreau indicates the extent to which he has refunctioned it.

He concludes the chapter by presenting us with an allegorical farmer named "John Farmer."

> John Farmer sat at his door one September evening, after a hard day's work, his mind still running on his labor more or less. Having bathed he sat down to recreate his intellectual man . . . A voice said to him,—Why do you stay here and live this mean moiling life, when a glorious existence is possible for you? Those same stars twinkle over other fields than these.— But how to come out of this condition and actually migrate thither? All that he could think of was to practise some new austerity, to let his mind descend into his body and redeem it, and treat himself with ever increasing respect.

Farmer Farmer wants a more contemplative life and a better bathed body, a sensual utopia for the entire personality. This utopia lies beyond "moiling," the orientation to surplus labor. It is a wish to undo the ascetic self-relation without which the notion of a self-regulating market society (in itself utopian) would be inconceivable. With an exceptional clarity, however, the passage shows that the post-renunciatory utopia will have an asceticism of its own, "a new austerity." The phrase may appear paradoxical, since Christian austerity is the opposite of the luxuriating pleasure that Farmer wants. But Thoreau imagines that this austerity will "descend into his body," economically redeeming it from its economy.

Thoreau describes a counter-austerity that resists the economic premises of labor even while it remains based on the ascesis of those economic premises. In the journal passage, where Thoreau also imagines a purifying austerity that would redeem his body and make it supple, he calls his model "the silent economy of nature." The term is hardly an accident. Thoreau sometimes uses "economy" simply to mean cheapness, but the word in this context implies more of political economy. It has the sense of a self-regulating system. Nature is a silent economy because it integrates itself through the counteracting functioning of its parts, like supply and demand. Even its disruptions, such as winter, serve a function and cannot violate Nature's integrity. Nature has no waste, no surplus that it cannot reinvest. When Thoreau says he loves the silent economy of Nature, he indicates that he wants to contemplate himself entirely, without encountering parts of himself that he cannot enjoy—in other words, without waste. The silent economy of nature, like his ascetic attitude in general, stands both for his desire to integrate himself as an object of contemplation and for the apparently contradictory desire to take pleasure in his waste, filth, and impurity. The dialectic of self-integration and self-dissolution can be summed up in two economic imperatives: have no waste; enjoy your waste. For this reason the journal passage suggests that the seasonal pattern of *Walden* represents not so much the mythic return that criticism used to celebrate so tiresomely, but rather the double movement of Thoreau's ascetics. *Walden*, after all, does not move from summer to spring. It moves from "Economy" to concluding images of flooding and metamorphosis, from the imperative of having no waste to the imperative of enjoying one's waste.

The same contradictory imperatives appear whenever Thoreau speaks more recognizably of sex. In one journal entry, he is led onto the subject of sex by describing the sight of an ideal woodchopper. "I could not behold him as an actual man; he was more ideal than in any picture I have seen. He refused to be seen as actual." From this vision of purity, an ascetic refusal, Thoreau immediately moves to a discussion of impure actuality and its refuse:

Nature allows of no universal secrets. The more carefully a secret is kept on one side of the globe, the larger the type it is printed in on the other. Nothing is too pointed, too personal, too immodest, for her to blazon. The relations of sex, transferred to flowers, become the study of ladies in the drawing-room. While men wear fig leaves, she grows the *Phallus impudicus* and *P. caninus* and other phallus-like fungi.

The rhymes which I used to see on the walls of privies, scribbled by boys, I have lately seen, word for word the same; in spite [of] whitewash and brick walls and admonitions they survive. They are no doubt older than Orpheus, and have come down from an antiquity as remote as mythology or fable. So, too, no doubt corporations have ever struggled in vain to obtain cleanliness in those provinces. Filth and impurity are as old as cleanliness and purity. To correspond to man completely, Nature is perhaps unchaste herself. Or perchance man's impurity begets a monster somewhere, to proclaim his sin. (January 30, 1852; III:254–55)

Here again, what Thoreau admires in nature is its economy. In the earlier passage, nature was purging filth. Here it produces filth. In both cases, what really drowns his muskrats is the economy of the operation. It enables him to see filth as something other than waste. Purity and impurity are coeval.

The peculiar tensions of the passage come from its axiomatic contradictions. Thoreau on one level thinks through the polar opposition of purity and impurity. The woodchopper had been attractive insofar as he was a chaste image of the purely ideal. And even in this passage Thoreau displays some anxiety about the impure, the monster begotten somewhere to indicate man's sin. He seems to advocate not an enlarged indulgence but a more sincere chastity. But by imagining the polarity dissolved in nature's economy, he anticipates enjoying pure and impure equally. The woodchopper's carnality, the man behind the fig leaf, displaced into outhouse graffiti and fungi, can be libidinally recuperated by anticipation, as the graffiti can be recuperated in the form of Orphic myth. Have no waste. Enjoy your waste. Thoreau reconciles these imperatives only in the perverseness of his economy. In order to enjoy your waste you must have no waste. In order to have no waste you must enjoy your waste.

In *Walden,* it is *the* economy that interferes with economy. An economically interested relation to the world makes waste. Sensationally alluring waste, to judge from a passage that occurs just after the Narcissus-like passages with which I began, in which Thoreau addresses the reflections of Walden pond. Walden, Thoreau says, "has acquired such wonderful purity, who would not regret that the comparatively impure waters of Flint's Pond should be mingled with it, or itself should ever go to waste its sweetness in the ocean wave?" The imperative to have no waste once again holds sway. Purity is threatened, very much in the paranoid manner, by mingling with an impurity in the neighborhood. Thoreau's self-contemplation in the face of Walden, implying a wasteless integration, thus leads to the horror of mingling waste, here luridly represented in Farmer Flint. "*Flint's Pond!* Such is the poverty of our nomenclature. What right had the unclean and stupid farmer, whose farm abutted on this sky water, whose shores he has ruthlessly laid bare,to give his name to it?"

The passage typifies Thoreau's critique of capitalism. It does not proceed in the register of political economy. The picture of Farmer Flint develops an economic critique only in its description of his self-relation. Thoreau says almost nothing, here or elsewhere, about the principles of a market economy. He says a great deal, however, about Flint's person and his waste. Flint is "unclean."

Some skin-flint, who loved better the reflecting surface of a dollar, or a bright cent, in which he could see his own brazen face; . . . who never *saw* it, who never bathed in it, who never loved it . . . who could show no title to it but the deed which a like-minded neighbor or legislature gave him,—him who thought only of its money value . . . —and would have drained and sold it for the mud at its bottom. It did not turn his mill, and it was no privilege to him to behold it. I respect not his labors, his farm where every thing has its price; who would carry the landscape,who would carry his God, to market, if he could get any thing for him; who goes to market *for* his god as it is; on whose farm nothing grows free, whose fields bear no crops, whose meadows no flowers, whose trees no fruits, but dollars; who loves not the beauty of his fruits, whose fruits are not ripe for him till they are turned to dollars. Give me the poverty that enjoys true wealth.

At first glance one might suppose that Thoreau criticizes dollars, or a monetary economy, or wealth, or greed. But the fundamental criticism is that Flint instrumentalizes his body. Where Thoreau looked for his own image in the pond's reflective surface, Flint looks for his in the dollar's reflective surface. The difference is that Thoreau adopts a posture of contemplative enjoyment toward both image and world, while Flint adopts an instrumental posture of self-interest toward image and world. Thoreau hopes to discover the unwilled character of his image; Flint wills the extension of his manipulated image into the world, to the point of naming the pond after himself. He wants his money to make him a mucky-muck. In an Ovidian manner his image magically betrays him. His person becomes subject to his own image and name, his fingers fixing in their instrumental grasp, his skin turning flint.

Flint cannot recuperate the useless world, the mud on the lake's bottom. It becomes waste because it gives Flint no pleasure. His farm begins to look only like waste, a muck-heap.

> A model farm! where the house stands like a fungus in a muck-heap, chambers for men, horses, oxen, and swine, cleansed and uncleansed, all contiguous to one another! Stocked with men! A great grease-spot, redolent of manures and buttermilk! Under a high state of cultivation, being manured with the hearts and brains of men! (195–97).

Like the pond, Flint has a uselessly and unpleasantly muddy bottom. (There may, by the way, be a buried image of sodomy here in the image of the fungus in the muck-heap; the connection between phallus-like fungi and privies appears consistently in Thoreau.) Flint's farm, in a typically inconspicuous pun, is said to have "abutted" the pond. This imagery of muck typifies Thoreau's treatment of anyone immersed in an economy. In the "Baker Farm" chapter, he describes yet another allegorical farmer, an Irishman named John Field, trapped in the cycle of production and consumption: "when he had worked hard he had to eat hard again to repair the waste of his system." That waste becomes stereotypically metaphorized in endless references to the Irishman's "boggy ways," "bog-trotting feet" (208–9). He becomes his bog. "The culture of an Irishman is an enterprise to be undertaken with a sort of moral bog hoe" (205–6). Despite the nationalist slur here, the problem, for Farmer Field as well as for Farmer Flint, is not much itself but the economic orientation that determines it as waste. Muck is the subject all the same; indeed, the point to be made about these passages is that they are simultaneously about the economy and anality. By way of contrast, Thoreau says of himself that he has "enhanced the value of the land by squatting on it" (64). Again, "I put no manure on this land, not being the owner, but merely a squatter" (54). Ours, he says in the journal, should be no "wiped virtue" (December 31, 1840; 1:214).

One could easily imagine that Thoreau criticizes Flint for having an instrumental relation to nature. But an instrumental relation to nature is at some level always a part of culture, and Thoreau has more to say about Flint than that he farms. Like other Concord farmers of the 1840s he was now farming in a market context. He therefore instrumentalizes not just the landscape, but himself. He does not simply manipulate nature, he manipulates nature out of a rational (universalizing, rule-governed) conception of self-interest. When he looks for his image in the surface of the dollar he betrays not an excessive narcissism, but a narcissism falsely limited by a market-mediated notion of self-interest. That is why Thoreau does not detail the farm's ecology. The farm figuratively metamorphoses into shit, but this is not a literal description of poor land use. It dramatizes Flint's unpleasurable self-relation. Flint fails to love the pond, does not bathe in it, does not see himself in it, does not taste his fruit, does not register the sublime of beholding, does not enjoy true wealth. Flint has waste because he cannot enjoy it.

The passage is therefore rhetorically paradoxical. It condemns Flint *as* waste because for Flint the world is waste. The rhetoric of the passage implies a desire to have no waste, no contiguity between men and excrement. At the same time, it argues for the recuperation of waste in an economy of contemplative pleasure. The playing out of these contradictory imperatives, however, helps to establish silently one of the main rhetorical effects not only of this passage but of *Walden* in general: a complete collapse of economic critique with a critique of sensual self-relation. It is possible to speak of Thoreau's erotic economy without analytically confusing these registers because in Thoreau they are identical. The articulated identity of these two registers, political economy and sensual self-relation, is what allows Thoreau's erotics to have a critical and utopian content.

In the passage about Flint, the identity of the economy and the body takes a form familiar to readers of Freud in the equation of money and shit. Flint's dollars turn to shit before our eyes. Freud accounts for the equation by explaining that a child understands its eliminations as gifts. Urine and shit are the occasions on which children encounter and understand the cultural meanings of saving, eliminating, purging, wasting, and hoarding. Although such terms get their primary associations from the body's eliminations and integration, the cultural meanings of a monetary economy will be learned in the same terms. Money retains anality's pleasure. Upon discovering the association of money and feces, Freud writes to Fliess, "I can scarcely enumerate for you all the things that I (a modern Midas) turn into—excrement."[6] His parenthesis says everything. A Midas who turns everything into gold deprives it of its value. It becomes equivalent to waste, since gold and waste get their respective valences only by virtue of the axiomatic economic condition of scarcity. Gold is gold only if other things are waste.

The elimination that separates waste from value means that waste is defined as surplus. If waste can be recuperated by an economy, it is only in the form of surplus, like Midas's uncontrollable proliferations. In Thoreau, the term that replaces waste is luxury. Within the economy, when Thoreau values purity, luxury appears as waste. He distinguishes precisely between economic necessity and luxury (9). He repeatedly uses "luxurious" as a synonym for "dissipated," and writes that one who "resigned himself" to the "luxurious" would soon be "completely emasculated" (36-37, 100). Luxury, he thinks, "enervates and destroys nations" (15). Luxury, defined as economic surplus, must be devalued and eliminated. By the same token, however, eliminations can be revalued as luxury. Thoreau consistently describes manured growth and the vegetation around privies as luxurious. In "Spring" he writes that the "excrementitious" oozing of the sandbank is "more exhilarating . . . than the luxuriance and fertility of vineyards." And the conclusion of "The Ponds," just after the passage about Flint's muck-heap, asks "what youth or maiden conspires with the wild luxuriant beauty of Nature?" (200). Economy allows Thoreau to turn gold, as waste, into shit; but it also allows him to turn shit, as surplus, into gold. The longing to revalue the waste of his body is what he has in mind when he imagines "mining" for gold: "My instinct tells me that my head is an organ for burrowing, as some creatures use their snout and forepaws, and with it I would mine and burrow my way through these hills. I think that the righest vein is somewhere hereabouts; so by the divining rod and thin rising vapors I judge; and here I will begin to mine" (98).

Nothing in Freud's remarks about money and excrement, however, would prepare us for the importance that a bodily economy has for Thoreau. Unlike the peasant folklore documented by Freud, *Walden* imagines that one's entire person must be subject to the logic of saving and wasting. It isn't just our money that might turn to shit. It's ourselves. "We are made the very sewers,the cloacae, of nature," Thoreau writes in his journal (May 12, 1850; II:9). In the "Higher Laws" chapter he writes, "I fear that we are such gods or demigods only as fauns or satyrs, the divine allied to beasts, the creatures of appetite, and that, to some extent, our very life is our disgrace" (220). In such moments Thoreau's economy resembles a familiar Christian ascetics of self-renunciation. Certainly it is the context of an ascetic self-relation that the poetics of impurity and waste have such extensive significance for Thoreau. But his economy has another side, entirely alien to the Christian ascetic tradition, in which the entire person can be revalued as excrementitious surplus. "What is man but a mass of thawing clay?" he asks in the famous passage about the fecal sandbank. Even in this utopian, luxuriating recuperation, the entire individual is subject to the economy of his ascesis. The economic operations of waste and surplus form more than a moment in the vicissitudes of the body, as they do for the Wolf-Man and Freud's peasants. They become the organizing principles of

Thoreau's erotics. His economy of self-integration and self-dissolution refers not just to flashes of lust, but to subjective experience in its entirety.

Thoreau brings to unbearable intensity a contradiction in the bourgeois subject that Barthes identifies in Werther:

> In Werther, at a certain moment, two economies are opposed. On the one hand, there is the young lover who lavishes his time, his faculties, his fortune without counting the cost; on the other, there is the philistine (the petty official) who moralizes to him: "Parcel out your time . . . Calculate your fortune," etc. On the one hand, there is the lover Werther who expends his love every day, without any sense of saving or of compensation, and on the other, there is the husband Albert, who economizes his goods, his happiness. On the one hand, a bourgeois economy of repletion; on the other, a perverse economy of dispersion, of waste, of frenzy (*furor wertherinus*).[7]

"A perverse economy of dispersion, of waste"—it could hardly have been said better. This, too, is a bourgeois economy, insofar as its very perverseness is owing to the other economy. The appeal of Werther, even to himself, depends on that monitory voice that marvels: "without any sense of saving or of compensation." Bourgeois life structurally isolates one realm from the other, placing an amnesia between all experience of the expense codified in the discourse of love and the inevitable, even quotidian return the self-regulation of the labor economy. The dispersion and waste of bourgeois love become merely compensatory. Thoreau says that the same is true of bourgeois art: "The best works of art are the expression of man's struggle to free himself from this condition [i.e., being the tools of our tools], but the effect of our art is merely to make this low state comfortable and that higher state to be forgotten" (37).

Thoreau's project consists of bringing to mind the full force of the contradiction between these two economies of ascesis and waste. The project of making that contradiction critical rather than compensatory remains paradoxical if not perverse, and I do not wish to normalize it in order to validate it as "critique," still less as redemption. A recuperative ascetics, though luxurious, would still be a purifying ascetics, leading John Farmer to "treat himself with respect." That phrase captures the dual movement of Thoreau's economy, since "respect" implies an unwilled reception of oneself, while the verb "treat" insists on a self-dividing, morally willed objectification. Only a self-alienated individual can treat himself with respect. The self-relation in this phrase finds its ideal image in Thoreau's Narcissus-like posture as the beholder of his own purifying reflection.

The need to have this relation to oneself appears as well from within the cultural history of capitalism. Social historians have emphasized the importance, in the decades spanned by Thoreau's career, of the rapid specialization of labor in a market context. Regardless of whether one labored for a wage or a salary, males at least no longer came by an economic role in the traditional manner. It became necessary for men to sell their services on the market for a role with which they did not fully identify. Identification with one's own labor was all the more difficult given the marked separation of the economic sphere from the home, since this meant that personal life was by definition separate from occupation. Men still had an occupational identity, and the now autonomous sphere of personal life promised a self-integration of its own. But the nonintegration of these two spheres is presupposed by the liberal market, which exists only if labor—manual and nonmanual alike—can be treated as a commodity. These changes took place at varying rates from the 1820s onward, but there is no doubt that Thoreau found in his economic context a relation to his own image that was simultaneously invested and alienated, anxious and anticipatory.[8] "All men want, not something to *do with*," he writes in "Economy," but something to *do,* or rather something to *be*" (23).

In 1847 Thoreau received a letter from the secretary of his class at Harvard, who was planning a tenth anniversary reunion and wanted a self-description from Thoreau. Thoreau wrote back:

I am not married. I dont know whether mine is a profession, or a trade, or what not . . . It is not one but legion, I will give you some of the monster's heads. I am a Schoolmaster—a private Tutor, a Surveyor—a Gardener, a Farmer—a Painter, I mean a House Painter, a Carpenter, a Mason, a Day-Laborer, a Pencil-Maker, a Glass-paper Maker, a Writer, and sometimes a Poetaster.[9]

The letter turns on Thoreau's nonidentity with himself—more precisely, a nonidentity between his personal self and his labor. That relation of nonidentity, far from being peculiar to Thoreau, is the disposition that enabled a liberal market society. It allows his labor to be a market commodity—a problem only more acute for the new middle class of nonmanual labor since the labor in question involved the entire personality. Thoreau's desire to contemplate his integrated self resists the instrumentalization implied by each of his occupational categories. At the same time, however, it reproduces the fundamental reflective relation to the ego that makes it possible to instrumentalize occupation in a market in the first place. He wants to treat himself with respect, but he still wants to treat himself. When he says "Walden, is it you?" he reimagines this instrumental self-relation of the market as contemplative. But it is still alienated and desirous. The subject who treats himself with respect is also the subject who can say, "I can almost say . . . "

The alienated but invested nature of this self-reflection makes it potentially erotic, overdetermining erotic self-relations, much as adolescence, which was emerging as a cultural phenomenon in this period, is understood as a period of sexual awakening, but is just as importantly a period of self-objectification in a context of voluntary association and career choice. In Thoreau's case, anxieties of self-integration occasion an erotics that can be not only narcissistically reflective but feminizing. In his letter to the class secretary listing his "monster's heads" Thoreau adds, somewhat flirtatiously, "If you will act the part of Iolas, and apply a hot iron to any of these heads, I shall be greatly obliged to you." He then worked this image into the third paragraph of *Walden,* where we learn that none of Thoreau's male contemporaries ever "slew or captured any monster or finished any labor. They have no friend Iolas to burn with a hot iron the root of the hydra's head, but as soon as one head is crushed, two spring up" (4–5). What isn't visible in the *Walden* version is that the hydra is oneself. We are hardly accustomed to think of Iolas and the hydra as bosom buddies, enacting through their scorching reciprocity an ascetic self-integration that will also allow a crushing self-dissolution. But that is the relation that Thoreau desires between men.

Integrating the ego had become normative for market culture, and only against the strength of this imperative does erotics come to be understood as self-dissolving. If the dissolution and waste of erotics is understood as feminizing for Thoreau because it undoes the ascesis of his self-regard, he can only imagine dissolution through a perverse economy in which that self-regard is maintained. In the following journal passage, he describes a visit from some reformers whose intimacy violates the asceticism of his self-regard. Their waste clearly threatens Thoreau, making him very nearly delirious:

They would not keep their distance, but cuddle up and lie spoon-fashion with you, no matter how hot the weather nor how narrow the bed. [One] wrote a book called "A Kiss for a Blow," and he behaved as if there were no alternative between these, or as if I had given him a blow. I would have preferred the blow, but he was bent on giving me the kiss, when there was neither quarrel nor agreement between us . . . It was difficult to keep clear of his slimy benignity, with which he sought to cover you before he swallowed you and took you fairly into his bowels.

"Bowels," here, are of course metaphoric for sympathy. But Thoreau literalizes the metaphor with considerable relish: "It would have been far worse than the fate of Jonah." He continues with what is easy to recognize as negation in the Freudian sense:

I do not wish to get any nearer to a man's bowels than usual. They lick you as a cow her calf. They would fain wrap you about with their bowels. [One] addressed me as "Henry" within one minute from the time I first laid eyes on him, and when I spoke, he said with drawling, sultry sympathy, . . . "I am going to dive into Henry's inmost depths." I said, "I trust you will not strike your head against the bottom."

By this point it is unclear who is in whose bowels, and Thoreau virtually acknowledges that he is describing sex when he adds that he prefers the more distant sexual method of the flowers, with their "beautiful reserve": "The truly beautiful and noble puts its lover, as it were, at an infinite distance, while it attracts him more strongly than ever." Thoreau wants a lover's regard to provide him with that integrating purity. But he still hasn't stopped thinking about those bowels. "I do not like the men who come so near me with their bowels. It is the most disagreeable kind of snare to be caught in. Men's bowels are far more slimy than their brains." And as though to anticipate my argument he concludes: "They must be ascetics indeed who approach you by this side" (June 17, 1853; V:264–65). Although Thoreau's ascetics outfits him with his wish to be immaculated beneath his skirts by another man, and although it provides him with the recuperative ideal of taking pleasure in waste and dissolution, the same ascetics makes it unthinkable that the other man would do anything other than integrate his image through recognition. His interest in these rectally aggressive men is greater, but he abhors them for exactly the same reason he abhors women. Their sympathetic identification violates the ascetic self-regard that he has taken over from market-mediated individuality.

Sympathy is economic trouble. "From the experience of late years," he writes in the year of Walden's publication, "I should say that a man's seed was the direct tax of his race. It stands for my sympathy with my race. When the brain chiefly is nourished, and not the affections, the seed becomes merely excremental" (VI:283; August 28, 1854). G.J. Barker-Benfield has shown that this economic thinking about individual boundaries and sperm spillage was common in Thoreau's America.[10] But the sperm/excrement equation, "merely excremental," is more typical of him. In "Higher Laws" he writes, "The generative energy, which, when we are loose, dissipates and makes us unclean, when we are continent invigorates and inspires us" (219).

Sex, for him, would have to be an ascetic self-relation that could recuperate waste, luxuriate in surplus. "The great art of life is how to turn the surplus life of the soul into life for the body . . . You must get your living by loving" (March 13, 1853; V:19). In formulations such as these, based in a market-mediated technique of economic self-relation, Thoreau's erotics takes on its new utopian importance. It now has the character of a demand for a transformed individuality, a transformed society. And it marks a turn away from both production and reproductive sex. That is why several of the chapters of *Walden,* including its "Conclusion," end with images of parthenogenesis. Erotics stands for an unrealized liberation from the productive economic orientation, a promise that comes through the paired themes of narcissistic reflection and luxurious anality.

I stress these transformations of Christian asceticism—leading simultaneously to narcissistic reflection, anality, and economic critique—in order to note that Thoreau's critical-utopian impulses come from within the cultural history of capitalism itself. It used to be thought that the valuable part of Thoreau had nothing to do with capitalism; it was his "fable of renewal," imagined in transhistorical terms.[11] In recent years Thoreau's reputation has risen and fallen according to whether or not he is seen as a successful critic of capitalism.[12] Either way, I would say, our criticism labors under a mistake. It is child's play to show the limits of Thoreau's critique. His social criticism cannot be said to employ even what would have been for the time an advanced understanding of social-economic systems. But we do not need to think of capitalism as having a bad inside and a good outside. We do not need nonhistorical reference points—like objective sociological knowledge, the intrinsic dynamics of sexuality, or humanistic values—in order to see a useful critical and utopian project in Thoreau's writing. Through his counter-austerity, an ascetics both inside and outside of capitalism, Thoreau imagines a utopia at once erotic and economic. More accurately, it is an economic utopia precisely because it is erotic, even because it is perversely erotic. And although consumer culture addresses itself to many of the same utopian longings I have described here, promising all of us a uniquely valuable subjectivity, limitless self-formation and non-ascetic pleasures, the perverseness of Thoreau's erotic economy is still ours and likely to remain so.

NOTES

1. *Eros and Civilization* (Boston: Beacon Press, 1966), 201. Further references to this edition will be parenthetical.

2. *Consciousness in Concord* (Cambridge: Harvard Univ. Press, 1958), chapter 7, passim. On the general subject of Thoreau's sexual biography, see Walter Harding, *The Days of Henry Thoreau* (New York: Dover, 1982); and Harding, "Thoreau and Eros," Raymond Gozzi, ed., *Thoreau's Psychology* (Lanham MD: University Press of America, 1983).

3. Thoreau, *Journal,* ed. Elizabeth Hall Witherell (Princeton: Princeton University Press, 1981–), 1:190 (October 17, 1840). Further references to Thoreau's journal will use arabic volume numbers for the Princeton edition. For material not yet available in that edition, roman volume numbers will be used, indicating the edition by Torrey Bradford and Francis Allen (Boston: Houghton Mifflin, 1906). All citations will be parenthetical.

4. The popular biography is Robert Richardson, *Henry Thoreau: A Life of the Mind* (Berkeley: University of California Press, 1986), which was moderately well-reviewed even though it reproduces a long-discredited myth about Ellen Sewall, while not dealing with any

of the questions raised by Jonathan Katz in *Gay American History* (New York: Crowell, 1976). The same objection can be made to Richard Lebeaux's two volumes of psychobiography: *Young Man Thoreau* (Amherst: University of Massachusetts Press, 1977), and *Thoreau's Seasons* (Amherst: University of Massachusetts Press, 1984). A more serious engagement with the questions of Thoreau's sexuality is made by Harding, "Thoreau and Eros," above.

5. *Walden,* ed. J. Lyndon Shanley (Princeton: Princeton Univ. Press, 1973), 186. Further references will be to this edition.

6. Letter to Wilhelm Fliess, December 22, 1897, in the Standard Edition, 1:273.

7. Roland Barthes, *A Lover's Discourse,* trans. Richard Howard (New York: Hill and Wang, 1978):84–85.

8. The literature on this subject is vast and well known, and my use of it here is intentionally broad. Two recent studies give useful overviews of the problems: Stephanie Coontz, *The Social Origins of Private Life* (London: Verso, 1988); and Stuart Blumin, *The Emergence of the Middle Class* (Cambridge: Cambridge University Press, 1989). The clearest statement of the theoretical issues of "personal life" involved in this history is Eli Zaretsky, *Capitalism, the Family, and Personal Life* (New York: Harper and Row, 1976).

9. Harding, *Days of Henry Thoreau,* 220.

10. G.J.Barker-Benfield, The Horrors of the Half-Known Life (New York: Harper and Row, 1976).

11. See for example Sherman Paul, *The Shores of America* (1958; repr. Urbana: University of Illinois Press, 1972); or, for a different version of the same assumptions, Stanley Cavell, *The senses of Walden* (New York: Viking, 1974).

12. Michael T. Gilmore, *American Romanticism and the Marketplace* (Chicago: University of Chicago Press, 1985); Leonard Neufeldt, *The Economist* (New York: Oxford University Press, 1989).

9.
Fear of Federasty: Québec's Inverted Fictions
ROBERT SCHWARTZWALD

Near the end of Denys Arcand's film, *Le Déclin de l'empire américain,* the viewer is situated on the shore of a placid lake, gazing across it toward an apocalyptically scarlet sun while a voiceover enumerates the telltale symptoms of imperial decay: a population that has contempt for its own institutions, a plummeting birth rate, a national debt that is out of control. And although the red-hued landscape may itself be taken as portentous of thermonuclear destruction, there is also something of import in the gaze which, heightened by the presence of linguistic difference, is not in the first instance that of someone within the Empire to which the title refers, but rather of someone on its margins. This situation may not be easily apparent to an American viewer, but it is undoubtedly crucial to understanding the particular derision which Arcand heaps upon his characters. For not only do they illustrate the very decadence that is at issue—and in this sense they are merely stand-ins for us all—but they are doubly diminished for being able to do no better than unwittingly participate in an inconsequential *ersatz* that stands in an essentially imitative relation to the Empire itself. Their sexual and political banter is just that, dissolved into a harmless "tongue in cheek" that authorizes the viewer to relax and enjoy what is finally impotent *commentary.*[1]

From what may be termed an "updated" anti-colonial perspective, Arcand's film brings severe judgment to bear on the fruits, both generational and material, of Québec's rapid process of modernization over the past three decades. And because *Le Déclin* has been widely shown and reviewed in the United States, it is perhaps a particularly appropriate place to begin a presentation on the sexual anxiety embedded in even the most radical discourses of Québécois anti-colonialism. I wish to explore these discourses today precisely because they are so exemplary of a rhetorical strategy that has been profoundly liberatory and yet, built on the very terrain of modernist preoccupations about subjectification, convey the tragic resiliency of homophobic tropes and their consequences.

But before continuing, I want to propose some of my own connections of place and time between the United States and Québec, among the first sites of European settlement in the Americas and yet little more than a blank slate to most of the population of this country. This is more than a little ironic, since New England and New York once lived in terror of the expeditions launched from New France. There are the somber tablets in Old Deerfield, Massachusetts, memorializing those "carried off to Canada" in revenge for the theft of a bell destined for the Iroquois church at Kahnawake. Almost a century later, bigoted tracts from Boston expressed satisfaction at what was believed to be the imminent eradication of Papism in North America in the wake of the French defeat on the Plains of Abraham in the fall of 1759. The "Conquest," as this episode came to be mythified in Québec, culminated what are known in American history as the "French and Indian Wars"; and "les Anglais," who appropriated the infinite Canadian wilderness, were known more precisely at the time as "les Bostonnais." Arguments over free trade aside, then, Americans do have a military and expansionist relationship to the north, as well as the south of this hemisphere, albeit a frustrated one: American revolutionaries could not understand why the French population of Québec would not join their cause, while their defeated Loyalist adversaries who moved north and demanded their reward from Britain could not understand why the "mother country" did not immediately proceed to forcibly assimilate the French population, or deport it as had been done earlier in Acadia. They would have to wait most of a century before the failed 1837-38 national uprisings against colonial rule—uprisings that cited Bolívar as a hero and received messages of support from the Chartists—led Lord Durham to declare the *Canadiens* to be a "people without a history or a literature," and indeed best assimilated into the great English race. Since then, this assimilation has been resisted, and it would be reasonable to claim that the earliest national histories and fictions of Québec are a direct result of taking up Durham's gauntlet.

But the fact remains that unlike the descendants of the other European colonial powers, the *Canadiens* never achieved sovereignty in the great age of American independences. Those who had explored and "discovered" much of the continental interior for Europe were increasingly excluded from dominion over these territories and confined instead to the St. Lawrence valley. Those of British descent gradually appropriated the appellation "Canada" wholly for themselves and created their hyphenated Other, the "French"-Canadians. In the century of great industrial expansion, these *habitants* became more, not less, rural. With this in mind, perhaps the following quotation will not seem so surprising:

> A society which had been conquered, bypassed by the creative movement of history, one which served only as a labour force for productive structures set up by others, which showed the marks, in impoverished bodies and impoverished spirits, of this exclusion, was a colony. The worthy response of a member of such a society who had awakened to his situation was anti-colonial revolution. (Reid, 1972, 22)

This is from a book published in New York by Monthly Review Press. The year is 1972, and yet the subject is not Africa, Vietnam, nor even the struggle of American Blacks. In *The Shouting Signpainters,* Malcolm Reid is offering instead a "literary and political account of *Québec* revolutionary nationalism." Ten years earlier, the English-Canadian poet Louis Dudek had already written enviously of the intellectual ferment among young francophone intellectuals in Québec: "This is powerful writing, exciting here, not the concocted controversial kind common to English-Canadianism, but passionate debate and persuasion for the sake of justice, for the sake of truth" (1962, 50). Dudek wrote in the full flush of Québec's "Quiet Revolution," a period of all-encompassing modernization in the 1960s and 1970s that laid to rest the century-long ideological representation of Québec as a piously Catholic, agrarian society. The tailspin in both church attendance and religious vocations; the decline of the birth rate in a few years from the highest to the lowest in the developed world; the expansion and taking charge of education, social services, and the development of new sectors of the economy by the State under the slogan *Maîtres chez nous* ("Masters in our own house")—all provided the concrete realizations for a modernity that represented itself as developmental, linear, and ruled by the inexorable laws of progress. But by far the most arresting aspect of this generalized contestation came from a layer of younger writers, who launched a journal called *parti pris,* after Sartre's imperative that in matters of social and political injustice sides must indeed be taken. The journal's motto "Laicism, Socialism, Independence" telescoped the specific tasks of Québec's Quiet Revolution with a social program and a political objective that took its inspiration from the anti-imperialist and anti-colonial struggles of the period: national independence in Africa, revolution in Cuba, and the civil rights movement in the United States. As a corollary, the challenge to English-Canadian anti-imperialists was not only to view Québec as a colonized society, but perhaps even more importantly, to regard the Canadian state and especially the federal government in Ottawa as colonial instruments that actively denied Québec its right to national self-determination.

Parti pris was not only a journal, but a publishing house that brought out novels, essays, and poetry that sought to "demystify" Québec's colonial situation, to provoke their readers into *assuming* their colonized status in order to transcend it politically. In the dialectic that was thus established, the pure modernists of the Quiet Revolution, caught up in their technocratic reveries, were as surely traitors to the nation as the agrarian nationalists who had preceded them, they who had taught the Québécois to be satisfied with a lesser lot in life, to believe that they had been "nés pour un petit pain" ("born for half a loaf").

The discourse elaborated in Québec, beginning with the appropriation of the anti-colonial writings of Sartre, Fanon, Mémmi, Bercque, Guevarra, Malcolm X, and others, came particularly to distinguish itself in literary practice. When, in the late 1970s, Fredric Jameson contended that "the only authentic cultural production today has seemed to be that which can draw on the collective experience of marginal pockets of the social life of the world system," he went on to draw up a list that included not only "black literature and blues, British working-class rock, women's literature, gay literature (. . . and) the literature of the Third World," but also "the *roman québécois*" (1979, 140). In so doing, he certainly exemplified a more generally felt need among Marxist critics to locate fields of literary practice, precisely under the shield of "authenticity," that could be secured from the destabilizing impact of anti-rationalism and the deconstructive methodologies thought to be allied with it. But at the same time, there was a recognition of an affinity between the interrogations enabled by a decolonizing discourse and the terrain of fractured subjectivity privileged in the postmodernist paradigm. How enabling this discourse has been, and how effective the leverage it provides may be best seen by remembering how current it now is for us to speak of the "colonization" of representation, of language, of sexualities. But for the anti-colonial writer, the manifold colonizations we have just listed were ultimately symptomatic and yielded before the primacy of a political moment in which the task was to constitute whole Subjects capable of finding a *way out* of the very fragmentation that constitutes the generative moment of postmodernist thought.

It is this preoccupation with unified subjectivity that led to a profound sexual anxiety in Québec's anti-colonial discourse, an anxiety which is *already* borne within the attempted synthesis of Marxist, existentialist, and Freudian theory that underlies the anti-colonial writings of the post-war period. But the figuration of this anxiety ironically marks what Eve Kosofsky Sedgwick terms "the *special* centrality of homophobic oppression in the twentieth century (. . .) its inextricability from the question of knowledge and the processes of knowing in modern Western culture at large" (1989, 55). How ironic—and instructive—it is that this epistemological heritage persists at the very heart of the anti-colonial imperative to think about subjectification outside the paradigm bequeathed by imperialism.

In Québec, this homophobic sexual anxiety accompanies a new nationalist project that wishes to effect a radical break with the conservative "agrarian" and clerically animated nationalism of the past; a nationalist project that is progressive in its social objectives, and that situates itself within the universalizing discourse of all the great anti-colonial movements of the epoch in question. In this anxiety, those found to be traitors or sell-outs to the cause of national revolution are gendered as passive/seductive men. They are illustrative of what Simon Watney demonstrates (1987) to be the radical antimony in homophobic representation of men who are both violated and craftily seductive, men who are first "corrupted," most likely in youth, and who then themselves seek to corrupt. The resiliency of this double-edged homophobic imaging is given form in the person of the *federast,* who appears as the butt (pun intended) of jokes that appear on the last page of *parti pris* under the rubric "Vulgarities." These are not easy to translate, but let me try:

They say there are a million *pédales* in Canada. *Conféderá(s)tion* seems comfortably seated indeed.

parti pris Grand Contest: Complete the following sentence: when a dog sees a rose, he uses his hose; when a federast meets one of his class, he aims for his . . .
(1964, 174)[2]

So original was the term that it stuck, so that in English-Canadian novelist Scott Symon's *Place d' Armes,* his perverse literary gift to his country in 1967, on the one hundredth anniversary of its Confederation (or Conféděra(s)tation, as the *partipristes* called it), it is repeated: "Better by far to be a Pédéraste than a 'fédéraste' " (in Martin, 1977, 30). In Symon's version, as Robert K. Martin points out, "fédérastes" are "pédérastes-manqués" (Ibid., 30): "the gelded Canadian who makes a career out of his self-castration in the Ottawa Pork Barrel." But Symon's facile derision is that of the outsider looking in; in the "jokes" of the *partipristes,* on the other hand, we can identify the main elements of a homosexual panic[3] that constitutes a significant undercurrent of intellectual discourse about decolonization in Québec: Québécois who function within the federalist framework are first the victims, and then the corrupted perpetrators of what is figured as a permanent violation by a salacious "fully grown" Canada against the waifish, innocent Québec. "Pédéraste," the word used to signify homosexuality, is not usually used in Québec, and, thus, its foreignness as a continental French signifier for homosexuality underlines the "exotic" or unrooted personality of the traitor/violator; the activity to which federasts give themselves over is compulsive, repetitious, and unproductive.

Now, what is particularly striking about these "vulgarities" is that Québec is, by any conventional standards, a very non-homophobic society. Québec was the first state jurisdiction in North America to adopt antidiscrimination legislation on grounds of sexual orientation, and this was done by the *nationalist* Parti Québécois government committed to sovereignty-association, a form of national independence. Far from stigmatizing gays as emblematic of "national alienation," the government spoke of wanting to protect and further the interests of all communities in an inclusive figuration of the nation. Therefore, received ideas about the disciplinary and necessarily exclusionary aspects of nationalist ideology cannot be applied in unmediated fashion, nor can glib references to a Catholic heritage explain homophobic imaging along the lines of a "repressive" thesis. In popular culture, homosexuality has served as an accepted metaphor for national oppression and continues to do so. For example, Michel Tremblay's early plays, in which Montréal's "Main" or tenderloin of drag queens and prostitutes alternates with the kitchens of lower working-class neighborhoods as sites for exploring the fears, insecurities, and damage wrought to the colonized psyche, are enduring popular successes. Yet Tremblay's work is not always enthusiastically received by critics and pretenders to high literature. Some have seen his use of *joual,* the French spoken in working-class neighborhoods of Montréal, as a desecration of the stage. But even other more "progressive" nationalists who defended *joual* regarded the popularity of these plays with alarm. When asked why there were no male characters in his plays, Tremblay responded "Because there *are* no men in Québec," and this is perhaps the statement that best represents the provocation to which many a revolutionary nationalist, but not Tremblay himself, felt compelled to respond.

For them, as we shall see, homosexuality signifies metonymically, in the guise of "authorized difference," to use Homi Bhabba's term (1984), that is, as the *presence* of an earlier intellectual élite composed of or tied to the clergy that entered into a compact with Anglo-Canadian capital to divide supervision over the colonized body of the Québécois; and then as a sign of the *absence* of an adequate relationship between the new generation of intellectuals and the people. Thus, the "people" are enlisted through projection as the source for the condemnation of the supposed lack of virility of traditionally nationalist intellectuals who, in turn, are culpabilized as the perpetrators of the people's continued alienation and "false consciousness."[4] However, in the wake of the defeat of the referendum on sovereignty-association in 1980, even more recent interventions that offer sophisticated critiques of this discourse demonstrate the resiliency of the tropes of homophobia. In a highly productive adaptation of Lacan, for example, essayist Jean Larose writes from the perspective of a nationalist intellectual wanting to insist upon the specificity and pertinence of intellectual theorization. Lamenting above all the collapse of a space for the elaboration of the Symbolic, a space properly belonging to "clerks" in the most generic sense of the term, Larose sees the collapse of the national independence project elaborated through the 1960s and 1970s as the occasion for the return of a rabid anti-intellectualism that thrives between the twin poles of an unmediated political Real and a cultural Imaginary that is increasingly a fantastic series of imagings bought from North American consumer culture. Québécois are the "passives" of their own discourse, he says, passionate about their passivity, and thus hystericized to the point where reflexion collapses in on itself: it's all "just for laughs," not to be taken seriously, a stance which immediately becomes figured through the association of homosexuality and imitation. Trying to account for the popularity of a Québec TV sitcom that features a homosexual hairdresser, Larose offers this junction as an explanation for an audience's unwitting self-deprecation: "Between the false and the true, the vulvic cavern gapes open, but just as a joke, for the anus is a joke vulva, not for real" (Ibid., 92–93).[5]

I now want to return to Arcand's film as a first site to explore this discourse of "phallo-national maturity." The film takes as its subject the intellectual petit-bourgeoisie that has benefitted from the educational reforms of the Quiet Revolution. In this highest grossing film of all time in Québec, the viewing public may be flattered to see not only the evidence of its own liberation from clerical discourse (here sex is spoken about at the top of one's voice), but also from the misery of a second-class existence. If many of my American colleagues were shocked to learn that the greatest success in the history of Québec cinema was a film about *professors,* this is because the gap between "ordinary people" and "intellectuals" in the United States is so established as to appear unbridgeable. But there are many Québécois of working-class origin who have a son or daughter, brother or sister or cousin who became part of the great secular corps of educators recruited in the 1960s and early 1970s. In Québec, one is still able to share in the major victories of social mobility garnered by one's friends and relatives to the extent that the entire society had gone through such a process in the post-war period. This complicity, Arcand seems to be suggesting, may be fatal.

With this in mind, I want to focus on a little-discussed aspect of the film, the representation of the gay character Claude. Although he may appear familiar as a gay icon to American audiences by virtue of his unbridled enthusiasm for cruising, his frank endorsement of sex with multiple partners, and especially because of the cloud of fatal illness that hangs over him, he is *precisely* for these reasons an unprecedented representation of a gay man in Québec cultural production. For although homosexuality, AIDS, and "promiscuity" have been repeatedly soldered and served up in this country, the fact is that contemporary representations of gay men in Québécois novels, television programs, and film by and large continue *not* to employ such figures.

A few examples from only the last couple of years: The television drama *Salut Victor!,* in which two elderly homosexual men meet in a comfortable retirement home, one helping the other recast his view of his erotic life from that of a series of private, doomed encounters to one that is openly and joyously assumed; or another television comedy, *Le Grand Jour* by the playwright Michel Tremblay, in which the families of the bride and groom muddle their way through the forgotten rituals of a church wedding under the ruthless condemnation of a video camera while one gay relative's date, a drag queen, is the only one who remembers how to play that old-time favorite, "The Angelus of the Sea." Both these programs have been aired as family viewing in prime time slots. A recent theatrical success has been *Les Feluettes,* a highly baroque historical drama set in a remote resort town where a local priest's fervor to stage Gabriele d'Annunzio's *The Martyrdom of Saint Sebastian* ignites a tale of love, jealousy, and vengeance among his schoolboys. And in Michel Tremblay's novel made into a film for television (also prime time), *Le Coeur découvert,* a middle-aged man sets up a household with a much younger lover and his son from a previous marriage, a son who is freely shared with the lesbian couple downstairs!

In Arcand's *Déclin,* however, viewers will recognize in Claude a typified Yuppie gay male. While the women work out at the gym and talk about sex, he enthusiastically leads the other men in preparing the evening's gourmet meal while they all . . . talk about sex. Indeed, the straight men seem anxious to include Claude in the conversation and use him as a willing foil for their derisive descriptions of female anatomy, bodily secretions, and scents. Under the signifier of decline, the heterosexual men in the kitchen are represented as *moving toward* Claude, engaging in a rapprochement in which the gender continuum has been tilted and the men sent rolling headlong down it toward him. Not that they want to sleep with each other or with other men; his ability to desire freely is what they covet, but if they only knew . . . if they only knew that he is pissing blood. It's the women in the entourage who have the right to know this, they whose menstrual blood is, even among these very men, cited as a curse. The gay man sheds blood as well, but in a topos of mimeticism that underscores a fundamental dissymetry; women's blood, a sexual "inconvenience," signifies life, while the blood of he who embodies for the straight men the possibility of limitless sexuality signifies death. This is the first, but far from the last occasion in this discussion where we will see homosexuality invoked as fatal mimicry. Of course, bloody urine is not a symptom of AIDS, although it may be read as a displacement of the fear of penetration and especially of the "bloody anus" reviled as AIDS' lair. In this film where Québécois intellectuals are represented as basking smugly in their "American lifestyle," it is charged with mortal signification as surely as Claude's never-articulated diagnosis becomes all the more ineluctable.

In one sense, the *Déclin* may be read as an *à rebours* restatement of the subject position of the modern Québec intellectual operating within the discourse of decolonization. Marc Henry Soulet has insightfully spoken about how, among this generation, "the motive of service is supported by an exacerbated sense of duty (. . .) What is foundational about the intellectual is the permanent duty to resolder the Québecois community" (1987, 61).[6] Arcand wants to present us with the portrait of a community united only in its dissolution, in its naive pursuit of individual happiness at the cost of its very propagation. This "missive" comes from a filmmaker who has never hesitated to lecture his audience *and* his colleagues. In the "Portrait du colonisé" issue of *Parti pris* from 1964, Arcand castigated Claude Jutra for the insufficiently exemplary character of his first and autobiographical film *A Tout Prendre*.[7] Arcand is upset that such an obviously promising filmmaker as Jutra cannot seem to bring himself to represent a "normal" heterosexual relationship in a film whose parodic and fractured construction is reminiscent of Godard. There *is* Claude's lover Johanne, the fashion model with no last name, who is disqualified because of her Haitian, i.e. foreign origin; she can only represent the flight of the Québécois man before his obligation to conquer and possess his *own* territory, to be personified in a physical and fruitful union with an indigenous woman. Arcand yearns for the day when "filmmakers will have forgotten their mamas so they can confidently undress the girl next door whose name is Yvette Tremblay or Yolande Beauchemin, in the full light of day, with an angle shot that's well in focus. (From) that moment on, we can think, like Jean Renoir, about having a cinéma that is free and at the same time fiercely national. A cinéma of joy and conquest" (1964, 97).[8]

But it is *this* Claude's avowal of his homosexuality that clearly upsets Arcand the most. The confession of desire for men, made to Johanne and described by Claude as "a source of hope rather than despair," is undoubtedly the most courageous moment of this film from 1963. Yet for Arcand, it cannot signify a true *liberation,* as a stable heterosexual relationship would. Far from marking a rupture with a chronic "infantilism," Claude's confession is assigned the status of a gesture of *revolt,* or antithesis, in the familiar tri-partite dialectic. Claude's coming out is a half measure and receives only the following guarded sanction from Arcand: "The only question is *to what extent* homosexuality is a *solid* sexual activity and in *which* way its practice may be linked to a special form of self-affirmation, once we take into account the overall context of our existence in relation to artistic expression" (Ibid., 97).[9]

Here we have a formulation that, while structured as a sanction for a particular practice, effectively devalorizes it. For, homosexuality would *not* be, "beyond a certain point," a "solid" activity; according to this formulation, it would be corrosive. As for the manner in which it is linked to the question of national affirmation, the formulation is at once impelled in the name of this affirmation to offer a certain tolerance, but only within limits left vague and, therefore, all the more amenable to control. In other words, homosexuality is admitted as a compensation in the face of Québec cinéma's inability to represent heterosexual eroticism without embarrassment, but it remains a deviation, or a "detour" in the truest sense. This essentially political criticism leveled by Arcand against comrade Jutra is augmented by another rhetorical formulation that further minimizes the very concession that has been granted. "There's nothing surprising," he says, "in the fact that the film appears to demand the right to be homosexual. In any case, our literature (. . .) had already made this demand before the last (World) War. There's nothing very new nor very immoral in this" (Ibid., 97).[10] It is true that several Québec pre-war novels do represent homosexuality in a variety of ways, but Arcand's contention is disingenuous because such works have up until recently enjoyed only marginal recognition, while their treatments of homosexuality have often been ignored altogether in whatever scant critical attention they have received. And as we have seen, in Arcand's own work, homosexuality is far from being banalized.[11] Instead, an entire component of the *Déclin's* reflection on the fatuousness of the "progress" realized during the Quiet Revolution is organized around having the audience see that the (straight) men in the film *cannot see* the meaning of their rapprochement with Claude; if women talk more about sex, it's because they still aren't satisfied at what they're finding, because they're faced with men who can't give them "what they want." Thus, the theatricalization of homosexuality in the *Déclin,* whether it be in the overdetermination of the physical symptoms of an illness (where "gay blood" is, in and of itself, emblematic of AIDS and death), or even in the impossibly choreographic representation of cruising on Mount Royal, betrays the silencing gesture behind a repressive tolerance that seems willing to admit the depiction of homosexuality as something "normal." In the 1960s, homosexuality for Arcand only exists in relation to a normative dialectic of ALIENATION-REVOLT-REVOLUTION, in which it is appropriately admissible only at the intermediate stage, as something "in between." In the 1980s, when Revolution and the question of national independence seem off the agenda and the materialism of the Quiet Revolution triumphant, gay men serve as beacons in whose shadows an entire society's dislocation may be discovered.

But this dislocation is not only a moral one, the product of a new middle class led too easily into temptation. Its origins lie much deeper in what the anti-colonial writers of Québec identified as an interrupted—or derailed— Oedipal itinerary. The *partipristes* saw themselves in constant danger of futilely combatting *false fathers,* those thrown up by the colonial situation itself, since the real Father in such a context can never be within the nation, whose very symbolic codes are disrupted and suppressed by the colonizing external authority. The anxiety produced by such a situation leads to the homosexual panic that rereads virtually all previous discursive engagements with national oppression as deceitful half-measures, as failures of manhood. These in turn become embodied in the figure of the homosexual.

At a colloquium on "Literature and French Canadian Society" held in 1964, novelist and essayist Hubert Aquin picked up from the observation of another participant, Michel Van Schendel, that one could see in much contemporary Québec literature "a subtle inversion of love relationships" (in Dumont and Falardeau, 1964, 165). Aquin agreed that this reflected "the particular conditions of colonization in Québec," and further affirmed that "(. . .) the large number of young modern priests and sacerdotal situations in our novels signify a survalorization of all human situations that have to do with inversion (. . .) This sexual deviationism seems to me to be the truest and inadmissible explanation for a literature that on the whole is weak, without brilliance and, in a nutshell, truly boring" (Ibid., 191-192).[12]

The most overt feature of this passage is, not surprisingly, its anti-clericalism. There is no doubt that for Aquin's generation, priests, or *pères,* must have indeed been the most prominent of "false fathers." Indeed, beyond familiar condemnations of the church's role in instilling fear and guilt among its followers, it is the role of *collaboration* assigned to the clergy in the colonial oppression of Québec that constitutes the most severe critique of the institution. The Church is represented as "wedded" to the Anglo-Canadian bourgeoisie in a marriage where it takes care of all womanly vocations, while at the same time effeminizing its own sons. "Men in skirts," was the derisive term for the priests. Yet, this in itself could not explain the slippage from the stigmatization of the clergy as a non-virile caste to the notion of generalized inversion that threatened the contestative prowess of an entire society. A further key lies in the intimate pedagogic relationship that existed until the 1960s between priests and boys. This clerical pedagogic tradition in a society where economic entrepreneurship was largely unavailable to the vanquished, constitutes an essential underpinning to the literary works called into question by Aquin's remarks.

In a novel from the late 1930s that would surely be typical of the genre for him, François Hertel's *Le Beau Risque,* a priest educates his young male students to become ardent nationalists determined to defend French-Canadian culture and the French language in the face of assimilationist threats. Here, the diegesis is firmly inscribed within a paradigm of initiation, education, and emulation that harkens back to a repressed pederastic model. The descriptive passages of the boys' physical development are offered from the point of view of the Father and unquestionably erotically charged. The cleric dreams of his students, stripped to the waist in their canoes in the woods, radiating strength, health, and masculinity. As the boys prepare to graduate and join the manly battle, he gracefully retires to the missions in China, fearing his own advancing age and spent energies would be only a discouraging example to his former students.

The irony is that the writers of decolonization are impelled to disavow the masculinist identification of nationalism in such a novel in tribute to an overriding imperative to differentiate from the clergy, their intellectual predecessors. And this is performed through a sharp demarcation of sexualities. Thus, Réginald Hamel in his *parti pris* article on "Eroticism in the Québec Novel" claims that *Le Beau Risque* "immerses us in the strange climate of homosexuality" (1964, 105). This slippage from a pedagogic to pederastic register, in which the novel is *named* as homosexual, is consistent with the self-representation of the colonized subject as a wayward son, vulnerable to seduction by a flattering but ultimately exploitative, "false father." Once seduced, these trained young men go on to become not the defenders of Québec independence, but true "fédérastes" like the "fifis" of Radio-Canada, the radio announcers on the French-language network with their European accents, or the "tapette" (the common Québec equivalent for "queer") Trudeau, as the former Prime Minister and friend of Hertel's is referred to in the manifestos of Front de Libération du Québec, the small cells of militants who blew up "Royal" mailboxes in the early 1960s and then reappeared to kidnap a British trade commissioner and a provincial cabinet minister in 1970.

But Hamel's labeling of Hertel's novel as "homosexual" is only a partial answer to Aquin's truly amazing call for "a systematic inventory of literary categories of inversion." In one of his earliest major essays, "The Cultural Fatigue of French Canada" (1988b), Aquin had already remarked on how the performing arts, in which the Québécois were "reputed" to excell, are an appropriate form of cultural expression for slaves precisely because of their imitative and repetitious character. It is through attributions of the ruses of mimicry and dulling repetition to the homosexual that this figuration of colonialism's tenacious grip is most insistent. These ruses serve, in turn, the larger strategy of dissimulation, in which the homosexual signifies the "enemy within," particularly heinous in the colonial paradigm. Once again, let us turn to Aquin to see how this soldering of dissimulation onto the figure of the homosexual operates: "This kind of inversion," he says, "which seems to me to have seriously contaminated almost the totality of our literature (. . .) takes care to veil itself through a diversified thematics. The literary categories of inversion (. . .) I would say, contain a majority proportion of stereotypes that in fact present themselves as cases of non-inversion. If there is a human situation generative of dissimulation, it is homosexuality, and I don't see why it would dissimulate itself less in literature than anywhere else" (1964, 191).[13]

Just as homosexuality is regarded as a potential in any situation, so too is the dissimulation it is now seen as *generating,* not merely representing, within society. How telling it is, therefore, that in Aquin's contemporaneously written novel, *Prochain episode,* the protagonist discovers that the traitorous double agent he must kill in order to further the national liberation struggle is in fact his *own* double—himself. Other critics including Fredric Jameson have already remarked upon the identity established in *Prochain episode* between the act of writing and that of shooting, both in the literal and sexual senses (1983). All are repetitive, reduced to masturbatory "shots in the dark," in a writing practice that fails to assuage its own anxiety about generating narrative. Beyond this substitution for narrative, however, the text signifies as a metonymic absence for genuine revolutionary action. In essays such as "The Art of Defeat"(1988c), Aquin complains about how previous intellectual generations, *posing* as liberators, lacked the necessary energy to carry through their revolt, and fell instead into a cycle of rhetorical excess and abjection that squandered the nation's chances for emancipation; in *Prochain episode,* the frantic attempts to generate narrative mark this failure through the collapse of time and the reduction of history to an undifferentiated aqueous medium in which the narrator struggles fruitlessly to "get to the bottom of things." Inevitably, he fails. The hero/narrator's bullets miss their target, and love with the elusive agent K (for Kébec!) is rendered impossible through her ultimate betrayal. Thus, the obsession for (hetero)sexual conquest that is so prominent in Aquin's novels, complete with its litanies of masculine connoisseurship, functions as a doomed compensatory mechanism. Its invariably unsuccessful resolution barely masks the homosexual panic that really fuels Aquin's writing.

But if colonized sons are dislocated and condemned to repetition, it is not only because of *false* fathers who may, after all, be unmasked, but more seriously because of the *absence* of fathers to whose authority they may submit in a decisive but unacknowledged moment of the Oedipal itinerary. In "The Colonial Oedipus," Pierre Maheu's contribution to the "Portrait du colonisé" issue of *Parti pris,* he urges, "(. . .) we have to come to terms with the fact that we are sons, that we are of flesh and situated in a specific manner, we have to accept that we are sons of women. This will lead us to make of women both our lovers and wives while we liberate ourselves from the Mother by surging forth once again from her breast, well armed for a new combat, a new confrontation: that of the free man who attacks concrete enemies head on, instead of the ghost of a Father" (1964, 29).[14] Yet, the triumphalism of this claim begs the question of whether a "true" father can ever be recovered. In this sense, the writers of decolonization resigned themselves to being *orphans,* but *anxious* orphans whose commitment to national liberation could not inscribe itself within a patrimony of successful struggle.

This anxiety is in fact present in much earlier works of fiction, often in the form of terminal lineages. In Albert Laberge's brutally anti-agrarian satirical novel from 1918, *La Scouine,*[15] the house built and prepared for the young married couple is abandoned, left to deteriorate in the winds and snows of winter.[16] This novel in fact figures the land as barren, and the countryside as diseased and unliveable. But even in the fictions of countless writers who supposedly subscribed to agrarian ideology, prospective couples find their futures truncated through murder and other tragedies with undeniable frequency.[17] With the demise of the *roman de la terre* and the rise of the urban novel in the post-war period, the unviability of love relationships in an authoritarian and conformist culture became a more explicit theme subject to psychological interpretation. Writers themselves were the first to postulate equivalences between these grim tales and their own rootless, sterile situation.

The anti-colonial writers both developed this analysis against their predecessors and attempted to circumvent their anxiety by figuring themselves as noble primitives (cf. Nepveu, 1988, 88–89) prepared to embark upon a project of (re)birth, or birth *tout court,* since, by definition, the colonial state is pre-historic. Unlike the African colonial subject, however, who has been taught about "his ancestors the Gauls" in schools designed to produce intermediaries between colonial masters and subject populations, the colonized subject in Québec really *does* have Gallic ancestors, but ones which have been implicitly "feminized" to the extent that a primitivist "Americanness" is identified with the virilizing effects of a successful anti-colonial struggle. The trope of virile "Américanité" versus feminine "Francité" also succeeds in accomplishing another necessary ideological reversal, of rendering "Canada," with its French origins, the site of castration, while making "Québec," the formerly feminized domestic space, that of the patriarcal homestead of the new national family. But this could involve only a further repression of the archaic, one that returns in the figure of the primitive himself as the "repressed of modernism," the "figure of a death that refuses to die" (Nepveu, 1988, 93). How deep a repression of the archaic is involved in this reversal is apparent if we recall the explorer Charlevoix's observations quoted by Jean Larose that

The Canadians, by which I mean the Creoles of Canada, draw their first breaths from an air of liberty that renders them most agreeable in the affairs of life, and nowhere is our language spoken so purely. One cannot detect even the slightest accent here. (in Larose, 1987, 22)[18]

The consequences of this "virilizing" imperative are further exemplified by the insistence on the part of some of the anti-colonial writers that *joual* was the authentic Québec language as opposed to the "effete" French spoken by the thoroughly colonized élite. But not all writers agreed so readily. Hubert Aquin understood the political motivation behind this use of *joual* to the extent that it exposed the attempts of the élite to deny the oppressed condition of Québec to the outside world and especially to itself. But he also understood that by claiming to speak *as do* the people, to claim to be representing the people in the texts of demystification, the proponents of *joual* were also making a claim *on* the people which was intimately bound up with their *own* self-representational concerns. Unlike many other writers, however, Aquin was troubled by the urge to appropriate "the people" for purposes of intellectual self-differentiation. He objected to the promotion of *joual* because it assumed that people did not understand the arbitrary nature of spelling (joual conventionalized new phonetic spellings based on "Québécois" ways of pronouncing words), and that it treated communication "as if we were dealing with illiterates" (1988d, 105). Aquin perhaps realized too well that "to give voice" to a people may be understood not only causatively, but transitively, as well. In such a moment, it becomes all too easy to see how the exhortation to no longer dissimulate (to assume the privileged identity of the oppressed subject) may be easily conflated with a supplemental requirement to abandon other subject positions which are figured as being "in conflict" or "peripheral," and whose forms of symbolic articulation are thus devalued. Thus, "faire parler," "donner la parole à," both suggest not only the crucial enabling potential of intellectually refracted discourse, but its disciplinary aspect, as well. For an intellectual's universality depends nonetheless on being able to speak from a specific site, itself constructed through a population coming to think of itself not only as united, but subject to a specific and delimited *jurisdiction*. As this happens, the informal *tactics* for finding a *modus vivendi* through the deprivations of national oppression, the manifold forms of "disguise" and "trickery" employed by "Natives" as so many forms of personal resistance, are abandoned in favor of an articulated *strategy* that itself re/devalorizes these older tactics as dissimulation and "evasion."

Once again, it is Aquin's work that seems most emblematic of this problem. Shortly before his suicide in 1977, Aquin expressed the burden he had assumed through a virilizing project that equated individuation with the obverse of a passively coded national condition. "Why expend such digital energy writing about nothing but oneself? Why not relax and simply become part of other people? It would be so much simpler, so much easier and—who knows?—maybe more uplifting. The exorbitant price of individuation can never be too loudly decried". (1988e, 117–118).[19]

Aquin's writing is far removed from those felicitous aspects of literary practice that derive from what Jean Larose describes as Québec's indecision, its hystericized inability to "choose." Larose regards these optimistically, consequences of irony, "an exquisite Québécois speciality. The mastery of a language and a writing that can play with regression, play out regression, so as to master it. Bi-continental, bi-sexual Québec, both affirmation and negation of the self, the play of movement fixed in an image" (Ibid., 176–177).[20] *Aquin's* irony, however, is tortured between images of national-populist revolution which he wishes to abet and those of the distinctions and autonomies engendered by modernity. His essays in particular betray a writer constantly torn between the imperatives of the "difficult" modernist text and the conviction that his readership is still colonized, fragmented in its Subjectivity *but in a "pre-conscious," "pre-modern" mode.* Aquin hoped and despaired for the day when writer and reader, in a bond homoerotically charged through its insistent reference to Antiquity, would confront the difficulties of the text together, finding in their symbiotic labors the catharses that classical texts once offered within themselves. Aquin desired this reader, for without the assurance of this communion with an educated representative of "the people," he saw writing as condemned to reinforce the colonial situation of the nation by merely providing a veneer of "culture" behind which exploitation would continue undisturbed.

In Hubert Aquin's writing and life, these conflicts worked themselves out in a complex and ultimately tragic manner.[21] In Arcand, as we have seen, the conflicts themselves have been adjourned in favor of derision and complicit self-deprecation. However, I want to end with a discussion of another contemporary text that seems to suggest an alternative mode of negotiating the sexual anxiety embedded within the processes of decolonization at the same time as it receives its impetus from the dissolution of the naturalized solidarities fundamental to its classical discourses. Yves Simoneau's film thriller *Year of Pouvoir intime: 1986*,[22] presented in the United States under the nicely polysemic title *Blind Trust,* presents us with the consequences of a bank robbery that goes awry when a series of traditional relationships fail to perform in the expected manner. Between fathers and sons, co-workers, and lovers, long established codes seem to break down and actions systematically produce the opposite of their intended result. Yet, the film is careful not to produce anxiety around the dissolution of these codes, nor to stigmatize its most conventionally marginal characters—gay men and a non-traditional "masculine" woman—as responsible for this breakdown. Rather, the film makes us ask, outside of convention itself, by what right would we expect these codes to function in the first place?

The final scene of the film is eerily reminiscent of the novels I discussed that undermined agrarian ideology with visions of abandoned nuptial homes and barren fields. Here, the boyfriend of the dead *gay* Brink's guard and the masculine ex-girlfriend of one of the thieves meet inside the ruins of a burnt-out church in the middle of a field to divide the haul from the theft. All others involved in the adventure have been eliminated along the way. The symbolism of the last scene is inescapable, coalescing into a single image evocations of the demise of the traditional rural way of life, its attendant religious practices, and the forms of sexual organization that accompanied these. But here there is no anxiety either about absent fathers nor aimless orphans, and unlike Arcand, Simoneau has not parachuted into commercial cinéma with disciplinary intentions for his audience. Rather, he is firmly situated within the genre of the thriller, comfortable with its conventions,and innovative in their articulation. The two survivors go their separate ways in mutual respect, and to the extent that these characters are symbolic, they remind me of Jean Larose's admonition to those who would like to believe they can evade a painful confrontation with modernity by entering it innocently, especially with the pretention to anti-colonial "authenticity." Being an orphan is not only all right, Larose reassures, it's the precondition for situating oneself, of "(. . .) affirming oneself as an outsider among outsiders, as an orphan among orphans, as a nation amidst international discord" (1987, 63).[23]

NOTES

I would like to express my appreciation to Sean Holland, Jean Larose, Robert K. Martin, Alain-Napoléon Moffat, Andrew Parker, and Bruce Russell, who talked through many of the ideas in this essay with me during its preparation. I am grateful for their critical observations and many valuable suggestions.

1. This marginal situation is suggested by Dominique, the head of the History department and author of a new book on historical notions of happiness: "Look, we're lucky to live on the edges of the empire. The shocks are much less violent. It must be said that the certain aspects of the current period may be very pleasant to live. And in any case, the way our minds work prohibits us from any other form of experience." ["Remarquez que nous, ici, nous avons la chance de vivre en bordure de l'empire. Les chocs sont beaucoup moins violents. Il faut dire que la période actuelle peut être très agréable à vivre par certains côtés. Et de toute manière, notre fonctionnement mental nous interdit toute autre forme d'expérience."] (Arcand, 1986, 144)

2. "Il y aurait, semble-t-il, un million de pédales au Canada. La confédéra(s)tion est bien en selle." / "Grand concours Parti pris: Compléter la phrase suivante: 'Lorsqu'un chien rencontre une rose, il l'arrose. Lorsqu'un fédéraste rencontre un émule, il. . . . . . ." And mocking the federal government commission on Bilingualism and Biculturalism holding sessions across Canada at the time: "La Confédérastie se fait embilinguer et biculer de jour en jour et de ville en ville. Au rythme actuel des séances de la B & B, on ne pourra la fêter qu'en 69 . . ."

3. Eve Kosofsky Sedgwick describes homosexual panic as "the most private, psychologized form in which many twentieth century western men experience their vulnerability to the social pressure of homophobic blackmail" (1985, 89). It is worth underscoring that in this definition it is "homosexual" that is the qualifier, i.e. the panic in question is not that of the homosexual, especially the "out" gay man, but rather of men who internalize this particular sexual anxiety and often aggressively deflect it onto gay men who are then held responsible for having generated it. Nevertheless, it is clearly more than an aside to register that some of *Parti pris*'s principal collaborators, who either themselves wrote or were at least aware of the "Vulgarities" we have discussed, came out in subsequent years and have since been active in the gay community and/or contributed to a substantial corpus of "gay literature" in Québec.

4. There is, of course, nothing new in these kinds of projections. They have been manifest over a whole range of social conflict, as the following quotation from the French socialist Henri Barbusse taken from a 1926 survey on the impact of homosexuality in French literature demonstrates: "The indulgence with which certain writers put their delicate talents at the service of questions of this kind, when the old world is in the grips of daunting economic and social crises and heads ineluctably toward either revolution or the abyss, does no honor to this decadent phalange of intellectuals. It can only reinforce the contempt which the healthy and young peoples' power holds for the representatives of these artificial and pathological doctrines, and which I hope will hasten the hour of wrath and rebirth." ["La complaisance avec laquelle certains écrivains mettent leur talent délicat au service de questions de cette espèce, alors que le vieux monde est en proie à des crises économiques et sociales formidables, et s'achemine inéluctablement vers le gouffre ou vers la révolution, ne fait pas honneur à cette phalanage décadente d'intellectuels. Elle ne peut renforce uque le mépris que la saine et jeune puissance populaire éprouve pour ces représentants de doctrines maladives et artificielles, et tout cela hâtera, je l'espère, l'heure de la colère, de la renaissance."] (1926, 178)

5. "Entre faux et vrai, l'antre vulvaire ouvert, mais pour rire, l'anus est une vulve pour rire, pas pour vrai."

6. "Ce mobile de service est supporté par un sentiment exacerbé du devoir (. . .) ce qui est au fondement de l'intellectuel réside dans le devoir permanent de refondre la collectivité québécoise."

7. Alain-Napoléon Moffat, who brought this film to my attention, has since written an excellent article, "*A tout prendre* de Claude Jutra: autobiographie filmique et rapport direct/fiction", forthcoming in *Québec Studies* 11 (Fall 1990/ Winter 1991).

8. "(. . .) les cinéastes auront oublié leur maman pour déshabiller sereinement leur voisine qui s'appellera Yvette Tremblay or Yolande Beauchemin, en plein soleil et avec une grande angulaire bien en foyer sur le caméra. (A) partir de ce moment-là, nous pourrons envisager comme Jean Renoir un cinéma libre en même temps que férocement national. Un cinéma de joie et de conquête."

9. "La seule question est de savoir jusqu'à quel point l'homosexualité est une forme solide d'activité sexuelle et de quelle manière sa pratique pourrait être liée à un état spécial d'affirmation de soi-même, compte tenu de notre contexte global d'existence en regard de l'expression artistique."

10. "Rien d'étonnant à ce qu'alors le film semble réclamer le droit à l'homosexualité. De

toutes manières, notre littérature (. . .) l'avait déjà réclamé avant la dernière guerre. Rien de très nouveau ni de très immoral là-dedans."

11. In fact, in a curious instance of the return of the repressed, Claude is described "neutrally" in the Dramatis Personae of the script as "single" (célibataire), this being his civil status just as Rémy is married and Pierre is divorced. Once again, a repression posing as a banalization . . .

12. "(. . .) l'inflation des jeunes prêtres modernes et des situations sacerdotales dans nos romans, signifient une sur-valorisation de toutes les situations humaines qui se rapprochent de l'inversion . . . (ce) déviationnisme sexuel me paraît l'explication la plus vraisemblable et la plus inavouable d'une littérature globalement faible, sans éclat et, pour tout dire, vraiment ennuyeuse."

13. "Cette sorte d'inversion qui me paraît avoir contaminé sérieusement la presque totalité de notre littérature (. . .) prend soin de se voiler elle-même par une thématique diversifiée (. . .) Les catégories littéraires de l'inversion n'ont pas été systématiquement inventoriées jusqu'à ce jour, mais quelque chose me dit que ces catégories sont très nombreuses et contiennent une proportion majoritaire de stéréotypes qui, précisément, s'annoncent comme des cas de non-inversion. S'il est une situation humaine génératrice de dissimulation, c'est bien l-homosexualité; et je ne vois pas pourquoi la littéraire dissimulerait moins que l'autre."

14. "(. . .)il nous faut en ce sens assumer notre être-fils, notre être-charnel et situé, accepter d'être fils de femme. Ce sera du même coup faire de la femme l'amante et l'épouse et nous libérer de la Mère en surgissant à nouveau de son sein, tout armés pour un nouveau combat, un nouvel affrontement: celui de l'homme libre qui s'attaque de plein front à des ennemis concrets, et non à un fantôme de Père." Obviously, there is much to be written about the figuration of *mothers* in the discourse of decolonization, and in fact many of Québec's most prominent women writers have engaged this question. The relationship of *l'écriture au féminin* to nationalism in Québec is a fascinating and crucial terrain which we can only signal in this essay.

15. "La Scouine," whose real name is Paulima, receives her sobriquet because "she pissed in bed. Every night she had an accident (. . .) and at school, because of the odor she exuded, her classmates gave Paulima the surname Scouine, a word without any signification, a vague interjection which takes us back to the very origins of language." ["Paulima pissait au lit. Chaque nuit il lui arrivait un accident (. . .) A l'école à cause de l'odeur qu'elle répandait, ses camarades avaient donné à Paulima le surnom de Scouine, mot sans signification aucune, interjection vague qui nous ramène aux origines premières de la langue."] (Laberge, 1972, 15)

16. "The rain, the cold, the humidity ate into it little by little, accomplishing their work of destruction (. . .) Like its master, the house was crumbling to ruins." ["La pluie, le froid, l'humidité, la rongèrent peu à peu, accomplirent leur oeuvre de déstruction (. . .) Comme son maître, la maison s'en allait en ruines."] (Ibid., 1972, 59). I am grateful to my graduate student, William Poulin-Deltour, for reminding me of this episode in his Master's thesis, "L'Image de la France dans le roman québécois." (University of Massachusetts- Amherst, 1989).

17. Lest this formulation appear too neutral, it should be pointed out that the corpse in question, in the works of male and female writers alike, is very often that of a woman. "For me, the image was scandalous, even obscene: a female corpse buried beneath the foundations of a structure, but who resisted the violence which had been done to her and refused to keep silent," writes Patricia Smart (p. 19) as she explains what fueled her recent study, *Ecrire dans la maison du père: L'Emergence du feminin dans la tradition littéraire du Québec* (Montréal: Québec/Amérique, 1988). ["Pour moi l'image était scandaleuse, obscène même: c'était celle d'un cadavre enseveli sous les fondations d'un édifice mais qui, résistant à la violence qu'on lui avait faite, refusait de garder le silence."]

18. "Les Canadiens, c'est-à-dire les Créoles du Canada, respirent en naissant un air de liberté qui les rend fort agréables dans le commerce de la vie, et nulle part ailleurs on ne parle plus purement notre langue. On ne remarque même ici aucun accent."

19. "Pourquoi mettre une telle énergie digitale à n'exprimer que soi? Pourquoi ne pas se relâcher et devenir les autres tout simplement? Ce serait tellement plus simple, plus facile et, sait-on jamais?, plus exaltant. On ne dénoncera jamais le prix exorbitant de l'individuation."

20. "C'est donc dire aussi: l'ironie, une exquise spécialité québécoise. La maîtrise d'une langue et d'une écriture qui peuvent jouer avec la régression, jouer la régression, pour la maîtriser. Québec bi-continental, bisexuel, à la fois affirmation et négation de 'soi', le jeu du mouvement figé en une image."

21. Early in the 1960s, Aquin had already refused to accept the "gregariousness" which Marc Henry Soulet claims is the natural state of Québec intellectual. The writer, he claimed, must freely choose unhappiness, both for his own sake and that of his people: In assuming my identity as a French Canadian, I choose unhappiness! And I believe that, as a conquered minority, we are profoundly unhappy (. . .) We have been taught to rejoice in this, as an invalid is taught to smile (. . .) May there also be writers and artists capable of following through on their unhappiness of expression! ["En assumant mon identité de Canadien français, je choisis le malheur! Et je crois que, minoritaires et conquis, nous sommes profondément malheureux. (. . .) On nous a enseigné à nous en réjouir, comme on dit à un infirme de sourire. (. . .) Que viennent aussi les écrivains et les artistes capables d'aller jusqu'au bout de leur malheur d'expression!"] (Aquin, 1977, 49-50)

22. Two recent discussions of *Pouvoir intime* are Gilles Thérrien, "Cinéma québécois: la difficile conquête de l'altérité". *Littérature* 66 (mai 1987), 101-114; and Henry Garrity, "Subversive Discourse in Yves Simoneau's *Pouvoir intime*". *Québec Studies* 9 (Fall 1989/ Winter 1990), 29-38.

23. "(. . .) s'affirmer en étranger parmi les étrangers, en orphelin parmi les orphelins, comme une nation dans la discorde internationale."

REFERENCES

Aquin, Hubert. "Le Bonheur d'expression." *Blocs erratiques*. Montréal: Quinze, 1977: 47-50. See also 1988a.

Aquin, Hubert. *Prochain episode*. Montréal: Le Cercle du livre de France, 1965.

Aquin, Hubert. *Writing Quebec*, ed. Anthony Purdy, trans. Paul Gibson, Reva Joshee, Anthony Purdy, and Larry Shouldice. Edmonton: The University of Alberta Press, 1988. (a) "Form and Discontent" first appeared as "Le Bonheur d'expression" in *Liberté*, III.6 (Dec. 1961): 741-743; (b) "The Cultural Fatigue of French Canada" first appeared as "La Fatigue culturelle du Canada français" in *Liberté* IV.23 (May 1962):299-325; (c) "The Art of Defeat: A Matter of Style" first appeared as "L'Art de la défaite: considérations stylistiques" in *Liberté* VII. 1-2 (Jan.-Apr. 1965): 33-41; (d) "Joual: Heaven or Hell?" first appeared as "Le joual-refuge" in *Maintenant* 134 (March 1974): 18-21; (e) "The Text of the Surrounding Silence?" first appeared as "Le texte ou le silence marginal?" in *Mainmise* 64 (Nov. 1976): 18-19.

Arcand, Denys. *Le Déclin de l'empire américain* (Film script). Montréal: Boréal, 1986.

Arcand, Denys. "Cinéma et Sexualite." *Parti pris* 9-10-11 (Summer 1964): 90-97.

Bhabba, Homi. "Of Mimicry and Man: The Ambivalence of Colonial Discourse." *October* 28 (Spring 1984): 125-133.

Dudek, Louis. "The Two Traditions: Literature and the Ferment in Québec." *Canadian Literature* 12 (Spring 1962): 44-51.

Dumont, Fernand and Falardeau, Jean-Charles. *Littérature et société canadienne-françaises*.

Actes du Deuxième colloque de la revue *Recherches sociographiques*. Québec: Les Presses de l'Université Laval, 1964.
Hamel, Réginald. "L'Erotisme dans les romans." *Parti pris* 9-10-11 (Summer 1964): 98-140.
Hertel, François: *Le Beau risque*. Edition définitive. Montréal: Fides, 1942.
"L'Homosexualité en littérature." *Les Marques* XXXV, 141 (15 March 1926): 176-216.
Jameson, Fredric. "Euphorias of Substitution: Hubert Aquin and the Political Novel in Québec." *Yale French Studies* 65 (1983): 214-223.
Jameson, Fredric. "Reification and Utopia in Mass Culture." *Social Text* 1 (Winter 1979): 130-148.
Laberge, Albert. *La Scouine*. Montréal: l'Actuelle, 1972. First edition 1918.
Larose, Jean. *La Petite noirceur*. Montréal: Boréal, 1987.
Maheu, Pierre. "L'Oedipe colonial." *Parti pris* 9-10-11 (Summer 1964): 19-29.
Martin, Robert K. "Two Days in Sodom, or How Anglo-Canadian Writers Invent Their Own Quebecs." *The Body Politic* (July/August 1977): 28-30.
Nepveu, Pierre. *L'Ecologie du réel. Mort et naissance de la littérature québécoise contemporaine*. Montréal: Boréal, 1988.
Reid, Malcom. *The Shouting Signpainters: A Literary and Political Account of Quebec Revolutionary Nationalism*. New York and London: Monthly Review Press, 1972.
Sedgwick, Eve Kosofsky. "Across Gender, Across Sexuality: Willa Cather and Others." *The South Atlantic Quarterly* 88,1 ("Displacing Homophobia") (Winter 1989): 53-72.
Sedgwick, Eve Kosofsky. *Between Men: English Literature and Male Homosocial Desire*. New York: Columbia University Press, 1985.
Soulet, Marc Henry. *Le Silence des intellectuels. Radioscopie de l'intellectuel québécois*. Montréal: Saint-Martin, 1987.
"Vulgarités." *Parti pris* 9-10-11 (Summer 1964): 174.
Watney, Simon. *Policing Desire: Pornography, AIDS and the Media*. Minneapolis: University of Minnesota Press, 1987.

Contributors

KIMBERLY W. BENSTON is Professor of English at Haverford College. His books include *Baraka: The Renegade and the Mask, Speaking for You: The Vision of Ralph Ellison* (ed), and *Faces of Tradition* (forthcoming). He is currently at work on a cross-disciplinary study of the Black Arts Movement.

LAUREN BERLANT teaches at the University of Chicago. She has written a related book on the cultural/sexual politics of national identity, *The Anatomy of National Fantasy: Hawthorne, Utopia, and Everyday Life*. This essay is part of an ongoing longer project about the sentimental identity politics of American "women's culture" since the 1830s.

VÈVÈ A. CLARK is Associate Professor of African and Caribbean Literature in the Romance Languages Department and American Studies Program at Tufts University. She is co-editor of the three-volume documentary biography and collected works, *The Legend of Maya Deren* (1985/1988), and author of numerous articles on Haitian Theatre, the Francophone African/Caribbean Novel, and Afro-American Dance. She is currently completing a study of Katherine Dunham's dance theatre entitled, "Modernism and Black Dance."

MAE GWENDOLYN HENDERSON is Associate Professor in the African American Studies Program and the Department of English at the University of Illinois at Chicago. She has written several articles on Black and Womens Literature and is author and co-editor of the five-volume *Anti slavery Newspapers and Periodicals: An Annotated Index of Letters, 1817–1871*. Her forthcoming work, *Speaking in Tongues, and Other essays*, develops a black feminist theory of reading.

SYLVIA MOLLOY is Professor of Spanish and Comparative Literature at New York University. Her work includes *La Diffussion de la littérature hispanoamericaine en France* (1972), *Las letras de Borges* (1979), *At Face Value: Autobiographical Writing in Spanish America* (1990) and many articles on Latin American literature and culture. Her novel, *En breve cárcel*, has been translated into English as *Certificate of Absence* (1989). She is currently working on decadence and the notion of "national health" in Latin America at the turn of the century.

MICHAEL MOON is Assistant Professor of English at Duke University. He is the author of *Disseminating Whitman: Revision and Corporeality in Leaves of Grass* and a co-editor of *Displacing Homophobia: Gay Male Perspectives on Literature and Culture*. He is currently engaged in a study of performance and sexuality in the work of Jack Smith, Andy Warhol, Charles Ludlam, and others.

ROBERT SCHWARTZWALD is Assistant Professor of French at the University of Massachusetts—Amherst and Director of the Five College Canadian Studies program. He has published numerous articles on Québec literature and cultural studies in Canada, the United States, and Europe. Recently, he guest edited "An/other Canada. Another Canada? Other Canadas," a special double issue of *The Massachusetts Review*. In Spring 1990, he was a Research Fellow at Concordia University (Montréal) in a group project on "L'Identitaire et l'Hétérogène", and is currently completing a volume on virility and nationalism in Québec literature.

HORTENSE J. SPILLERS is professor of English and Women's Studies at Emory University. The co-editor with Marjorie Pryse of *Conjuring: Black Women, Fiction, and Literary Tradition*, she has written a number of essays, reviews, and short fiction that have variously appeared in periodicals and anthologies of black and feminist criticism. At work on a monograph that examines the claims of gender against specific historical orientations—*In the Flesh: A Situation for Feminist Inquiry*—she is attempting to establish groundwork on African-American women and the culture critique.

MICHAEL WARNER is Associate Professor of English at Rutgers University. He is the author of *The Letters of the Republic: Publication and the Public Sphere in Eighteenth-Century America,* and co-editor (with Gerald Graff) of *The Origins of Literary Studies in America*. A companion piece to the essay in this volume is forthcoming in *Raritan*.